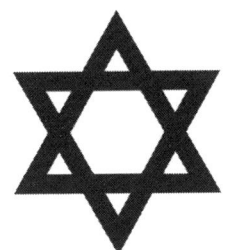

The Hidden Star of Yehudah

HADASSAH'S JOURNEY FROM CAPTIVITY
TO QUEEN ESTHER OF THE PERSIAN EMPIRE

Gale Ard

The Hidden Star of Yehudah by Gale Ard
© Copyright March 2022

All rights reserved.

Cover by Michael McDonald/*artfx2@gmail.com*
Layout by Gale Ard/*ard.design@mac.com*

ISBN: Book 978-0-578-38503-7
ISBN: E-book 978-0-578-38504-4

Scripture quotations marked (CSB) are from *The Christian Standard Bible*. Copyright © 2017 by Holman Bible Publishers. Used by permission. *Christian Standard Bible*®, and CSB® are federally registered trademarks of Holman Bible Publishers, all rights reserved.

Scripture quotations marked (ESV) are from The Holy Bible, *English Standard Version*® (ESV®), copyright © 2001 by Crossway, a publishing ministry of Good News Publishers. Used by permission. All rights reserved.

Scripture quotations from The Holy Bible, *New International Version* NIV® Copyright © 1973, 1978, 1984, 2011 by Biblica, Inc.™ Used by permission. All rights reserved worldwide.

Scripture taken from the Holy Bible, *New King James Version*®. Copyright © 1982 by Thomas Nelson, Inc. Used by permission. All rights reserved.

Scripture quotations marked (NLT) are taken from the Holy Bible, *New Living Translation*, copyright © 1996, 2004, 2007 by Tyndale House Foundation. Used by permission of Tyndale House Publishers, Inc., Carol Stream, IL 60188. All rights reserved.

Scriptures marked (KJV) are taken from the Holy Bible, *King James Version,* and are public domain.

Scriptures that do not show a version have been modified to show Hebrew names of God. Book, chapter, and verse are given.

Image page 254-255: Petter. Anton. Dútsk: König Ahasver verurteilt Haman zum Tode. Image/jpg. 1979. Ankauf Hedwig Dankner, Wien. https://commons.wikimedia.org

Image page 274: Aert de Gelder (after) - Esther and Mordecai. Image/jpg. October 5, 2015. https://commons.wikimedia.org

Author's photograph: Lynn Galloway Sims

Printed in the United States

Dear Reader,

Hadassah was forced from her home by men following orders and taken into a place where she lost all rights and freedom of choice. Today we call that *abduction* and *trafficking*. Her being taken was not because she chose to enter a beauty contest, nor was it by choices that she and Mordecai made. The selfish, ambitious, and evil choices of others often bring the innocent into captivity of heartbreaking and devastating circumstances. This explains the events and results in lives that are often hard for others to accept or understand. The results, however, are determined by how one faces the captivity.

The message of *The Hidden Star of Yehudah* will hopefully encourage any one of us who find ourselves entrapped in circumstances or situations that have nothing to do with the consequences of personal choices. Esther's captivity resulted in deliverance for her people. But, would she have chosen that path? The outlook was bleak and uncertain—for Esther it was a path against God's plan for a Jewish maiden. The result of deliverance was obviously by the will and purpose of Hashem. But in her captivity, she made choices to submit her life to God in trust and in complete submission for the outcome. That is the definition of righteousness and servanthood. Esther's story is one of submission and trust—even if she died.

Special appreciation to Rosalyn Small a graduate of Lee University and a lover of all things Hebrew. She helped me with the vocabulary I included in the text that is Jewish/*Yeduhi*.

Also, many thanks to Dorothy Easterly for editing the book and helping me to make it easy to read.

Thanks to Genie Byrd for her encouragement, support, and connecting me to Dorothy Easterly.

Thanks to Michael McDonald for the beautiful cover.

I trust that before you read this book, you will read the book of Esther in the Bible. Much of this book is from my own imagination and at times a bit of inspiration.

Shalom,
Gale Ard
gale.ard@icloud.com

Vocabulary

Shushan - Susa, also called Shushan, modern Shush, capital of Elam (Susiana) and administrative capital of the Achaemenian king Darius I and his successors from 522 BCE. It was located at the foot of the Zagros Mountains near the bank of the Karkheh Kūr (Choaspes) River in the Khuzistan region of Iran.

Yehud - singular Jew

Yehudah - the place of Judah in the promise Land

Yehudi - Jewish; plural **Yahud**

Yehudim - the Jews as a collective people

eema - mother

abba - father

boker tov - good morning

boker or - good morning to you, or light of the morning

Torah - the Law, first 5 books of the Old Testament

dod - endearing word for a close relative, especially an uncle or cousin

Adonai - the Lord

Hashem - the substitute in place of God's Sacred Name

Elohim - God, as a title

melek - king

Mashiyach Melek - Messiah King

baht - daughter of God; also bat

El-Elohe-Yisrael - the God of Israel

Avram/Avraham - Abraham

Yitzkak - Isaac

Yaco - Jacob

Kiddish - a blessing to sanctify the Shabbat

achot - sister; *achayot* - sisters

ach - brother; *achim* - brethren

aleicha shalom - peace to you

toda raba - thank you

Shabbat - a day of rest to commemorate God resting on the seventh day after he made the world. *Shabbat* begins on Friday at sunset and lasts until sunset on Saturday. It is a time for family and community, and during this time services at the synagogue are well attended. No work is to be done on Shabbat.

Shabbat meal - dinners are usually multi-coursed and include bread, fish, soup, meat and/or poultry, side dishes, and dessert. It is held every Friday at sunset until after dark on Saturday. Work and travel is stopped on this holy day. The *Kiddish* is the prayer during Shabbat.

Kiddish - the Prayer of Wine prayed together during Shabbat meal.

Mezuzah - ("doorpost") a piece of parchment in a decorative case and inscribed with specific Hebrew verses from the *Torah* (*Deuteronomy 6:4–9* and *11:13–21*). These verses consist of the Jewish prayer *Shema Yisrael*. A mezuzah is affixed to the doorpost of Jewish homes to fulfill the *mitzvah* (Biblical commandment) to "write the words of God on the gates and doorposts of your house" *(Deut.9:6)*. Whenever passing through the doorway, many people touch a finger to the *mezuzah* as a way of showing respect to God and often kiss their finger after touching the *mezuzah*.

Mithra - the Persian god of the rising sun, contracts, covenants, and friendship. He also oversaw the orderly change of the seasons, maintained cosmic order, and was responsible for bestowing divine grace on kings, legitimizing their rule, and, as a protector of the faithful, was also invoked by warriors before battle and so became known as a god of war. The best-known and most popular god.

Angra Mainyu - the evil, destructive spirit

Baga - Persian god of good fortune and wealth

Shema - refers to a couple of lines from the book of Deuteronomy (6:4-5). It became a daily prayer in Ancient Israelite tradition. The *Shema* gets its name from the first Hebrew word of the prayer in Deuteronomy 6:4, "Listen, Israel, the Lord is our God, the Lord alone." The lines in Deutoeromony 6.4, and lines from Deuteronomy 6:4-54 were combined with other passages from the Torah (Deut. 11:13-21 and Num. 15:37-41), and prayed in the morning and the evening. One of the most influential traditions in Jewish history. It also serves as the Jewish pledge of allegiance and a hymn of praise.

Hazan - an official of a Jewish synagogue or community of the period when the Talmud was compiled. **Talmud** is the central text of Rabbinic Judaism and the primary source of Jewish religious law.

Tallit - a fringed garment worn as a prayer shawl by religious Jews and Samaritans. The tallit has special twined and knotted fringes known as **tzitzit** attached to its four corners.

Sheol - in the Hebrew Bible a place of darkness to which all the dead go, both the righteous and the unrighteous regardless of the moral choices made in life; it is a place of stillness and darkness cut off from life and from God.

Shemitah - means *release*; it refers to the seven-year cycle when all field work stops so the land can rest. Also, loans are forgiven. September 7, 2021 - September 25, 2022 will mark the dates of the next *Shemitah*.

Especially for You

To my seven loves:
Merritt Jenkins
Eleanor Jenkins
Eli Jenkins
Ava Jenkins
Chloe Mosely
Arden Mosely
Leo Mosely

To Hashem
Who inspired me and gave me so much joy while writing
Hadassah and Mordecai's story with the insight
that He gave. Thank You for the Word of God
who inspires, comforts, teaches, and
gives purpose for our lives.

To Larisa
Who loved the Word of God and dilligently taught it
and lived it until Jesus called her home.
Tell Esther I am an admirer. I will see you both soon.

To Sallie
My talented and gifted singer, writer, photographer, and
teacher of children. I love you, my sweet girl.

To Flemon
Who washed dishes, vaccumed floors, bought grocries, and learned
to make grits, so I could spend more time writing.
I love you, Sug. You are my inspiration.

Table of Contents

Prologue	9
1. Shushan	11
2. The Ten Thousand Immortals	13
3. The Invitation	18
4. The Refusal	27
5. Dark Days	39
6. The Plan	44
7. The Collection	48
8. The Post	51
9. The Light	66
10. The Chosen	69
11. Gaining Favor	84
12. The Tenth of Tebeth	91
13. The Image in the Mirror	104
14. Accepting the Crown	109
15. The Day of Small Things	112
16. The Plot	115
17. Messages	119
18. Rescued	129
19. The Parade	134
20. The Meeting	140
21. The Report	145
22. The Prince	153
23. Setting the Date	156
24. A Momentous Day	161
25. The Decree	165
26. Sackcloth and Ashes	170
27. The Tailor	177
28. The Mission	186
29. My People	190
30. The Garden	200
31. The Reply	203
32. An Appointed Life	208

33. Rending the Veil 215
34. The Battle Plan 221
35. The Third Day 228
36. The Scepter and the Gallows 233
37. A Matter of Record 240
38. Haman's Big Idea 245
39. The Temptation 248
40. The Queen's Request 252
41. Shattering Secrets 258
42. The Postscript 263
43. The Reunion 264
44. Rumors and Gossip 268
Epilogue 273

The Names of God

Elohim - My Eternal Creator
El-Shaddai - My Supplier
El-Olam - Everlasting God
El-Jireh - My Provider
El-Rophe - My Healer
El-Nissi - My Banner
El-Makadesh - My Santifier
El-Shalom - My Peace

El-Shammah - My Abiding Presence
El-Gibor - The Mighty God
El Elyon - God Most High
El-Elohe-Yisrael - the God of Israel
El-Roi - God Who Sees
El-Tsidkenu - My Righteousness
El-Rohi - My Shepherd
El-Sabaoth - the God of Armies

Prologue

Hadassah's eyes flew open and the room was now dim with only the dawning sunlight filtering through her window. *What was that? What happened?*

She pondered the dream. She remembered the faceless men; she remembered the shame and embarrassment of being naked and frightened; she remembered the cords of gold woven with thorns; she remembered the darkness—the light! *What was the light?*

The horror of the dream was overshadowed by the awareness that something—*a light*—had entered her? *What was it?*

She closed her eyes and waited for the presence of the light to return. The memory of it was strong, the brilliance of it unforgettable.

What were the words? Her mind could recall Mordecai reading similar—*no*—*those same words* . . . words from the scroll of Jeremiah's prophecy.

As she lay there, she repeated the words and felt the liquid light deep inside moving like a river.

The thoughts and feelings were dark, tormenting, foreign and evil. He shook his head trying to make them stop. He ran his hands through his hair and pulled with his fingers; he groaned and looked upward. He groaned and looked upward, He hoped that like Avram he would see three strangers coming to give him a promise and a chance to make a bargain with Elohim to rescue the righteous from Shushan and the palace while fire and brimstone fell from heaven and consumed them. But all he saw were people up and down the street bowed to the ground. Coming straight at him was Haman, leading a horse and two eunuchs. Mordecai hoped they were coming to take him to the dungeon where he could stay and die.

That's what I deserve, he thought, *for all this chaos is my fault*. He stood up as Haman stopped and stood in front of him.

"I'm ready," he said softly. "I've been expecting this."

"Really? That's strange. How did you know I was coming?" Haman's tone was flat, painful, sarcastic.

"Well, Haman, because I deserve it. The decree, the fear among my people, the sackcloth and ashes, the prayers—all of it is because I would not shame Hashem by bowing to you. This is the work of Hashem."

Haman felt shame and a weakness wash through him at the thought that a god he had scorned and disregarded and spoken against might be real, one that could actually be behind all of this.

"What about Bigthana and Teresh? What about the message you sent to the king, the one I hand-delivered? Is that why you deserve it?"

"Yes," Mordecai said softly and his head dropped. "Let's just do what has to be done. You have me where I am supposed to be, so do what you have been commanded to do. I will not resist you."

Without another word, one of the eunuchs moved to Mordecai and said, "Raise your arms."

Mordecai obeyed and felt himself engulfed in a robe. Looking down at it, he was completely confused.

"What is this?"

"It is one of the king's robes," Haman said. "Now, get on the horse."

Without a word, with the help of the two eunuchs Mordecai was lifted to mount the huge beast. Mordecai noted that the crest of the king was on the horse's head. He became overwhelmed by the realization that he was about to be paraded before the town square while his acts against the king and his people were being proclaimed. He closed his eyes as Haman led the horse to the main street. With no one else to call upon for help, he silently cried out to Hashem, the one he had just doubted and accused. He knew that if Hashem were not real, nothing was.

Chapter One

Shushan

> *There was a Jewish man in the fortress of Susa whose name was Mordecai son of Jair. He was from the tribe of Benjamin and was a descendant of Kish and Shimei. His family had been among those who, with King Jehoiachin of Judah, had been exiled from Jerusalem to Babylon by King Nebuchadnezzar. This man had a very beautiful and lovely young cousin, Hadassah, who was also called Esther. When her father and mother died, Mordecai adopted her into his family and raised her as his own daughter.* (Est 2.5-7 NIV)

Hadassah yawned, blinked, stretched her legs, wriggled her toes, and took a deep breath. The rooster outside her window was doing a fine job of announcing the day. The singing birds in the trees were in contest with him, and he was not to be beaten. The smell of baking bread filled her small room. She had prepared the dough the night before, and she knew Mordecai had fired the oven. The very aroma was mouth-watering.

Hadassah closed her eyes and listened to the melodious cadence of Mordecai reading aloud in soft intonations. She was awakened to that pleasant sound every morning. Pulling herself quickly from the covers, she slipped into her clothes.

"I'm missing it again," she mumbled to herself.

She drew back the woven drape that divided the small room from the living area. For a moment she stood taking in the view that had been hers every morning for twelve years since Mordecai had brought her to live with him after her *eema* died in childbirth. Abihail, her *abba*, who was Mordecai's uncle, had died earlier. A warm happiness filled her at the sight of her beloved cousin, and she breathed deeply to capture the scene one more time.

"Ah, *boker tov*, sleepyhead," Mordecai glanced her way.

"*Boker or, Dod*. What have I missed today?"

"Our people have been delivered from Egypt," he replied.

"Are they at the Red Sea now?"

"Yes."

"And Pharaoh is hot on their trail?"

"Yes, Little Myrtle Tree," he replied with a slight smile as he used her name's meaning. "You remember well."

Cousin Mordecai read their *Yehudim* history from the scrolls of the

Torah every day, even though as a scribe he knew almost every word from memory. He treasured the scrolls of the scriptures more than anything he owned. Only Hadassah was as precious to him.

"*Dod*, why do you read the same words from the scrolls over and over. Do you not already know every word?"

"I read them because I love them. They are Adonai's words to us; we are his people. These are the words penned by Moses to remind us we are the chosen people of Hashem. We belong to our creator, Hashem, the Elohim of Avraham, Yitzkak, and Yaco. We have a rich heritage, and He has appointed us to be different from the other nations around us to show forth His name, His glory, His provision, and many times His deliverance. I read our *Yehudim* history to give Him thanks every day that we are His, and He is our *melek*. One day He will come to us as our *mashiyach melek*, and set up His kingdom and we will live with Him."

"But we are not in *Yehudah*, *Dod*. We are here in the province of Shushan! We are surrounded by people who are not *Yehudi*. Perhaps He will come and we will not know it!"

"Remember His promises, *Baht*. We will know when He has come. It is true; we are not in *Yehudah*, but we are not enslaved here in Persia as our forefathers were when they were brought here after Jerusalem was destroyed. Thanks to King Cyrus who made a decree when he became the Persian king that gave us permission to return to Israel if we desired. He also made it possible for us to remain and live in peace with the people here. We are blessed to live freely, to live and worship as *Yehudim* here. Now our present king, Ahasuerus, is not like those early kings that bound us as slaves."

"Like Pharaoh!" exclaimed Hadassah.

"Like Pharaoh, like Nebuchadnezzar, like Belshazzar, and others. We have our own village quarters, our own leaders, our own worship, our own Elohim. We are blessed to work, to own land and to live; so we live our lives to give glory to Adonai. Wherever we are, we are His. Whatever our conditions, we live for Him. We worship Him! We represent Him! We live for His name's sake and glory."

"I want to live to give El-Elohe-Yisrael, (the God of Israel) glory, *Dod*. I want to know everything in the scrolls. I missed some of the reading, but please read to me now. I want to hear again about the Red Sea parting and the cloud and the fire and . . ."

"Very well, but you must stop talking to hear, *Baht*." ✡

Chapter Two

The Ten Thousand Immortals

The Ten Thousand Immortals were the elite force of the Persian army of the Achaemenid Empire (c. 550-330 BCE). They formed the king's personal bodyguard and were also considered the shock troops of the infantry in Persian warfare. They are among the most famous fighting forces of the ancient world. (https://www.worldhistory.org/Persian_Immortals/)

Hadassah wove her way into the crowded market with her basket on her arm and her eyes searching for her best friend, Sara. Sara was also an orphan. They had shared stories of how their *abbas* had died, and Hadassah knew Sara's *eema* had died giving birth to her just as Hadassah's *eema* had. So the girls felt like sisters and were as close as *achayot* could be. Sara lived with her *eema's achot* and her husband, and sometimes she felt sorry that Hadassah did not have an aunt and a large family of cousins like she did. However, Hadassah didn't really feel the loss as Sara feared because the women of the village had cared for Hadassah since the day she had come to live with Mordecai. They made sure Hadassah had clothes and was instructed in the ways of a proper *Yehudi* woman. Many of them had tried to take Hadassah as their own, but Mordecai's heart had been bound to the small infant the moment he laid eyes on her. Now he could not imagine his life without her.

"Sara!"

Hadassah knew there was no way Sara could hear her over the noise of the vendors and shoppers, so she quickened her pace to catch up with her. When she did, she yanked on her head covering to get her attention. Startled, Sara whirled around ready to box the ears of a naughty boy and then burst into laughter when she saw her friend.

"You almost got your ears boxed! I thought you were Nathan!"

Sara kissed her on each cheek and bumped her shoulder against hers.

"My basket is almost full and if you had been that mischievous prankster, I may have dumped it all!"

"Not Nathan! It is just I!" laughed Hadassah.

Although Sara was almost finished with her shopping, she accompanied Hadassah to each booth and helped her choose items. At one sheltered booth, they stood transfixed as they watched a pottery artisan working clay on a spinning stone wheel powered by his foot on the pedal below. Intent on his design, he did not notice their curious quietness and intensity as they admired his fast and nimble hands beginning to form his medium into a pot. Suddenly, he used his hand to squash the creation back into a wet mass of clay, kneading it again and remolding it.

The girls knew this potter was famous for the most elaborate and exquisite designs. Even Queen Atossa, the queen mother, had at times sent her eunuchs, or attendants, to purchase his beautiful work. Hadassah knew his name to be Uriel ben-Avram. Hadassah also knew his son Ezra was his apprentice and would one day take over the business. Hadassah glanced around the booth to see if Ezra were in sight, but he was not.

Uriel and Mordecai were close *Yehudi* friends. On specific days of the week, these two respected leaders sat at the palace gates. They offered resolution in disputes among citizens who had issues not serious enough to go before the court of the regents. Their efforts were often sought out and greatly appreciated, especially among the poorer citizens in the village.

In Mordecai's every day business, beyond his service as a scribe for the temple servants, he wrote contracts, deeds, and other legal documents for Shushan citizens in his booth at the palace gates.

Uriel paused to refill his water jug and sprinkled some on the clay. As the girls stood and watched transfixed, he created a beautiful pot. When he paused a moment, he glanced up to take in his two observing admirers.

"*Shalom*, Hadassah. I see you have brought a friend."

"*Aleicha shalom*, Uriel ben-Avram. This is my friend Sara."

"*Shalom*, Sara."

"*Aleich shalom*, Uriel ben-Avram," Sara replied with a slight blush.

While Uriel focused again on his current project, Hadassah turned her thoughts to Uriel's family and particularly to Ezra.

Hadassah was acquainted with Uriel through the *Shabbat* meals she and Mordecai shared with him, his wife Rachel and Ezra. Hadassah also suspected that Mordecai and Uriel had discussed the possible arrangement for Hadassah to be wedded to Ezra on her fifteenth birthday. Hadassah felt a bit bewildered by the idea of leaving Mordecai and her home to live with Ezra, of whom she knew very little, and what she did know about him was unsettling. She secretly hoped the day would not come when it was decided that she would be wedded to him. During times when Uriel's family had meals with them, Ezra had looked around their small home with eyes of derision. Further, he had also refused to pray the *kiddish* when they prayed it together. She knew this because she had peeked one eye to watch him. She had not told Mordecai her feelings about Ezra, and hoped it would not become necessary. It might disappoint him since he was using his best judgment in his choice for her future.

Hadassah knew Ezra regretted his *Yehudi* nationality because only boys of Persian nobles could be in the king's army of the Ten Thousand Immortals, a fierce force of three million strong, or so it was claimed. One day when she and Ari's twin daughters, Hannah and Rivka, were waiting to meet up with Sara in Ari's market booth, she had overheard Ezra, Babak and Parviz a few feet from Ari's business. The boys were resting after unloading a wagon of fruit for Ari's stand. Hadassah remembered Ezra explaining to Babak and Parviz what he had learned from one of his Persian friends who had an uncle in the Ten Thousand Immortals.

"I'm telling you the truth!" Ezra had said. "When a boy is born he is taken away from his *abba*! By the time that boy is five, they start training him to be a warrior!"

"Why would a family give up their baby?" asked Babak. "Elohim wants *Yehudim* to have many children, not give them away!"

"That's why only Persians can be in the army. Cyrus made it that way so *Yehudi* could keep their sons. Actually, the *eema* gets to nurse the baby, but she has to go to the Fort of Shushan to do that. The *abba* is paid to let the boy be taken and made into a warrior. It's actually a great honor for a man's son to be taken and trained. Once the boy is taken, the family doesn't even claim him as their son."

"I wouldn't want to leave my family!" said Parviz. "Maybe getting money from giving your child to the king's forces is something many people feel like they have to do. But I can't imagine why!"

"Well, Parviz, it is an honor to be selected! And sometimes people pay their taxes that way! It's better than being turned into a eunuch, a slave, or even a farmer or a merchant!" Ezra said with sarcasm. "The training is a lot of hard work, long days, and strict rules; but they are taught archery, hand-to-hand combat, how to survive in the forest and in deserts, and how to train a wild horse! Also, they must practice standing guard, and make long, tough marches. When the boy is fifteen, he's trained in every way to kill and destroy other soldiers!"

Ezra's excitement was building.

"That sounds like a lot of tough training to be called an Immortal!" Babak remarked, shaking his head.

"Well, actually, at first, they are placed in the lesser forces, the Sparabara or the Takabara."

"What's the difference?"

"The Sparabara are the shield bearers, and although the king's army is taken from every province, they must be Medes or Persians. They are the front line in battle to form a wall of protection in front of the archers. The Takabara are the javelin throwers. They often carry light axes called the *sagaris* as sidearms."

"What kind of men are these?" asked Parviz. "Do they serve the king or Mithra, the warrior god?"

"Both," replied Ezra.

"So when do they become part of the Ten Thousand Immortals?" asked Babak.

"Since the Ten Thousand Immortals are the elite, most trained forces, the Sparabara and the Takabara are the replacements when an Immortal dies or retires, if they live long enough. They keep putting men in to replace others so the number never decreases. That also keeps the legend that they never die—thus, immortal!"

Hadassah had heard enough. She had moved away so she couldn't hear any more of such a life. *I guess I'll never understand boys*, she had thought. She often saw the boys in her village pretending they were part of the legendary elite force. The idea of battle and killing was so horrifying to her, she could not imagine anyone as gifted as Ezra wanting to make that his life. But in every opportunity he had, Ezra recounted and celebrated the many victories by the forces that had brought the empire to its current expanse.

Hadassah raised her eyes from Uriel's wheel to note one particular shelf of pottery behind Uriel that showed great skill and talent. Obviously, the pieces were created by Ezra since the pots included designs of weaponry and war. Hadassah suspected these pieces sold quickly and were in great demand by anyone connected to the military. *Why can't he just be content to build his reputation as his* abba *did?* She wondered.

Uriel paused a moment and continued his conversation with the girls.

"I know your parents well, Sara. You come from a very large and honored family. Your *abba* is a real craftsman. Highly respected."

"*Toda raba.*" Although Sara lived with her *eema's achot* and husband, Sara did not mind that they were referred to as her parents. She had no other guardian and she had been with them since birth. However, she was a bit surprised that this man who was considered one of the wealthiest in the village knew her family. She mumbled her thanks for his kind words and gave a slight bow.

Uriel grinned at her action. She was known to be a sweet, obedient, and adored young girl. He also knew she was promised to Nathan the carpenter's apprentice. He could not help but feel pity for her. With such a beautiful character and face, the limp that she carried from her difficult birth was known throughout the village. Of course, it was not an issue for Sara. Fortunate for her that she did not know Uriel's thoughts, or she would have blushed even more, and might have wondered if he saw her as unacceptable. Even though in times past she had suffered teasing and whispers, she knew that when she was betrothed to Nathan all of that would disappear. Nathan's parents and hers had agreed in the union when she was six. At that time also, Nathan was old enough to begin watching Sara's *abba* in his wood shop with the plan that at twelve Nathan would be Daniel's apprentice. Although she often teased her *abba's* lanky, dark-eyed, carpentry apprentice and pretended that he was just someone annoying, the truth was she had loved and admired Nathan for as long as she could remember. She was confident she would be Nathan's bride and the *eema* to his children. That was her dream and confidence.

Uriel ben-Avram began the wheel's spinning again and the girls moved on to finish their shopping, each one lost in her own thoughts.

Chapter Three

The Invitation

And now I will tell you the truth: Behold, three more kings will arise in Persia, and the fourth shall be far richer than them all; by his strength, through his riches, he shall stir up all against the realm of Greece. (Daniel 11.2 NIV)

In the third year of his reign Ahasuerus gave a feast for all his officials and servants. The army of Persia and Media and the nobles and governors of the provinces were before him, while he showed the riches of his royal glory and the splendor and pomp of his greatness for many days, 180 days. (Est.1.3 NIV)

On Friday, Mordecai opened the door to welcome Uriel, Rachel, and Ezra. Each one placed a hand on the *mezuzah* mounted on the doorpost then kissed that same hand before they entered.

As Hadassah watched, she slipped her hands down the front of her dress to smooth away any untidy wrinkles or flour spots still lingering from her day's preparation for the *Shabbat* meal. Small sweat beads still clung to her forehead, and she quickly wiped them away with a small towel. At the same time, she watched Ezra to see if he might have changed from the month ago when they came for *Shabbat*. The only change she observed was a slight appearance of fuzz on his upper lip. He in return did not even glance her way, but instead gave his full attention to the conversation between Mordecai and Uriel.

Ezra's parents had warmly greeted her before the men huddled and began quietly talking. Rachel cheerfully offered Hadassah a bundle of flowers from her garden for the table, talking non-stop as she arranged them in a vase. Hadassah watched her survey the table and the food, and lastly, inspect Hadassah with obvious approval. All the while Hadassah's ears were straining to hear the conversation about which the men seemed to be so engrossed. She could not interpret the expressions on their faces, but she knew they were not talking about the usual topics. Rachel's oblivious and happy chatter, her gushing compliments on the table, and of course, the latest gossip, completely drowned out the men, much to Hadassah's chagrin.

Once around the table, Mordecai led the *Shabbat* prayer service that Hadassah loved so much.

THE INVITATION

"*Baruch Atah Adonai Eloheinu Melech ha'olam asher kidshanu b'mitzvotav vitzivanu l'hadlik ner shel Shabbat.*" (Blessed are You, Infinite One, who makes us holy through our actions and honors us with the light of Shabbat. Blessed are You, Adonai our Elohim, Ruler of the universe, who commands us to kindle the light of Shabbat.)

As she listened to Mordecai's rich voice, she closed her eyes and felt a deep, sweet presence of peace and purpose that always accompanied the sharing of the meal. The celebration of creation as recorded in the *Torah* was a weekly favorite of hers since she knew why there was a beginning of all things, and why *Shabbat* ended in rest. This was important to Hadassah who longed to understand and know everything she could about Hashem.

That evening when the meal had ended and the guests were gone, the house was quiet again. Hadassah sat before Mordecai and asked, "*Dod*, what were you and Uriel and Ezra discussing tonight when they arrived?"

"Maybe I will tell you tomorrow," Mordecai slightly shut his eyes and she knew that was a signal to her to be dismissed. She sat for a pause and determined she could not wait. So instead she used her irresistible tactic.

"Is it good news? Is it about our village? What, *Abba*? Please . . . tell me?"

Mordecai opened his eyes and stared at her with a slight curl of his lip. She knew when she called him *abba*, she would not be denied an answer.

"It is not women's business," he replied in resignation.

"But *Dod*, I'm not quite a woman yet . . . so I will listen and be quiet."

He raised his eyebrows, hesitated, and then stated, "Ahasuerus is going to war again. He's preparing to go to Greece."

She drew back her head and with a slight frown between her dark eyes she said, "War? But why? Since he became king when his *abba* died, he has already faced and won an uprising in Egypt and a rebellion in Babylon. He already has over a hundred provinces conquered by King Darius. It has only been three years! Why would he go to war with Greece, *Dod*?"

"Ah, *Baht*, it is a long story. Perhaps we should wait until another day."

"*Abba*, I am not tired. It is still early and you will be busy tomorrow with your writing. Please, tell me why the king and the Immortals are going to war with Greece. I know King Darius went to war against Athens and Plateau when they attempted to intervene during one of our province's revolts."

"Oh . . . you know about that? Something that happened that long ago?"

"Yes, *Dod*." She gave him a teasing grin and turned her head to one side to look at him sideways.

"You told me about it when you were hired to make a map for Aziaha the merchant. You started showing me places in the empire and told me about some of the important events of those places."

"You learn well, Hadassah! I'm impressed! Do you not remember that the province that revolted was in Ionia? It was Athens and Eretia that sent forces to support the revolt. They actually captured and burned Sardis, one of the most important cities in the empire, but there were heavy losses for them, so they had to retreat. Because they dared to assist in a revolt against the empire, Darius vowed he would burn down Athens and Eritrea. In fact, it is rumored that Darius shot his arrow upward and cried out, 'Zeus, may it be granted to me to take vengeance on Athens!'"

"Zeus? Why Zeus? Why would he appeal to a Greek god?"

"Simply because Zeus is the supreme god of the Greeks. So Darius appealed to him for permission and favor to attack Athens so Zeus would not give them the victory. Also, if you can believe it, Darius appointed one of his servants to say three times every day before the evening meal, 'Master, remember the Athenians!'"

"How ridiculous! Why not call on Mithra? After all, he is considered the most powerful warrior against the forces of darkness! Or why not Angra Mainyu? He is the god of chaos and disorder!"

"*Baht*, King Darius was sure that Mithra and Angra Mainyu were already going to give him victory. I'm sure he had made sacrifices and ordered the priests to pray, so he didn't see the need to appeal to them. His sorcerers and astrologers would have given him assurance that the victory was imminent."

"All of this praying and sacrifices to gods that don't exist. Gods that can't see, hear, or speak! Using the heavens and sorcery to determine events. What a pitiful mess, *Dod*!"

"You're right, Hadassah. Many disasters have come to men that put their trust in such things. Because of the prophecies of his seers and astrologers, when that first invasion against Greece ended by the Immortals crushing the Ionians in the battle of Lade and ending the revolt, it seemed the sorcerers and astrologers were right. I'm sure Darius rewarded them well."

"You said, the first invasion. Why did King Darius attack Greece a second time?"

"Remember, Darius had vowed to destroy Athens and to completely take over Greece. The word of a Persian emperor cannot be broken. So when he planned his second attack, he and his commanders decided to attack by sea. They sent a naval force under the command of Datis and Artaphernes."

"I don't understand. Why attack by sea? Is Athens a port?"

"The forces needed a location close enough to plan a strategic attack. A string of small islands in the Aegean Sea was close to Greece, so they invaded and overthrew the islands to give the army a position for close range against Athens and Eretria."

"Oh, that makes sense."

"They were able to capture Eretria, but when they landed in Marathon, which is the closest port to Athens, the much smaller Athenian army marched to Marathon to confront them there rather than give the Immortals a chance to ride their horses into Athens. The Athenians knew that their numbers against the huge forces of the Immortals required strategy over size."

"I'm sure! Just the number of the Immortals would make the strongest army flee or surrender! Isn't that true, *Dod*?"

"It is, *Baht*. You have pointed out one of the reasons the empire is so large. When a town or city knows a force of ten thousand is coming, most of the people just submit. Ahasuerus depends on that."

Mordecai gave her an admiring look. She was not only a lover of history, but she had a sharp mind to discern and understand.

"What happened at Marathon, *Dod*? Did the Athenians out-smart them?"

"The Athenian commanders chose a location they knew to be full of marshes and mountains, and also one with a tight passage between them. Their strategy meant that the poor terrain would prevent access for the Persian warriors on horseback, so only the Persian foot soldiers would be able to join in the battle. Still a lot to face! So they divided their small army and planned to block the only two ways to get in and out of the area. When the Persian infantry rushed in, the Athenians had them surrounded. When the Persians realized their position was at a disadvantage, they rushed in a panic for their ships. The Athenians had the clear advantage and killed thousands of them. This humiliating defeat led to Darius' foolish vow to burn Athens."

"So King Ahasuerus will complete his *abba's* vow. Do you think he will burn Athens?"

"Actually, I think the Athenians have learned something valuable about the Persian Ten Thousand Immortals."

"Let me guess . . . the Persians can be defeated! Right?"

"You are right! Athens proved that the Immortals can be defeated. Also, it's clear that size is not always the determining factor . . ."

"Like David against Goliath!" Hadassah's eyes shone with the thought.

"Right. Since they won a battle over an army with ten times the number of warriors, it seems to me the Greeks will depend more on strategy than numbers. That's a new, unexpected problem for the Immortals. They have always won due to their numbers and psychological methods."

"I know the battle you refer to, *Dod*. The battle in Egypt, when the Persian commanders released thousands of cats in front of their forces and the Egyptians—who worship cats—wouldn't fight because they were afraid they might kill a cat! The Egyptians were defeated by cats!" Her bright eyes and face were filled with laughter at the memory.

Mordecai laughed. "You remember exactly what I was referring to, *Baht*. When the Persian army came up with that plan, it was a stroke of genius. It just proves that when idolatrous gods are involved, anything can happen!"

They both laughed at the foolishness of the Egyptians for allowing a clowder to defeat them.

Hadassah's face suddenly clouded over and her dark brows drew together.

"What's the matter?" Mordecai asked as he suddenly realized how late the evening was getting and wondered if she was suddenly afraid after all this talk of war.

"But it will not come here, will it, *Dod*?" Her eyes wide with alarm. "We will not be in the war. Will we?"

Hadassah's face grew pale at the thought. She had never seen war, but she knew well the stories from Mordecai's scrolls. The images of men, women and children dying from battles, of cities being burned, of populations being taken into captivity and carried into foreign lands. These were vivid scenes in her mind from the historical scriptures in the scrolls, even some of the history of *Yehudah*! Even more, in fact, Hadassah also knew her own people's history of how *Yehudi* relatives had been taken as captives to Babylon by Nebuchadnezzar's armies years ago. Because of the Babylonian siege and invasion of Jerusalem after King Jehoiakim rebelled against the Babylonian rule, the great city of David had been overthrown. The great temple of Solomon, and the city had been destroyed. Only the very poorest and a few appointed leaders had been left in Jerusalem.

"Surely El-Shalom (the God of Peace) will keep war from us here!" Hadassah shuddered at the possibility of war.

"We will trust in Hashem that war will not come here from the Greeks. Ahasuerus is sure that he will be victorious. Since his *abba's* death, he has been setting up new commanders throughout the empire to build his Immortals into an army larger than any empire has ever seen. It will be a

THE INVITATION

mighty force like none other. In fact, he is celebrating his victory before he leaves. For almost eight months now the nobles, princes, and his province leaders have been at the palace drinking, eating, singing, dancing, and playing war games to celebrate the victory."

Hadassah's eyes showed her surprise.

"I knew a palace celebration was on-going, but I didn't know why. It seems very strange to me that a celebration would happen before the battle! King Ahasuerus must be very brave and certain of victory."

Mordecai looked intently at her and inwardly admired the ability of youth to believe that the foolish ways of men could possibly be reasonable. Her innocence hid from her the facts that the king's purpose was based on pride and the rash arrogance of his father. Mordecai knew the cost of this extravagant celebration would land on the backs of the working people of the provinces.

"Do you know when he will leave?"

"I only have an idea based on the current celebration that is to go on for another four months. But tonight an invitation to another banquet, only for the citizens of Shushan, has been sent. Our conversation you were trying so desperately to hear while Rachel was talking was about this invitation."

Mordecai noted that Hadassah's face blushed and she lowered her eyes; but curiosity caused her to sit up a bit taller and lean toward him.

He continued. "The men will celebrate in the king's gardens. Another banquet invitation was sent out to the women. It will be held in the palace in the presence of the queen. These banquets will last for seven days, so I can only assume the king will leave sometime shortly after that."

Hadassah's mouth was open in surprise.

"*Dod* . . . everyone is invited? The women, too? Will you attend the king's banquet? Will Uriel, Rachel, Ezra, and Ari and Elizabeth and Joseph and . . . "

"I cannot speak for the other men and women, but I will not be attending. No doubt the king intends to make quite a show of his treasure storehouses, the expansion of his power and majesty, his plan to defeat the Greeks, and of course, his generosity. I have no interest in displays that are for the purpose of promoting a man's pride and giving glory to idols."

Hadassah silently regarded his gentle face and considering her cousin's character and wisdom, she inwardly acknowledged that she should have known his response without asking. He was much too serious to be attracted to such an event. But the palace! A banquet! She fought back the urge to object to his decision.

"Oh, I wonder what a banquet with the queen would be like?"

Hadassah's eyes were closed, her voice suddenly dreamy. But since she had never been in the palace and had only seen it from afar, she couldn't imagine the scene.

"No, Little Myrtle Tree," Mordecai warned. "You do not want to go to one of the queen's banquets. It is not like our *Shabbat* meals, our religious festivals, our wedding celebrations, or the celebrations during one's birth month. These types of banquets are filled with too much wine and too much food, vulgar and immoral behavior. Even the conversations of the women would be inappropriate for one such as you to hear, even if you were old enough to attend."

"Oh, but I would so like to see what the women in the village describe. They tell of wondrous gardens and passageways with beautiful hangings, woven in white, green, and blue threads held by purple and gold cords on silver rings from marble pillars! The village women say that even the banquet goblets and pillowed beds around the tables are made of gold with silver bases supported on red, blue, white and black marble." Hadassah was breathless with the description. Her eyes had a far-away look in them.

Mordecai's eyes closed, but his heart suddenly felt heavy in his chest. He wondered who these idle and gossiping village women were that had put such images into the head of his young, virtuous, and innocent cousin. She had been taught the scriptures. She loved the celebrations of their people and was well-versed in the blessings from El-Tsidkenu (God our Righteousness) to those who kept His law and judgments. The ease of following after the idolatrous and immoral nations was clearly written in the scrolls, and Hadassah and he had shared many conversations about the disastrous results of following after them. To hear her now speaking of the palace, the riches and the celebrations of which she could not imagine, was to him a sad realization. He also knew from the writings of Solomon the foolishness in the heart of young men, and surely of young women, too.

"Perhaps when you are married, you will be able to make your home a palace, *Baht*, if such things are still important to you."

"I love beautiful things, *Dod*, but I love being here with you more. So I will forget about those palace gardens, walls, and banquets. I guess I just get carried away with the imagination of it all sometimes."

"Yes, imaginations will do that! Perhaps you should stay away from those gossiping village women who prattle about the palace goings-on they hear from their daughters who are palace servants."

Hadassah burst into laughter to hear her cousin say that about the women, or anyone for that matter. He was such a wise and just man, and if he said to stay away, well, maybe she would.

"Tonight I will stay far away from them, *Dod*. I will sleep in peace and arise early enough to hear you read from the scrolls that tell us the joy and blessings of Hashem. I am ready for the *Shema*."

They each laid their right hand over their eyes and together prayed the same prayer they offered every night and morning.

> "Shema, Yisrael, Hashem Eloheinu, Hashem echad."
> ("Hear, O Israel, Hashem is our God, Hashem is One.")

Then in undertones, they continued the recitation,

> "Baruk sh'mo kevod malcuto le'olam va'ed."
> "Blessed be the name of the glory of His kingdom forever and ever.
>
> "You shall love Hashem your God with all your heart, with all your soul, and with all your very being. And these words which I command you today shall be upon your heart. You shall teach them thoroughly to your children, and you shall speak of them when you sit in your house and when you walk on the road, when you lie down and when you rise. You shall bind them as a sign upon your hand, and they shall be for a reminder between your eyes. And you shall write them upon the doorposts of your house and upon your gates.
>
> "And it will be, if you will diligently obey My commandments which I enjoin upon you this day, to love Hashem and to serve Him with all your heart and with all your soul, I will give rain for your land at the proper time, the early rain and the late rain, and you will gather in your grain, your wine and your oil. And I will give grass in your fields for your cattle, and you will eat and be sated. Take care lest your heart be lured away, and you turn astray and worship alien gods and bow down to them. For then Hashem's wrath will flare up against you, and He will close the heavens so that there will be no rain and the earth will not yield its produce, and you will swiftly perish from the good land which Hashem gives you. Therefore, place these words of Mine upon your heart and upon your soul, and bind them for a sign on your hand, and they shall be for a reminder between your eyes. You shall teach them to your children, to speak of them when you sit in your house and when you walk on the road, when you lie down and when you rise. And you shall inscribe them on the doorposts of your house and on your gates—so that your days and the days of your children may be prolonged on the land which Hashem swore to your abbas to give to them for as long as the

heavens are above the earth.

"*Hashem Elohim spoke to Moses, saying: 'Speak to the children of Israel and tell them to make for themselves fringes on the corners of their garments throughout their generations, and to attach a thread of blue on the fringe of each corner. They shall be to you as tzitzi, and you shall look upon them and remember all the commandments of Hashem and fulfill them, and you will not follow after your heart and after your eyes by which you go astray—so that you may remember and fulfill all My commandments and be holy to your melek. I am Hashem, your God, who brought you out of the land of Egypt to be your Abba; I, Hashem, am your Abba. True.*"

Hadassah's eyes shone bright with the words. She smiled at Mordecai and with that she kissed him and said, "*Aleicha shalom.*"

To which he replied, "And peace to you, my *Baht.*"

Mordecai's offering of peace to Hadassah was not as powerful as he might have hoped, for once she was in her bed, sleep left her as she pushed out all thoughts of far away war. From her active and vivid mind came images of palaces and golden goblets and women in fine apparel lounging around tables filled with every imagined royal food that an innocent and simple village girl could imagine.

✡

Chapter Four

The Refusal

In the third year of his reign Ahasuerus gave a feast for all his officials and servants. The army of Persia and Media and the nobles and governors of the provinces were before him, while he showed the riches of his royal glory and the splendor and pomp of his greatness for many days, 180 days. And when these days were completed, the king gave for all the people present in Susa the citadel, both great and small, a feast lasting for seven days in the court of the garden of the king's palace. Queen Vashti also gave a feast for the women in the palace that belonged to King Ahasuerus. (Esther 1.3-5, 9 ESV)

As soon as the invitations were received, the normally routine community life around Mordecai and Hadassah was disrupted by the preparation, discussion, and anticipation of the palace banquets. In some quarters disagreements loomed as some men argued against the possibility to use the occasion to defile themselves. Others feared loss of reputation and position if they refused the invitation. A majority of the younger men thought one would be simple-minded to reject such a once-in-a-lifetime opportunity to attend a royal banquet. Many of the women of the village became overwhelmed by the idea of being in the presence of the queen in her finery compared to their simple and modest attire. Suddenly hidden stashes of silver and gold were found and used to purchase rich embroidered fabrics, while daily chores were pushed aside as much as possible for the more important, and certainly more exciting work of designing, sewing, and other womanly concerns.

Sara and Hadassah, as chores would allow, spent much time discussing their own opinions and ideas about the upcoming event. They struggled with the fact of their young age and at times fretted that those who were slightly older would be allowed entrance into the palace. The two also considered and discussed at length Mordecai's warning to Hadassah and wondered how the experience would affect the men and women of their village. Only time would give the answers, so the two were left to their positions of helping the more fortunate prepare for a week of unknown sights, sounds, food and conversations.

—————— הַפְסָקָה ——————

Queen Vashti observed her guests in small huddles discussing ideas, news, and information related to shared interests. The sounds of laughter, polite chatter, and loud eruptions from some of the more boisterous women who made enough noise to draw attention to themselves, filled the room. The positions and occupations of their husbands and sons were the most important topic as egos and vanity grew throughout the week. Some prideful wealthy noble women used obvious tactics to make sure the quieter more modest women were ignored—just to let them know their place and how unimportant they were. The simple village women huddled in awed whispers with nervous giggles and sweaty palms awaiting their turn to converse with the queen. Because of the large number of them, a simple greeting, a few words of introduction, and a polite bow would be all that time would allow. Minds rehearsed, discarded, and reworded an anticipated private meeting with her.

Most of the women were stunned by her beauty and poise even though it was rumored that she was a vain and evil woman. Many of the women in the room knew Vashti had slaves that were *Yehudi*, and they also were aware that she treated them with disdain. Some, if not all of them wondered about her background and how she had come to be the queen of the greatest empire in the world.

However, Vashti was determined that no one in the kingdom would ever know that she was the daughter of King Belshazzar. During his rule, the mobs of Medes and Persians attacked the kingdom and murdered Belshazzar in his bed. Vashti, unknowing of her father's death, rushed to her father's quarters where she was kidnapped by King Darius. No one would ever know that Darius had pity on her, and instead of the sword, gave her to his son Ahasuerus as wife.

Compared to the women in the room who had planned with much effort and detail their own attire for the banquet—and yet were poorly dressed—the queen was the epitome of grace and composure, even dressed in what most would consider quite revealing and most certainly for the purpose of showcasing her most enviable qualities. After seeing her appearance first hand, much of the gossip that had been spread in the village was confirmed. However, in spite of her beauty, charm, and look of refinement, everyone knew she was just one of many wives that Ahasuerus had in his harem, and the idea and mystery of that life made many of them confused, some of them shocked, some of them embarrassed by their thoughts, but all of them undeniably curious.

On the seventh day, when the heart of the king was merry with wine, he commanded Carkas, Mehuman, Biztha, Harbona, Bigtha, Abagtha, and Zethar, the seven eunuchs who served in the presence of King Ahasuerus, to bring Queen Vashti before the king with her royal crown, in order to show the peoples and the princes her beauty, for she was lovely to look at.
(Est 1.10-11 NIV)

Quite a different scene and atmosphere was happening in the garden. Usually a scene of natural beauty and peace with quite a bit of royal grandeur mixed in, it was now a raucous and drunken arena of unrestraint. The king had given the men the approval to drink as much or as little as they desired, which was quite the unusual opportunity for craftsmen, farmers, and shoppe owners who only enjoyed wine with a meal or an occasional celebration in a simpler setting. So by now, on the last day of this banquet of overeating, too much wine, and conversations that had gone from courtesy and politeness to brashness, bragging, and even disputes about positions, wealth, and generational lineage, the contentious conversation arose as to which man had the most beautiful and desirable wife.

An especially loud and unruly group of younger and recently married men were arguing with some other very inebriated older men. The dark trained eyes of the squadron of Immortals that encircled the men were watching every move, ready in a moment to drag the offenders out. Even over the din, laughter—and occasional vomiting—the boisterous argument drew the attention of King Ahasuerus, his royal regents, satraps, and personal attendants. The men were loudly proclaiming explicit and vulgar comparisons on their brides' and wives' beauty and bodies, and each man's outrageous comparison was designed to overshadow the previous man's description. This unseemly and inappropriate drunken display dismayed and even embarrassed some of the more reserved men in the room, but still proved to provide amusement to most. In minutes the atmosphere was more like a sports arena than a royal banquet, even a raucous one.

Not to be outdone, Ahasuerus signaled to Zethar, one of his seven eunuchs, to quieten the roar. Once he could be heard, the king staggered to his feet, raised his goblet and announced, "I, Ahasuerus, King of the Persian and Median Empire have the most beautiful wife in the world. Her beauty is greater than that of any woman alive—now or ever!"

Stupidly, a loud but invisible challenger shouted, "Prove it!"

Whistles, laughter, and more challenges arose with the foolhardy courage that only comes from the result of too much wine, extended celebrating, and a loosening of the tongue. A nearby Immortal grabbed the fellow by the scruff of the neck and held him with his feet off the floor while he struggled to breathe. Finally, Farzad, the squadron leader, gave the signal to let him down. After all, there were many more in his same appalling condition.

Vice-Regent Memucan leaned over to Ahasuerus and quietly whispered.

"King Ahasuerus, do not let this debate go any further. Send your eunuchs into the palace and have them bring the queen to the garden so the men may see her beauty that is beyond any they have ever seen. Already you have displayed your wealth, palace, grounds, and throne to be the most glorious. Now display to these peasants—that dare to speak of the common women of the village—what a royal treasure you own in Queen Vashti."

Before Ahasuerus collapsed back onto his throne, his clouded mind received the message from Memucan, so he held up his staff and loudly declared to his eunuchs.

"Carkas, Mehuman, Biztha, Harbona, Bigthana, Abagtha, and Zethar go into the palace to the royal ball room and command Queen Vashti to present herself to me in the audience of my people of Shushan. Tell her to come prepared to prove to these present that she is more beautiful and desirable than any these poor, deprived men have ever seen. Farzad, you and your men attend the eunuchs!"

A sudden, unexpected quiet settled over the room as Farzad and six of his men snapped from their positions and followed the seven eunuchs. When the squadron and the eunuchs reached the archway to exit the garden, a deafening roar of cheers erupted.

"Bring more wine!" roared Ahasuerus.

Immediately, servants with urns and pitchers of wine began filling the goblets of the cheering, drunken men.

Snide and vulgar comments and suggestions floated among the crowd, but only loud enough for those in close range to hear—which would have resulted in their heads being removed if said loud enough to be heard by the king. They could not believe that the woman whose very name meant "beautiful" would soon make her appearance. The more

THE REFUSAL

respectable among the crowd stood stunned, but they remained curious enough to see how it would all play out.

Standing by the king, Memucan silently congratulated himself for his achievement. Queen Vashti had often ignored and belittled him. Once she even requested that he leave the king's presence when she entered. This was just the kind of opportunity for which he had waited, and he smiled with satisfaction at the simple villagers who had unknowingly provided it.

But Queen Vashti refused to come at the king's command delivered by the eunuchs. At this the king became enraged, and his anger burned within him. (Est 1.12 ESV)

Inside the palace, the double doors to the queen's banquet room were abruptly thrown open. The harsh sound of the guards marching on marble floors brought the women in the room to a hushed and startled quiet. Close on the heels of the seven burly Immortals were the king's seven personal attending eunuchs. Bringing up the rear, the queen's eunuch waddled, red-faced and fearful that he would face harsh words, and maybe even punishment since he had been unable to keep these unexpected "guests" from entering. Many of the women scrambled for veils and coverings that had been discarded in the privacy to which they were accustomed. Other more brazen women in the crowd, tried desperately to catch the eyes of the king's guards with the intention of some idle, flirtatious behavior.

Vashti's eyes flashed with indignation at the interruption as the men quickly took their positions before the platform of her throne. The eunuchs stood in two rows of three with Carkas and Farzad positioned in front as the spokesmen. The guards were behind the eunuchs in the same formation standing in full military attention.

She stood to her full, elegant height to look with disdain upon the intruders. The reputation of the Immortals did not matter to her, nor did the position of the eunuchs. She fully believed she held power over their lives.

"Explain yourselves! Carkas! Farzad! What is the meaning of this? What do you mean by coming into my banquet uninvited?"

Carkas, who appeared completely unfazed by her demeanor, bowed, straightened to his full height, then began in an unmodulated, slightly nasal, loud voice.

"We are here by the king's orders, My Queen. You are commanded to put on your royal crown and come to the palace garden."

The queen rolled her eyes to meet the eyes of the guardsmen and noted there was an air of satisfaction and swagger in their demeanors. *They are enjoying this! Memucan!* she thought. *He is the one that put Ahasuerus up to this ridiculous command.* Vashti gritted her teeth at the thought and had visions of him on a gallows impaled by a spear pushed through him from the bottom of his torso to the back of his head. She took particular note that Carkas said she was instructed to wear her crown. She understood that Ahasuerus intended that the crown was all she was to wear.

Queen Vashti irately noted the nonchalant attitude of the eunuchs regarding the command. Knowing by now all the king's guests in the garden would be quite drunk and unruly, the idea of going into the garden to be ogled—and with no covering at all—was completely out of the question. No woman with any self respect would want men, especially drunk men, leering at her. She was in disbelief that King Ahasuerus would command her to do this.

"I will not!" she exclaimed. "The very idea is outrageous!"

The women in the room quietly gasped behind their veils, and with wide-eyed admiration mixed with the shock of understanding the request wondered at the queen's brave, if not reckless refusal. This was not something they had ever expected to witness.

The seven eunuchs took the news without emotion; they were simply delivering a message. But perhaps even more shocked than the women were the seven guardsmen who suddenly felt some of their previous bravado begin to wan. Facing an army intent on ending lives was easy, but they began to realize they were no match in a battle with Queen Vashti.

Suddenly unsure how to proceed, Vashti noted that Carkas was satisfied with her refusal. However, the squadron leader Farzad questioned the refusal in a calm and reasonable tone.

"Do you mean you are refusing a royal command, My Queen?"

With complete disregard for possible consequences, she blasted, "Absolutely, Farzad! I will not shame myself by going into a room with drunken men to parade myself. I am shocked that my husband would ask that of me! That would put me on the level of a harem woman or worse. It is certainly not appropriate or acceptable for a queen! I won't do it! Now get out!"

For a brief moment Farzad considered warning her, but since she held power greater than his, and since she had dared to use such a disrespectful tone with him, an Immortal leader, he dismissed the idea. *I'm*

THE REFUSAL

just a messenger, he thought.

As Carkas and the eunuchs filed out of the room, the guards followed in a much different manner than they had entered. The women silently arranged their positions to form an aisle. As each Immortal passed through, they could look in the faces of men who for the first time had been given a refusal to a command, and that by a woman. The women were already forming a conversation they would deliver and repeat often to their husbands, sons, and other male relatives of what they had just witnessed. However, they also had a clear foreboding that the scenario was not over. As soon as the men were gone and the doors shut again, the women gathered around their queen in stunned, silent admiration and awe.

As Farzad shut the doors of the queen's banquet room, he looked at each of the eunuchs in silence. Mehuman, Biztha, Harbona, Bigthana and Abagtha, Carkas and Zethar noted the beads of perspiration on Farzad's forehead and lost hope that he would deliver the message to Ahasuerus.

The guardsmen were mumbling in disbelief and shock.

Finally, Farzad spoke. "We have a message to deliver. Form up!"

Without orally responding, the six guards positioned themselves into two rows of three behind him and proceeded toward the garden with straight backs, eyes forward, with the eunuchs in tow. There was definitely a less than enthusiastic desire to return to the garden.

In every man's mind questions raged and jawlines hardened as the men considered the king's response.

How will he react? What will he do? Why did Memucan suggest this? Was he deliberately trying to get us killed? Did he know what she would do?

With obedient, yet somewhat uneasy anticipation, the guards continued grim-faced in proper military fashion, the clip of their heels keeping pace with their heartbeats. The eunuchs walked silently behind them, each one still in disgust and shock because the queen had refused their king's command. They knew the message to be delivered could result in a turn for the worst. One thing they all knew, they must not show it in their countenances.

> "Therefore, if it pleases the king, let him issue a royal decree and let it be written in the laws of Persia and Media, which cannot be repealed, that Vashti is never again to enter the presence of King Xerxes. Also let the king give her royal position to someone else who is better than she. (Esther 1.19 NIV)

As they entered the garden, the deafening sound of the guests' debating and their drunken laughter suddenly stopped, replaced by a tense anticipation. Every head turned, every eye searched for the prize that was not present.

King Ahasuerus put his goblet down. He turned to watch as the guards took their posts again and the seven eunuchs approached.

Then with the ease of a man who had never been denied, he asked, "Well, Carkas, where is she?"

Six stoned-faced men held their breaths. Each one could sympathize with Carkas' hesitation, yet each of them hoped he would respond quickly and get the matter ended.

Ahasuerus glared at the eunuchs who stood stone straight with shoulders squared, and eyes locked on some point just above the king's head to avoid the king's icy stare. They knew what was coming, so they braced for it.

"She isn't coming, Sire."

Carkas spoke in a lowered voice with the hope that only the king, that grinning Memucan, and a few of the closest regents would hear. The silence in the room was now deafening. The mood was tense with curiosity. Every ear was strained to hear the report.

And every ear in the room clearly heard the king's response.

"What do you mean, she isn't coming, Fool!"

The ease and slackness of Ahasuerus' face was instantly replaced by dark, scowling lines; his blood-shot eyes turned black with anger.

"Is she ill? Is she dead? Explain yourself!"

A murmur from the crowd was evident of their attention.

"Sire, a moment alone perhaps?" Carkas' quiet tone was politely strong, but compelling.

To Carkas' relief, the king nodded his head and made an unfruitful wave toward the guests to resume their gaiety. Carkas, the other six eunuchs, and Memucan formed a tight wall between the king and the guests so only they would hear Carkas' message.

Still in hushed tones, Carkas reported.

"Sire, she refuses. She said it was humiliating. She said you were treating her like a harem woman or worse."

Strangely, Ahasuerus had a quick jerk in his neck that resulted in a reaction much the way one might respond to a quick slap. Then in sequence his jaw hardened, his lips tightened, his eyes narrowed, and his nostrils flared.

At the same time, Memucan gave a sudden quiet gasp followed by a small cough to cover the reaction, then cleared his throat and spoke as though abashed.

"Ah-hem. My pardon, King. Forgive me."

On the inside Memucan was jumping up and down like a dog greeting his master. He struggled lest his face reveal his thoughts.

The wench refused! I can't believe it! The gods be praised! The arrogant wench refused a command!

With steely calm and with a voice that reminded the eunuchs of snow on frozen mountains, Ahasuerus finally spoke.

"She said that?" He clenched his jaw. "Get back to your duties!"

To which the seven eunuchs, as quietly and as quickly as possible, retreated. The whispers among the guests were heavy with confusion.

Sitting near the king were Memucan, Carshena, Shethar, Admatha, Tarshish, Meres, and Marsena, the seven princes of Persia and Media that advised the king, wrote the laws, and saw that they were dispersed.

King Ahasuerus with his eyes still in narrow slits, and surprisingly more sober, turned and spoke to them through his clenched teeth.

"What is the law concerning a queen that will not obey the command of the king?"

The seven men rolled their eyes at each other, their heads not turning, not quite sure what to say.

Finally, Shethar, the eldest among the regents answered flatly and with authority.

"Sire, never has a queen disobeyed a king; only a woman desiring to be severely beaten would even dare to disobey her husband."

As vice-regent and the schemer behind the current dilemma, Memucan in what seemed to him a stroke of genius, leaned forward and spoke only loud enough for the king and his other six princes to hear.

"My King! The queen has not only wronged you! She has wronged all the princes, and all the people in every province of your empire! Everyone will surely report this! Especially the women! They will be emboldened to despise their husbands when this is known! Those with her in the palace witnessed the chamberlains delivering your command and heard her refusal! Now our wives and all the women of Persia will say the same to us! It will spread every where! This will cause much contempt and wrath among the women and their husbands."

Ahasuerus lost all control in that moment. His bellicose response echoed and bounced against the marble columns and even the beautiful woven hangings could not diminish the volume of his outrage.

"You . . . ! You fool! You advised me to do this and now you dare to suggest that my kingdom will regard me as weak or despised? I'll hang you for this! I'll be the joke of my whole empire! She has disgraced me and has planted the seed to destroy my kingdom! I cannot let these men or women leave the palace until something has been done to divert this disastrous result! Advise me, Fool! Give me the solution so I may save face before the palace and the empire, and before this rebellious woman's refusal is spread abroad!"

At this outburst, most of the men in the garden set goblets down and lost the mind to make any word or noise. Heads were about to roll and not one of them dared at that moment to draw attention to himself.

"I have a plan, Sire," Memucan said confidently and hoping inwardly that it would be received.

He continued to present his ill advice to be rid of Vashti in a tone and volume so that every ear could hear. This was his moment to save the king.

"We must not allow this deed to go unpunished. If it pleases the king, let a royal commandment be made and written into the law of the Persians and Medes so it cannot be changed. Decree that Vashti may not come before King Ahasuerus ever again. Therefore, her royal estate and all that is hers by her position will be given to another that is better than she. Be rid of her, Sire, and every man will applaud you, and every woman will fear to disobey her husband."

Ahasuerus' head tottered as he contemplated the plan. *He would show her. He would show all the women in the empire of the great King Ahasuerus that a king, a husband, a man must be obeyed!*

Memucan saw the king's face relax, a sign that anger was subsiding and resolution was setting in.

When Memucan realized that in the king's present drunken state, he may not remember any of these events in the morning, he continued.

"And when the decree is written, it shall be published by written decree and delivered to every province throughout all the empire. Then all the wives will give their husbands honor, both the great and the small."

The king now bleary-eyed and desperate for sleep looked into the faces of his seven princes. He looked into the faces of the now waiting, silent guests. Each prince nodded with approval, relief, and satisfaction. The men in the room saw it too, and waited for the outcome.

"Excellent, Memucan," Ahasuerus slurred loud enough for all to hear. "I knew I could count on you. I so decree. Let it be done, and the sooner the better. Start by announcing it here and now in the palace garden before my guests; and announce it in the royal palace before the women, as well!"

But in the garden no announcement was necessary, for the crowd broke out into a cheer, clapping, and slapping each other on the backs and chanting.

"King Ahasuerus! King Ahasuerus! God of the Medes and Persians!"

Memucan felt the swell of satisfaction and pride that he was finally to be rid of the vile-tempered, beautiful but arrogant queen. He marched through the cheering crowd of men while also noting their faces of admiration. He signaled for Farzad and his five men to follow. When they reached the palace entrance, Farzad opened his mouth to ask the question in every man's mind, but Memucan spoke first.

"Farzad, you and your men are ordered to attend me to the queen's banquet. I have a message to deliver."

Of course, King Ahasuerus had not ordered Memucan to deliver the message, but never one to lose an opportunity to put a woman in her place—especially one ranked above himself, Memucan led the six guardsmen to the banquet room to deliver a message and witness what he knew would be a demoralizing and humiliating scene. And he couldn't wait to get there.

———————הפסקה———————

That evening in every village home, and especially in the *Yehudim* quarters, the events of the final day of the king's banquet were discussed. The women who had been in the banquet with Vashti were crushed and sorrowful that their beautiful and courageous queen with such modesty and grace was so rudely and cruelly treated. Her gracious invitation to the palace was an event they would never forget; nor would they ever forget the results of the king's command.

The men who attended the king's banquet—those who in their drunken condition had ignited the fire that led to the banishment of a woman of strong character and obvious modesty—were somehow quiet and reserved that evening. Perhaps it was due to the severe headaches, or the distress and upset in their stomachs. Maybe it was some guilty, conscious awareness of what had been done to a woman who instead of being honored was the object of the most shameful and disrespectful behavior.

Hadassah lay in her little room with eyes wide open, her temples and cheeks wet with tears. Even with all of Mordecai's efforts to keep the gossip and tales from her, Hadassah had heard enough to know that some of the men in their *Yehudim* quarters had participated in—or witnessed—events that dishonored the queen, and by their behavior, dishonored *Melek*, their *King*. Mordecai did not have to remind her of his warning that such events and celebrations were not times of beauty and joy, but rather times when men became fools, and often came away hurt or even destroyed. When she had asked him about the wisdom of what Ahasuerus had done, Mordecai replied that even kings could be unreasonable and wrong. She came to realize that the king was a man of pride and haste, and yes, capable of unreasonable actions. She reasoned that perhaps this was due to ill advice.

Hadassah closed her eyes, not to sleep but to say a prayer of thanksgiving to El-Mitkadesh (God our Sanctifier) that she was not present to witness such revelry. In confidence and assurance of her lineage as a humble but royal maiden from the line of King Saul, she determined in her heart she would live her life as a queen of Hashem.

"I will honor you, My *Abba* and *Melek*. I will worship only You and live as a blessed and reverent daughter of Avraham, Yitzchak, and Ya'acov," she whispered.

With that, Hadassah, wiped away her tears, closed her eyes and slept in peace.

———————— הפסָקה ————————

After the hangover while still feeling the need to kill someone, the king confirmed his plans to assemble the Immortals to invade Greece. Confident that the proposed letters concerning Vashti's rebellion were being written in the language of each of the 127 provinces, he made the command for the royal messengers to deliver the letters throughout the empire. The regents had worded the decree to make sure all man in every province were granted by royal command to rule in his own house.

With a detached satisfaction that Vashti had been properly punished, imprisoned, stripped of her position and possessions, and his reputation saved, King Ahasuerus determined that in one week he and his capable, heavily armed Ten Thousand Immortals of cavalry, navy, and infantry would take Greece and burn Athens. His foreign sources had reported that only one-tenth of the Greeks would face his forces. Most of the Greeks had declared themselves neutral or had already surrendered to him.

Let the Athenians and Spartans meet me! My forces will conquer them, burn Athens, and wipe them out!

✡

Chapter Five

Dark Days

Pride goeth before destruction, and an haughty spirit before a fall. (Pro 16.18 KJV)

The day was dark with clouds as Hadassah left the market and headed home. She was certain her own dark mood was the reason for the weather. With Sara married and busy in her new home with Nathan—"Naa-tha-a-a-n," she said with a wagging of her head—Hadassah felt lonely and forsaken. She had other friends and some distant cousins, but none like Sara. She and Sara finished each other's sentences, enjoyed the same things, and before Nathan had taken her off to be his wife, they had been practically inseparable. A smile, although one could say a sad smile—if there is such a thing—formed on her lips.

She remembered the wedding. Everything seemed to be going wrong the three weeks before the long planned, long-awaited event. A sickness came into their village and for a week it looked as though the wedding would have to be postponed. When Sara succumbed to the sickness, she lost so much weight her dress was suddenly too big. Her *eema* was in a flurry to alter it to fit her slender body again. Before that, the rains did not come for two weeks and all the flowers were dying—flowers that were to create archways, decorate the tables, and go onto Sara's veil and in her hair. Ezra, who had been working frantically to create new goblets for the wedding, cut his hand on the tool that he used to divide the clay, and he would not be able to work until it healed. The final straw was when word was sent to the family that the price of wine had increased due to the drought, and suddenly the wedding budget was strained.

When the anticipated day dawned, however, the wedding party was a huge success despite the obstacles. All of the guests and the wedding party were recovered from the sickness. The experienced gardeners had saved enough flowers to make the square beautiful and filled with fragrance. Hadassah and Mordecai paid the caterer as their private, anonymous gift to the couple. To add blessing to the couple's home, Hadassah had purchased the *mezuzah* to be placed on the door's frame. Inside the *mezuzah* she placed Mordecai's beautifully scripted copy of the *Shema*. Sara's dress fit her again, and Uriel ben-Abram came out of retirement to finish Ezra's goblets in time for the wedding meal. Rabbi Joseph ben-Gideon, the *hazan*, later said Hashem had started the couple off with difficulties so their patient and steadfast faith in Hashem Elohim could be manifested.

Two weeks later Hadassah went to see Sara in her new house that Nathan and Daniel, Sara's abba, had built. Since Nathan was from a large family of twelve, he and Daniel had been blessed by many hands to help build the home he and Sara now owned.

After Sara welcomed her best friend, or more, her *achot*, she proudly showed her each piece of furniture in the home also made by Nathan and Daniel. Sara made the home her own by using the many gifts from the women in the village. With her typical gratitude and humility, Sara pointed out the multi-colored woven rugs, the beautiful vases, soft velvet cushions, skillfully woven wall hangings; each item was a treasure. Since Sara was also from a big family with eight children, she was more than capable in the kitchen that was well stocked with supplies for the new couple. Her home was not only a display of Sara's taste, but it also showed just how much she and Nathan were loved by all who knew them.

Before she left, Sara invited Hadassah outside to the plot of land behind the house they were preparing for grape vines, a vegetable garden, a large flower bed, and an outside area for entertaining. All of it was evidence that Nathan was not only a carpenter, but he also had an eye for design and a knowledge for gardening.

As she slowly walked alone deep in thought toward Mordecai's and her home, Hadassah realized how very blessed Sara was. She could not deny that Nathan was a good man and a hard worker, although she was still unhappy that now Sara belonged to someone besides her. Daniel had spent fourteen years teaching Nathan carpentry and structure, and he had proven to be an eager and gifted learner. Additionally, Hadassah was sure Nathan loved Sara; she was not a wife just by parental contract, she was his beloved.

Hadassah, one year younger than Sara, prayed each day that El Jireh (God our provider) would bless her with a husband and a home of her own. She secretly hoped it would be a large home so Mordecai could live with her. He was a faithful, loving, and righteous man, and she could not imagine living without him.

Right after Sara and Nathan married, Hadassah finally told Mordecai of her lack of desire to be wed to Ezra. Mordecai took the news better than she expected. She suspected her confession was not news to him.

For Sara's wedding, Daniel and Anna, Sara's parents, had invited Mordecai's relatives who lived outside of Shushan. This gave Hadassah the opportunity to meet cousins she had never seen. During the week long wedding celebration with dancing, singing, wine and eating, she was given an opportunity to see them, and once she did, she had to admit she had come from some healthy and well-formed stock.

Any guilt she may have felt about wanting to break her betrothal to Ezra was relieved when Mordecai informed her that Ezra had his eye toward one of her cousins. When Ezra saw Hadassah's dark and beautiful cousin Ruth at the wedding, it was obvious that Ezra was completely smitten. During the week Ruth was in Shushan, Hadassah saw her often inspecting pottery in Ezra's shop, however, she never bought anything. Before her family returned to their village south of Shushan, Uriel met with Mishael, Ruth's *abba* and the marriage contract was made. There would soon be another wedding.

When she entered the house and called to him, she found Mordecai in the kitchen. He appeared to be uneasy about something.

"*Dod*, what's the matter? Is something wrong?"

"Nothing wrong here, *Baht*, but news has arrived by messenger from the army. Ahasuerus' forces made their way to Hellespont, which is a narrow body of water that must be crossed to reach the East and Greece. The report received at the palace today is that after Ahasuerus ordered his men to build a bridge across the waters, a storm followed and shattered the bridges."

"That must have been a terrible storm!"

"It may have been a bad storm, but it is said that the first bridge was very weak and poorly constructed. That storm was not as terrible as what Ahasuerus did! He beheaded all the men who designed and built the bridge, then ordered his soldiers to whip the waters three hundred lashes. After that, they threw red-hot shackles into the waters to punish and enslave them."

Hadassah's mouth dropped open.

"He beheaded them? All of them?"

Mordecai nodded gravely.

"But *Dod*, He enslaved waters? Whipped waters? Three hundred lashes ... *on water?*"

Even in her shock at the king's behavior, Hadassah suddenly struggled to restrain her desire to laugh that one could be so foolish.

"But *Dod*, water cannot be punished or whipped or enslaved! It is water!"

"Oh, I know, *Baht*, but that just shows the character of a man who sees himself as a god. He has forgotten he is a man. His cruelty to his men and his arrogance against nature shows a man unable to control his temper."

Mordecai continued.

"The men finally were able to build a bridge that would withstand horses and men, so they could cross over. The messenger reported they had a victory over the Greek states at Thermopylae, so they torched Athens, and overrun most of Greece."

"Oh, no! Those poor people!"

"Do not fret! The Athenians were prepared and wisely had vacated the entire city."

"Oh, it all still sounds just awful."

Hadassah shook her head with her eyes closed tightly to block out the mental images.

"Shall I continue, Hadassah? Shall I not tell you the rest?"

"You must tell me, *Dod*. I have to know."

"After the destruction of Athens, the king's navy suffered a severe defeat in Salamis. For the second time, the Greeks out-maneuvered the Immortals by catching them in a strait and destroying most of the naval fleet. The king has decided to turn the fight over to Mardonius, so he can return to his summer palace here in Shushan. He is tired of war."

"*Dod*, isn't Mardonius the husband of Artozostra, the sister of King Ahasuerus?"

"Yes. So now his sister's husband is in charge of the army. May El Gibor (the Mighty God) provide safety to His people in Shushan and keep the war far from us. The king's arrival will not be a joyous homecoming."

Mordecai rubbed his eyes and let out a deep sigh.

"Ah, *Dod*! A man with his pride will surely take the defeat harder than another."

Hadassah's face showed the horror of the news. All of Shushan had been convinced the army was well-equipped, under the best leadership, so victory had been assured. To hear a report of loss and humiliation for their arrogant and rash king was not only shocking, but it had an air of doom in it.

"Yes, I fear his pride will precede a great defeat," Mordecai wearily sighed again.

"All of Shushan is stunned. It has been a long three and a half years since the big celebration at the palace. There will not be a celebration when he returns in a few months. A deep sadness and quiet hangs over the palace like a dark cloud."

Hadassah considered her own spirit's depression as she put away market items. For dinner she made a salad with large fresh olives, sweet mandarin oranges, juicy plump grapes, crisp apples, black raisins, and the mixed, freshly picked leafy greens. The delicious salad tossed with spices, wine and olive oil took care of her hunger, but the darkness in her spirit went even deeper with the news from Mordecai.

After they prayed the *Shema* together, Hadassah retreated to her small bedroom. As she lay on the smooth cool linens, and stared at the ceiling, she wondered in her heart about the result of the defeat and continued war in faraway Greece and what it might mean for the people of the Shushan province and possibly the entire empire of the Persians.

✡

Chapter Six

The Plan

Some time later, when King Ahasuerus's rage had cooled down, he remembered Vashti, what she had done, and what was decided against her. (Est 2.1 CSB)

The summer palace had a blanket of heat, gloom and stifling quiet over it. King Ahasuerus hid himself in his house and took to demanding more wine than usual, often to the point that he left off eating and instead slept too much. Those serving his needs slipped quietly in and out of his presence serving with meticulous care and dread to avoid the verbal bashing and threats. His royal attendants and vice-regents suddenly found there was much to do in the gardens, villages, and furthermost parts of the province.

Queen Mother Atossa had arrived from Babylon soon after her son returned from Greece. She was well-acquainted with the impact and lasting effects of a loss in war. However, rather than soothe her son, she soon realized he was in no mood for her efforts. In fact, on some of her attempts to see him, he refused to open the door. She decided that while she was in Shushan she would resume her previous position over the harem. She had noted the eunuchs' slackness of control and determined that she would soon have things whipped back into proper shape.

After three weeks of his dreadful mood and the subsequent atmosphere, Ahasuerus summoned Memucan. When he received word to appear, Memucan took a deep breath, smoothed his hair, set his jaw, and proceeded to meet the king. Silent and shaded eyes followed Memucan through the hollow halls, down the stairs, up the stairs, across breezeways, through the garden and finally toward the king's house where Ahasuerus had hibernated since returning from Greece.

Outside the gilded double doors, the door keepers Bigthana and newly promoted Teresh, solemnly watched Memucan approach. Without a word or expression, they opened the doors to give him admittance, grateful they were not going in with him.

"O King. You called for me?"

Memucan tried to make his voice and countenance assured and easy. "You know I did. Else you would not be here."

Ahasuerus' voice was cold and sarcastic, his words slightly slurred. His look was disheveled, and Memucan wondered if the king had the power to kill with a stare. His knees suddenly felt weak, and the assurance he was faking suddenly seemed pointless.

"My King, what service do you need of me?"

The voice was calm, but the heart was pounding and suddenly the room became too warm. A rumble from his stomach caused the king to snort.

"What do I need? What do I need?"

The volume increased and the two doormen standing at attention outside the door cast knowing glances at each other.

"I'll tell you what I need, Fool! I need Vashti! I need to see her face! I need to hear her voice! I need her to ease me in my darkness! What have you done to me?"

"But, Sire, . . . you have a harem full of women . . . of all . . ." Memucan backed up as Ahasuerus rose from his couch and leaned forward.

"I don't want another woman or concubine, or any woman from the harem. I have sent for the best of them and none are as beautiful, as intelligent, as . . . comforting. I want the most beautiful woman in the empire. The one you persuaded me to banish. The beloved wife you and the regents forbade to come back into my presence. I want her!"

He glared at Memucan with blood-shot eyes.

"It's the law, Sire. It cannot be changed . . . to change the law would make the king . . ."

"Make me what? Fallible? Weak? Look at me! I am shamed by the war. My army is shamed. The bodies of the Persian dead are on the hills of Greece. I am alone and I need Vashti! She would know what to say. She would know how to ease my mind, my spirit, my body."

Ahasuerus sat—no, fell back onto the couch.

"My King, there is a solution. Vashti cannot return, but I know what to do."

Ahasuerus rolled his black eyes to Memucan's face; his mouth a twisted scorn of disgust and hatred.

"What do you know?"

"Your empire is vast. You have been gone for four years while young, beautiful girls of Shushan and your vast kingdom have matured. Shushan alone is full of virgins. Beautiful, pure, delicate virgins. Perhaps another Vashti is right here!"

One eyebrow rose on the king's forehead as he looked at his vice-regent. "What is your plan? Tell me speedily."

"You must order your most trusted men to go through the villages and select the most beautiful, unblemished virgins. They will bring them here, we will put them in perfumed baths, and use scented and softening oils for their purification. We will dress them in the finest attire the empire has to offer. Then one by one they will come to you, one each night for you to choose the best, the most beautiful, most desirable to be your queen. If none of them are satisfactory nor can equal Vashti, we will expand our search until we find just the right one to become your queen."

Silence was heavy; the king was motionless. He remembered that Darius had often had men to collect maidens for the harem and for his pleasure; but when Darius had brought Vashti from Babylon to be his wife, Ahasuerus had not used his power to bring more maids into the palace. When he needed another woman, the harem had plenty of them. *This is one arena in which I am sure I can successfully conquer,* he thought.

Memucan noted that the king's eyes were closed and he wondered if the king had fallen asleep, or perhaps entered the gates of the dead. A sudden upturn of his chin showed sudden alertness.

"Yes, Vashti be hanged! She is not the only beautiful woman in the world. Your plan Memucan . . . how long will this take?"

Memucan realized anew that the king was not a patient man, and he had already made it clear that he needed a replacement here and now. But Memucan also knew that what he was suggesting was not a here-and-now plan. Just the purification process would require a year.

"Sire . . . ," his voice had a slightly pleading tone to it, so he cleared his throat and tried again.

"Ah-hem, . . . Sire, it will take some time. I can choose the men most qualified and dispatch them immediately to begin the gathering of the young women and girls, but the training and purification of them will take some time."

He watched Ahasuerus' face anxiously. "These women will need to receive instruction on living as a queen, and they will need myrrh, oils and perfumed baths which will take time."

"I want only the best. I want only the most beautiful; and I mean from head to toe. I want the smoothest, softest, clearest skin, the most perfect shape of body, the clearest eyes, straightest nose, fullest mouth, and the voice . . . it must not be the voice of a crying goat or the cackling of a hen . . . but musical, soft and melodious. The hair must be thick and soft, the teeth straight, white and none missing or crooked. As they come in, compare them to the statue of Vashti. They must not be less. Can you find that? In all my empire, does one like that exist?"

The last two sentences rose until Ahasuerus was practically yelling as a man in desperation.

For just the slightest moment Memucan felt that his answer may be his death sentence, so he swallowed hard and pushed out every doubt and confidently answered.

"Of a certainty, Sire. One and many more. Your most difficult decision will be to choose between so many. Our eunuchs will be instructed to teach them in the ways to please you, and the women will comply with desire and enthusiasm at the thought of becoming Queen of the Persian and Median Empire."

"For that I will wait. I will reacquaint myself with those of the harem until then; and with the anticipation of my Queen, I will wait. Make it happen, Memucan, and don't disappoint me or I'll have your head."

"Yes, My King."

And with that bold promise, Memucan forced himself to walk toward the doors displaying great assurance in his body language that he was able to produce what he had promised. However, once outside the doors, he exhaled all the air in his puffed up ego and wobbled down the hall as the two eunuchs Bigthana and Teresh watched in curiosity as to what the muffled voices behind the door had been about and what assignment Memucan had been given.

✡

Chapter Seven

The Collection

> *And let the king appoint officers in all the provinces of his kingdom, that they may gather together all the fair young virgins unto Shushan the palace, to the house of the women, unto the custody of Hegai the king's chamberlain, keeper of the women; and let their things for purification be given them . . . :* (Est 2.3 KJV)

Memucan and Farzad began organizing and preparing the appointed men to find at least four hundred beautiful virgins that would meet the king's requirements. With the statue of Vashti as their visual for comparison, the men understood the mission but wondered if it were possible. Commander Farzad took the lead over the troops to instruct them in the procedures for collecting the girls.

"You will take every girl from thirteen to twenty years old. Under no circumstances shall you lay a hand on any one of them with the result of scratches, bruises, cuts, or broken limbs. Take care that you do not take lustful advantage of any of them. You do not know which one may one day be your queen, and if you trespass your duty, you will be made a eunuch or hanged! If it takes two to manage a difficult one, so be it: but watch yourselves. Once you are confident you have every one who is qualified of that age, you will make a preliminary examination of them. If you see defects, missing or broken teeth, growths, scales, or rashes on their exposed skin, leave them in the village. They are not acceptable."

"Sire, how will we determine if they are indeed virgins?" asked one hopeful. "Some of them will greatly desire to go with us, and many of them may lie."

"That is not your responsibility!"

He glared at the fool and wondered if he should be relieved from duty.

"The royal physicians will determine that once they are in the palace. Feel free to inform them, however, that anyone found not to be a virgin will be punished severely. Any questions?"

When no one responded, he asked, "Do you understand me? Are you clear on your instructions?"

"I am," he replied meekly.

One burly man from the assembly asked, "What if they resist us? The younger ones will surely be afraid of us."

Farzad was prepared.

"As to the resistance, if you feel it is needed, you tell them how beautiful they are. You tell them about the life of ease and royalty, the palace beauty, the servants. You tell them their life will be filled with wine and food and beauty."

Farzad saw the reaction of his words on the men who knew full well that what Farzad was describing was not even close to the full story. These men were the relatives of the eunuchs of the harem that the Queen Mother was presently supervising. They knew what harem life was like. The younger girls would be subjected to the tyranny of many of the concubines and wives, and would most likely become the personal slave to one of the wives who held more influence and power over the others. Many would be trained for seductive dancing for the king's entertaining of guests, and others would be trained for helping with chores. Some would have the responsibility of caring for the children. And if they rebelled, or failed to fulfill expectations, they may be sent off to become the wife or slave of a regent or satrap in another province or given as a reward to a guardsman, or worse, killed. These girls would never again go shopping in a market, or tend a garden, or take a walk with a friend. They would never see their families again, and some of them who were pledged to a man for marriage would be taken from him, never to have a home or children. And then there was the Queen Mother. Their life under her would be determined by the competition to win her favor. The men had seen the results of those who did not.

As the men contemplated their duty, one suddenly asked, "What if a father, a man betrothed, or a brother should try to intervene?"

"We have that taken care of," said Farzad firmly. "Any man that interferes with the king's business, will be fined, punished, imprisoned, or hanged. Now prepare yourselves to do your duty."

———————— הַפְסָקָה ————————

With the announcement of the incoming maidens, the news was announced in the harem that Shaashgaz the eunuch would soon become the chamberlain over the concubines since Queen Mother Atossa would be returning to Babylon after her two month visit with her son after he returned from battle.

When the women of the harem heard that she was returning to Babylon, some were suddenly alarmed that she might be taking some of them with her to be reduced to slaves and attendants. Queen Atossa ruled with a harsh hand over her subjects and the idea of having to come back under her control was not good news.

Hegai, a eunuch that served the king and had been assigned to oversee the arrival and training of the maidens, was informed by other eunuchs that the previously used house for captives was in need of repair and updating if young maidens were coming to live in it. Hegai, with Queen Mother Atossa's assistance—and with her sudden decision to delay her departure—were overseeing the work of getting the house cleaned and refurbished. Between the two of them, and after quite a bit of dissension, a decision was made to rename the building The House of the Maidens.

Meanwhile, in The House of the Women, the concubines' quarters, hopes and dreams among them were dashed with the news that virgins were to be collected so Ahasuerus could select one as Vashti's replacement. This news brought relief to the older more settled wives, bitterness to the younger ones, and among those who had borne children of the king, rage and jealously arose like a volcanic mushroom. However, when the women remembered that it would be more than a year before any of the maidens coming in could be presented to the king because of purification rituals, and when they also realized that until that distant time some of them would be called to attend the king, suddenly the opportunity to win the king's affection and desire renewed the hope that one of them might still win the crown.

Once The House of the Maidens was well under way, news arrived from Babylon that Queen Atossa must return as soon as possible. To Hegai's relief, she was soon gone, but not before she promised she would return when the first collection of maidens was completed.

✡

Chapter Eight

The Post

When the king's command and edict became public knowledge and when many young women were gathered at the fortress of Susa under Hegai's supervision, Esther was taken to the palace, into the supervision of Hegai, keeper of the women. (Est 2.8 CSB)

Under the cover of darkness, during the evening of the third day after Memucan's plan was accepted, the order was initiated. Copies were made by the palace scribes. The couriers on horseback began to post the decree written by Memucan in every booth and shoppe and along the entrance gates of the cities. This was all approved by the regents and stamped with the king's royal seal.

"BY THE DECREE OF KING AHASUERUS:

ALL MAIDENS OF THE AGES OF THIRTEEN TO TWENTY OF EXTRAORDINARY BEAUTY, MANNERS, AND OBEDIENCE WILL BE TAKEN TO THE PALACE FOR THE SELECTION OF ONE TO BECOME THE QUEEN AND WIFE OF KING AHASUERUS. ANY RESISTANCE TO THIS DECREE WILL RESULT IN IMPRISONMENT, LOSS OF PROPERTY, FINE OR DEATH."

In the early morning quiet as the sun was warming the day, the sounds of feet on stony ground could be heard. Men were talking among themselves, and some of them were softly singing. Their sons greeted one another; some of them sighing at the thought of another long day. The usual sounds of a normal day were soon quieted as the merchants began to see the post. The men who had arrived to open business windows, raise screens and awnings, and prepare for the business of the day suddenly grew quiet as they read the posted decree and realized their world had suddenly taken an unexpected turn.

Ari, a neighbor and young friend of Mordecai, had started his morning as usual before the dawn with the *Shema*, a light breakfast, and a goodbye kiss on the upturned face of his wife, Mibtahiah. Stepping through the doorway, he placed his finger on the *mezuzah*, kissed his finger, and with an easy pace, headed for the market street. Once there he would open it for business, handling the early morning customers until Mibtahiah arrived with their children to take over the booth. Afterwards, he would attend the noon prayers and the reading from the *Torah* with the men.

Mibtahiah stepped to the doorway.

"We will see you soon in the market! May Adonai bless and keep you!"

After she saw Ari turn and wave, she turned to join her daughters.

"Ladies, let us make the bread for the day!"

Like most of the other shoppe owners' wives, Mibtahiah shared responsibilities in the booth with Ari. Hers included the cleaning, keeping the fruits and vegetables in neat arrangements, determining which items of foods needed to be replenished and those that needed to be removed. Socially, she especially enjoyed getting news from the other wives and from the merchants that traveled from their various markets with goods and news from afar.

Mibtahiah's children stayed with her in the back of the booth where they were learning math, writing, and reading. They were also learning how to apply their skills to make records of the business profits. In the afternoons when Ari returned to resume the booth's business, Mibtahiah would walk her boys to their place of congregate worship to receive teaching by the rabbis on the scriptures and to receive assignments of memorization of prayers and passages from the *Torah*. Later in the afternoon, she and the girls would return home to prepare the evening meal.

When Ari reached his shoppe, the posted message was unknown to him, but it had completely changed the atmosphere, priorities, and routines in the marketplace. Some men had abandoned their booths and rushed home. Others sent word to their wives and daughters. *Yeduhi* owners turned pale, and their mouths suddenly went dry from fear. A sick feeling overcame them as they recalled the captivity and slavery experienced from generations to generation.

Ari found the post nailed to his door. As he read it, his mind resisted the words, and refused to comprehend the message. A muddled confusion swam and clouded his mind. He placed his hand against a post and shook his head hoping to clear his mind of its meaning. As his heart raced, he fought to breathe. His knees weakened, but by now his mind was rushing ahead for thoughts, any thoughts, to somehow stop the words he had read from happening.

"Mordecai! I must go to Mordecai."

THE POST

―――――― הַפְסָקָה ――――――

Mordecai did much of his work as a scribe in his home in a small room lined with shelves containing scrolls, ink and nibs. He was not due to join Uriel and the other elders at the city gates for at least a fortnight. Since he did not need to go into the market that morning, he had started the oven for baking and chosen the scroll for the day's reading. While waiting for Hadassah to join him for the reading and the morning *Shema*, he went outside to gather the hens' eggs.

When Ari reached the door of Mordecai's house, he frantically began calling for him. With no answer from within, he turned his attention to the outer gardens and the coops.

Even before Mordecai saw Ari, he heard him.

"Mordecai!"

As Ari frantically searched the garden, and before he could call out again, he saw Mordecai step out of a coop.

Looking toward the house, Mordecai saw Ari—pale, trembling, and his outer garment ripped down the front. Immediately, Mordecai recognized the all too familiar *Yehudim* sign of mourning. In alarm, Mordecai thought, *Ari's wife Mibtahiah has died! Or maybe one of his children is severely hurt or sick!*

Ari's voice was hoarse; his face was smeared with ashes, and his beard and hair were disheveled.

"Mordecai!"

Ari began sobbing with deep groans as he began to beat his chest with his fist. He fell on his knees and bent his torso forward.

By now Mordecai was completely bewildered, but his compassionate heart immediately knew something was very wrong. He dropped the eggs, rushed to his young friend and held him against himself.

"Ari, what's happened?"

"The decree . . ." he stammered. "The girls! Mordecai! Do you know?"

"What, Ari?" By now Mordecai was feeling the same panic expressed on Ari's face even though he had no idea of the source.

"Please. Come inside, sit down. Let me get you a bit of wine to help you."

"Wine?" he sobbed. "No wine will help, Mordecai! They are going to take our daughters!"

"Who? Who do you mean, Ari?"

Mordecai gripped Ari's shoulders to support him, and wondered in a dizzying moment if indeed the Greeks were invading, killing, and capturing their women and children.

"King Ahasuerus . . . has ordered that . . . our virgins, . . . our young and beautiful maidens . . . be taken to the palace for one of them to be chosen as . . . the new queen!"

His sentence stammered out, ending in a rising cry of anguish.

Mordecai saw Hadassah standing in the doorway. Her eyes were large pools of fear and shock at seeing Ari in his condition. She heard some of what Ari said.

"Hadassah! Go inside! Please! Leave us!"

For a moment Hadassah hesitated and remained with hands frozen in a white-knuckled grip on the door frame. Then wildly looking around the yard and back at the two men, she yanked herself inside and shut the door. Leaning breathlessly against it, her heart filled with fear as her thoughts began wildly spinning in scenes of her last conversation with Mordecai.

Mordecai continued to support his friend as he managed to lead him into the house and seat him.

Ari, through bleary eyes, saw Hadassah standing in the doorway between the main room and hers. At the sight of her, he bowed over in a groan that sent shivers down her spine.

Wild-eyed in fear and confusion, Hadassah searched Mordecai's face with unspoken horror.

Ari fumbled inside his garment and pulled out the crumpled post he had ripped from his door. He handed it to Mordecai with pleading eyes and waited as Mordecai read it.

Hadassah watched as Mordecai's face lost all color. She noted the distinctive sag of his body as if a great weight suddenly fell upon him. He laid his hand on Ari's shoulder and spoke, drawing from some inner source of strength.

"My friend, we must remember El-Sabaoth (The God of Hosts) is the one we call upon when a flood of the enemy comes against us."

Ari's eyes flew to Mordecai's face hoping he had a better answer, an explanation, some reason for this sudden action being taken by the king.

"Mordecai, can we know if this is perhaps the work of Hashem? Perhaps He is bringing judgment upon Shushan for the wickedness, the idolatry, the hatred. Can it be blamed on the sins of Ahasuerus against the villages and cities he has overtaken with his blood-thirsty, power-driven armies?

Is Hashem sending the enemy against us for our own failure to obey Him? Should we have left Shushan when the last captives were allowed? Are we caught up in Hashem's wrath against this arrogant, over-reaching empire to be brought down for its demise!"

Ari's words came in a rush of anguish and ended in uncontrollable sobbing.

Mordecai understood his questions. Every descendent of Avraham knew that when the wrath and punishment of Hashem was sent against the wickedness of a nation, the righteous were caught up in it and suffered, as well.

"Ari, my friend, let us take great caution against believing this evil plan to take our maidens is by the purpose of Hashem as a punishment. Let us trust Him and account this as a vile and immoral plan devised by man. We must put our hope in El-Gibor (the Mighty God) to work for our protection and favor. He is El-Shammah (the God who is present) even now.

"Go home, Ari, to your wife, your two daughters and your sons. Send your sons to gather the other boys of *Yehudim*, and instruct them to call our *achim* to meet. We will call for the elders and men who serve Hashem to unite in prayer and seek the face of Hashem. This is a sudden attack against our children, but we cannot just lose our faith in Hashem Elohim."

Ari, still overcome with shock and grief, pushed himself up from the chair with one hand on the table to balance himself. He searched Mordecai's face with bleary, bloodshot eyes to perhaps draw some strength from him. Then with shoulders rounded, and his head sagging, he walked slowly to the door and turned.

"It will take great faith to meet this, Mordecai, be it from Hashem or from our enemies."

Once Ari was gone, Hadassah rushed into the arms of Mordecai.

"*Dod*! What does this mean? What has happened?"

Mordecai holding her close to his chest, closed his eyes and laid his head on hers. She could feel his heart racing, and noticed his ragged breathing. She reached for his hand to take the post, but he tightened his fist to hold it.

"I will tell you, *Baht*. But you must give me a moment. My thoughts are troubled."

As the two stood silently holding one another, there was the faint sound of wails and even screams coming from the nearby homes. The news was spreading fast. Hadassah raised her eyes to search Mordecai's face and he noted her eyes were even darker in her pale face.

"Please, *Dod*, do not keep me in ignorance any longer. I know it is terrible news. I know Ari said it was against the children. What have we done, *Dod*? Are we to be slaughtered for some offense against the king?"

"No . . . . No, Hadassah. It is not a death threat we are receiving. Please sit. I will read the message again, and this time you will hear it, as well."

Mordecai opened his hand and took the now completely crumpled and wadded post. He spread it out before him on the table, inhaled deeply, and with a steady voice that even surprised himself, he began to read.

───────── הַפְסָקָה ─────────

As the same post that Mordecai was reading to Hadassah was being read in the homes of the Persians, the effect on their population was very different, although just as extreme.

Many of the Persian maidens accepted the news with hopeful, breathless excitement of being taken to the palace. It would mean an escape from the simple life of home, market, and the ordinary existence they lived. In these homes, the daughters were encouraged by the family to accept the news gladly as a wonderful, once-in-a-lifetime opportunity. It was stressed to them, that even if the young maiden was not made the queen, the chance to live in a palace with servants, prepared foods, and luxurious surroundings should become the focus. Also, it was known throughout the community that the families of harem wives and concubines were regularly given gold, food, and other benefits as long as the women fulfilled her duties.

In other Persian homes, daughters had already been promised for marriage by contract. In some cases the marriage was already sealed by exchange of money or land. To keep the betrothed daughter from being released from the contract, it was decided that she simply must no longer be a virgin. When it suddenly became clear to the maid that it was more beneficial for her to be deemed not a virgin, confessions abounded—which under any other circumstance would have brought about severe punishment. Instead, these confessions were received with rejoicing and relief. *Money and lands would be preserved! Thanks be to the gods for a daughter without virtue!*

However, betrothed Persian maidens who had managed to keep themselves free from youthful lust were more unsettled. A vile plan was devised and agreed upon between her parents and her betrothed's parents.

To ensure the king's men would not take her, she simply must no longer be pure. Many of these maidens fled to their private quarters, and fell across beds, or on the floor, or simply stomped their feet and threw items in rage. Suddenly, the elaborate wedding and long-awaited celebration was to be replaced by what previously had been forbidden and shameful. For them, the chance to become the queen was suddenly being ripped away by a planned act of a rushed and unceremonious appointment.

Of course, there were also some betrothed Persian maidens that suddenly felt relieved that promises made by fathers of lazy or quite undesirable sons for other reasons would soon be broken. The very idea of possibly becoming a queen made many of these maidens quite giddy.

———————— הַפְסָקָה ——— ———

After Ari's boys recruited other *Yehudi* boys to help announce the meeting of the *Yehudim*, the crowd was large and the reactions to the post were varied, but all were highly emotional.

The first reaction of the outraged *Yehudi* men was to consider a planned exodus much like their forefathers had done from Egypt. However, while they discussed this idea, it became apparent that Moses was not there to lead them, or to bring forth plagues or angels of death. As the awareness of the imminent action being taken by the royal forces was being discussed and fully realized, the men knew escape without being quickly discovered was an impossibility. There were just too many of them. The idea to select those maidens most likely to be taken and to assist them in leaving Shushan hoping to reach Jerusalem was also declined. They would need royal passage and protection that they just did not have, and because of the decree it would not be given. Of course, there was also the obvious problem: every man thought his daughter the most beautiful, and therefore, she should be among those selected to be sent to Jerusalem.

The betrothed men were horrified at the thought that not only were their betrotheds to be taken, but also the other women who were of marriageable age would be gone. Heads huddled to whisper solutions directed toward attempts to keep their young maidens from becoming concubines who would be hidden away for the rest of their lives. However, the pagan plan to remove virginity was not included in the possible solutions from the *Yehudim* since Hashem had commanded stoning for such unholy unions.

Many times, during the meeting, there were those who raised their voices and made prophetic proclamations of miraculous deliveries to convince the others they were speaking the word of Hashem. The older and wiser elders used their knowledge of the scriptures, and in many instances good sense, to respond to those prophets with warnings against proclaiming words which they called foolish, filled with lies, and blasphemy. When these attempts failed, less devout *Yeduhi* fathers and men raged in anger suggesting the men take up arms to confront the men and defend their daughters.

"And how do you suppose we shop-keepers, shepherds, farmers, potters, and scribes defend our daughters against the Ten Thousand Immortals?" asked one man, who like Ari had ripped open his outer garment and had ashes on his head.

"We cannot! We will all be killed, and then what of our sons and younger daughters, and our wives?" replied a man from the middle of the room.

"There must be something we can do!" cried a young father. "Will we allow our daughters to become concubines, seductive dancers, and possibly even slave women for pagan men to use as prostitutes in their idolatrous worship?"

As Mordecai stood with those he knew and trusted as the most devout among them, he waited for the silence that gradually settled over the men. Eventually, in mute resignation, they finally accepted that the situation was hopeless. In the background and in the silence among the men, the whimpers and softly sobbing women could be heard.

Mordecai pulled out a scroll he had tucked in the belt underneath his ripped robe and carefully unrolled it as bleary-eyed, desperate and exhausted men watched. Then he began to read:

"*Blessed are You, Hashem Elohim, God of the universe.*

"*From the word of Hashem . . .*

'*Go, find where he is,*' *the king ordered,* '*so I can send men and capture him.*'

The report came back: '*He is in Dothan.*'

Then the king sent horses and chariots and a strong force there. They went by night and surrounded the city.

When the servant of the man of God got up and went out early the next morning, an army with horses and chariots had surrounded the city.

'*O, my Lord, what shall we do?*' *the servant asked.*

THE POST

'Don't be afraid,' the prophet answered. 'Those who are with us are more than those who are with them.'

And Elisha prayed, 'O Hashem, open his eyes so he may see.'

Then Hashem opened the servant's eyes, and he looked and saw the hills full of horses and chariots of fire all around Elisha.

As the enemy came down toward him, Elisha prayed to El-Nissi (the God our Banner), 'Strike these people with blindness.'

So, He struck them with blindness, as Elisha had asked."

(2 Kings 6.13-18)

The room was quiet as Mordecai ended his reading. Some of the men closed their eyes as the understanding of the words sank into their spirits. Others frowned and looked around the room in confusion.

"What does that mean? How does that relate to us?" demanded Emmanuel. "Who in this room is Elisha? Are we going to see chariots and horses of fire?"

Mordecai searched the eyes of the men in the room to see if he saw any flash of understanding or humor at the question from the one man in the room whose name meant *God with us*. In many eyes, he only saw complete and utter incomprehension.

"It means, Emmanuel, that Hashem is with us. He tells us not to be afraid. We are surrounded by the horses and chariots of fire even if we can't see them!"

"But that was Elisha, the great prophet, the miracle worker! I don't see how those words should comfort us in this situation."

"Then I pray that Hashem will open your eyes, Emmanuel, so you can see that we are the chosen people of Hashem Elohim. Chosen to be a sign to nations that He is our One True Melek. As was shown to the servant in this scripture from the account in the Chronicles of the Kings, He is El-Shammah (the God who is Present) and His armies surround us."

"So, what? How do we protect ourselves? Are you suggesting we do nothing? That we just pray our eyes are opened—so we can see what? Horses and chariots of fire?"

Emmanuel's tone was bitter and angry.

From someone in the back came the question, "Why must we do anything? Why can't we accept that what the king is doing is a thing that will be pleasing to Hashem?"

When it was realized the questions came from Caleb, murmurs arose among the men like a sound of wind. The sound grew to a thundering storm of yelling out opinions, questions and threats directed toward Caleb and to anyone else that held the idea that their daughters being ripped from their homes was a good idea or the plan of Hashem.

"What do you mean, Caleb?" yelled Ari over the crowd's roar. "Why would our daughters being taken into a pagan palace be pleasing to Hashem? It was Hashem that commanded that we not give our daughters to foreigners who do not worship Him. Has He suddenly changed His mind? Will He suddenly include gentile pagans in His plan?"

Every head turned to Caleb for his answer.

"It's just that some of us are not sure it would be wise to disobey the king. We put our families in danger if we do not submit. The history of our people is filled with sudden and vicious attacks against us! Our women with child, ripped open; our children and youth taken from us into foreign lands to be slaves, thrown into fires, and used for all manner of evil. Do we want that to happen here in Shushan? I say, let the soldiers take the maidens! At least they will be alive, well fed, and educated. And none of us will be killed!"

"You can say that, Caleb! Your daughters will not be taken! They are not beautiful!" announced Jabez with sarcasm.

Some of the men broke out into laughter at the response.

"What Caleb is saying sounds a lot like the report of the spies sent into Canaan by Moses!" said Rabbi Joseph ben-Gideon. "He is saying that Hashem is not strong enough to protect us. He is saying that El-Shaddai (the God sufficient for our needs) is sending judgment and wrath upon us. He is saying we should be glad our maidens are to be taken from us!"

Murmuring agreement arose from some, and others shook their heads in disagreement.

The rabbi continued.

"I encourage all of you to remember . . . those acts of judgment came upon our forefathers when they worshiped idols, offered their children to Moloch, worshipped Baal, and committed gross immorality. Judgment *only* came after Hashem raised up prophets to warn them and to tell them judgment was coming. After all, He is full of mercy and compassion. He is El-Elohe-Yisrael (the God of Israel) who has chosen us as His own."

Mordecai stood solemnly wondering how Hashem could possibly continue to put up with such as were in the room. *Truly, He is Mercy and Compassion,* he thought. He waited until any other outbursts might happen. For the most part, the men were quiet and somber, and heavy sighs and quiet sobbing and groaning seemed to be the only other responses.

"Men, *achim*," Mordecai searched their faces, "the time has come for us to obey the word of Hashem, our *Melek*. Either we can trust that regardless of what is about to happen He will take care of us, or we can choose to respond in ways that clearly show that we have put our trust in Ahasuerus, his strong men, or our own devices.

"As for me, I will return to my home and anoint my daughter with oil, put on sackcloth and ashes and turn to prayer. I will pray and commit into the hands of Hashem Elohim this evil plan the king has decreed for his own pleasure and will. I will pray that instead of what is intended by the plan, the results will be turned to bring glory and salvation to us and will reveal that we are Hashem's people. If Hashem chooses, He can blind the eyes of the captors so that our daughters are not desirable, and thus, will not be taken. Or perhaps He will cause them to find fault in our daughters so that they will be rejected.

"With my trust in Hashem I am sorrowful concerning this decree, but I am confident, and yes, expectant in El-Gibor (the Mighty God) to do great and mighty things because of it."

With that Mordecai returned his scroll to his belt and turned to leave the men.

Once outside, Hadassah joined him in the shadows. Her face was pale and streaked with tears, her eyes pools of wonder and fear that reflected the brightness of the full moon. However, when she grasped his arm, he felt it firm and strong like he knew her to be. He also felt a pang go through him as he looked at her perfect skin, her well-formed, full mouth, her lustrous, long black hair, and her beautiful dark eyes. He could not help but think that of all the young women in Shushan, surely Hadassah was the most beautiful. He fought against the pull of his will to crumble into dismay.

The two of them walked the short distance to their home, and as they reached the doorway, Hadassah finally spoke.

"*Dod*?"

Mordecai touched the *mezuzah*, then kissed his finger. He waited for her to do the same.

"Yes, *Baht*…?"

"Do you think I will be . . . ," her voice broke, " . . . taken?"

They stepped through the doorway and inside the dimly lit room. He put his arm around her and pulled her under his *tallit*.

"Only Hashem knows at this point, *Baht*, but unless the men are blind, or struck down by the angels of Hashem, you certainly fulfill the kind of maiden they are coming to take."

She wrapped herself around him and pressed herself into his chest.

"Oh, *Dod*, I do not want to be taken! I am a *Yeduhi* woman with the dream of becoming the *eema* of *Mashiyach Melek*! But if I am locked away in a palace of pagan idolatry, and used by a pagan king, my virginity taken, my shame, disappointment and sorrow will be more than I can bear!"

She sobbed and wept against him as he stood holding the most precious gift he had ever been given. Tears flowed from his eyes and ran down his beard, and it was all Mordecai could do not to fall on his face, hold his abdomen like a woman in labor, and cry out to Hashem.

She wept until exhaustion overtook her and quivering jerks of her body came when there were no more tears. She continued to hold on to him, until her soul and body calmed. Suddenly she realized they were still standing just inside the door. She pulled away from him and wiped her face.

"Tell me how I must prepare myself, *Dod*. We do not know how much time we have before they come, and I am gone—never to see you again. Tell me what I must do."

Mordecai sank into his chair, wiped his face and blew his nose, and looked at her upturned face now full of determination to meet whatever was coming. Amazed that she still had the mind to realize that this was something neither of them had ever faced—nor were they prepared to face—his mind tried to focus on her request. *Yes, how must she prepare?*

Mordecai, unlike most of the *Yehudi* in Shushan, was more experienced with the palace routines, deliveries, couriers, and authorities. He already knew some of what she was going to encounter if chosen by the guards.

"The most important advice I can give you, *Baht*, is to trust in Hashem. He will be with you. In times of doubt and fear, He will bring back to your mind the scriptures of wisdom, instruction, comfort, and promises. Repeat them to yourself in prayers and meditations, and let them give you strength, hope and promise. Do not believe that El-Shammah (the God who is present) has forsaken or forgotten you. Refuse to believe or follow after the teachings or ideas of those who worship the Persian gods, or those who have been brought as captives from Egypt, or from other provinces where idols are worshipped.

"Do not become ashamed because you believe in El-Shaddai (the God who is sufficient to provide all your needs). If Hashem in His benevolence allows you to be taken to the palace, be what you are—a chosen vessel of Hashem. Be His witness. The thoughts of Hashem Elohim are higher than ours, so trust Him to lead you.

"Having said that, I must warn you—do not tell anyone you are *Yehudi*. Do not tell them your real name, nor who I am to you. Hadassah, it is important that they believe you are Persian, and if they suspect you are *Yeduhi*, or related to me, you may be mistreated. Many of our neighbors who have daughters in service in the palace tell me that they are treated with cruelty. One man in particular comes and goes from the palace that I suspect would harm you if he knew you were my daughter. And I am sure there are more than one!"

"But will the men not know those of us who are *Yehudi*?"

"Those men are coming to take virgins. The post told us what they are after. They don't care who the maidens are. The maidens' nationality is unimportant.

"Stay as quiet as possible. Keep your head down; speak only when spoken to; and remember, if you see another girl mistreated you must not object or try to intervene. I know that goes against everything in you, but your life depends on it. Do not show any anger or arrogance. Follow their instructions unless you are told to do something against the name of Hashem. If that should happen, Hashem will act on your behalf."

"Do you think they will... uh..., remove our clothing? Will they..."

"I suspect the men are under strict orders not to hurt any of the girls they take, but if any one should cause them a problem, they are men that are not accustomed to disobedience or even eye-to-eye contact. I feel sure you—if you are taken—or any of the other girls who are taken will be examined for obvious, visible flaws, injuries, or marks of any kind once you are in the palace. The men will only judge which girls to take by what their own eyes deem to be suitable. You may have to show your arms and possibly your feet, but I can't imagine they will spend much time examining the girls. They have too many to take. But I must warn you..."

Mordecai struggled with what he was about to say. He knew she was modest and would be extremely embarrassed by what he needed to tell her.

"Be prepared for the men to ask you if you have lain with a man. At some point you will be examined to determine if you are a virgin, but it will be after you are taken to the palace, and then only by the palace physicians or midwives. They will not take your word for it. Other young women may even be severely punished or killed if they lie to the fact that they are a virgin. So, prepare for scenes of mistreatment or even abuse."

The images in Mordecai's mind caused him to suddenly feel nauseous and faint.

Her eyes never left his face. She somberly took it all in. They sat looking into each other's eyes: fearing the possibilities, imagining the worst, hoping for it not to happen. They memorized afresh the shape of the other's face, the lines, the way the light shone on hair, and the depth of the eyes.

In a whisper she said, "I don't want to go, *Dod*. I don't want to leave you. I don't want to miss the morning *Shema*, the reading of the scriptures together, our sharing of the meals, the *Shabbat*, seeing Ezra and Ruth's marriage . . ."

Her voice suddenly cried out, "Oh! Do you think they will take Ruth? She is beautiful! Oh, Ezra must be terrified!"

"I think that Ezra is on his way tonight to wed Ruth, at least that is what Uriel told me as I was leaving the temple. They are so close to the marriage date; they will marry as soon as Ezra arrives—hopefully before the arrival of the king's men. In a few weeks, they will have the wedding feast in the country where she lives. Hopefully, they will come back here in a few months so Ezra can resume his business with Uriel."

"What if the king's men find out? Will they hurt Ezra? Will they punish Ruth? Oh, *Dod*, the world has suddenly turned upside down!"

"You cannot make it right, Hadassah. You must trust Elohim to take care of those we love. That is what I must do for you, as well. I start now."

He arose from his chair with a determination to see that she was committed into the faithful hands of Hashem. He took the oil and poured it over her head; then, spread the *tillit* over the two of them and began his prayer in the rhythm and intonation that she knew so well. She listened more intently, determined she would never forget her cousin's voice or his beautiful prayers from scripture.

> *"I lift up my eyes to the mountains—*
> *where does my help come from?*
>
> *My help comes from Hashem Elohim (The Eternal Creator)*
> *the Maker of heaven and earth.*
>
> *El-Shammah (God is Present) will not let your foot slip—*
> *He who watches over you will not slumber;*
>
> *Indeed, El-Rohi (God our Shepherd) who watches over Israel*
> *will neither slumber nor sleep.*
>
> *El Roi (the God who sees) watches over you—*
>
> *El-Nissi (God our Banner) is your shade at your right hand;*
> *the sun will not harm you by day,*
> *nor the moon by night.*

*El-Sabaoth (the God of Armies) will keep you from all harm—
He will watch over your life:*

*El-Tsidkenu (God our Righteousness) will watch over
your coming and going both now and forevermore."* (Psa 121)

Peace settled over them and seemed to fill the room. Neither of them knew what the future held, but they did know the One who held them. Standing motionless under the cover of the *tillit*, Mordecai began the prayer that closed and started every day...

"Shema, Yisrael, Hashem Eloheinu, Hashem echad."
("Hear, O Israel, Hashem is our God, Hashem is One.")

Then in quiet undertones, Mordecai and Hadassah continued the recitation in unison,

"Baruk sh'mo kevod malcuto le'olam va'ed."
("Blessed be the name of the glory of His kingdom forever and ever...)

✡

Chapter Nine

The Light

Ahasuerus sent dispatches to all parts of the kingdom, to each province in its own script and to each people in their own language, proclaiming that every man should be ruler over his own household, using his native tongue. (Est 1.22 NIV)

Mordecai did not sleep. Instead he went into his garden where he poured ashes on his head, knelt with his forehead to the ground and poured out his grief before El Roi (the God who sees) for Hadassah and the other young maidens of *Yehudah*. For this evil plan to remove so many of them would have a powerful impact upon the population of the *Yehudim*. Mordecai knew that the plan of Lucifer was and had always been to wipe out Hashem's chosen people so *Mashiyach Melek* could not come. He determined in his heart that he would not forsake her, but he would be present around the palace daily.

Hadassah struggled to regain the peace she and Mordecai had felt during prayer, but instead weariness finally dragged her into a restless sleep filled with dreams. She saw frightening scenes of young maidens being pulled from the arms of parents by faceless men who stripped veils and clothing from them and replaced them with filthy, stained, garments in tatters. Tasseled ropes woven from fine gold, intertwined with thorns bound them, leaving their arms and hands bleeding and covered in blood. They were thrown into a dark pit and from time to time, one maiden would be pulled from the others. Those left in the darkness could hear her crying and begging in muffled tones of indiscernible words.

Suddenly, she was out of the pit and back in her room which was flooded with light so bright she could not fully open her eyes. She shielded her eyes with her hands and tried to allow only enough of it through her fingers that possibly she would see its source. She could not. She felt the light on her skin—much like the sun, only it was not heat that she felt, it was like a liquid moving over her, through her, bringing with it a calming and a strength she could not understand. In her mind she wondered if she had died in the darkness and now was in *Sheol*. She tried to speak but her mouth could not work and words would not form. She lay still and allowed the light to move from the room into her being until she herself became melted into the light. From all around her and from within her, she heard a whispering wind of words.

> I know the plans I have for you;
>   plans to prosper you and not to harm you,
>   plans to give you hope and a future.
> When you will call on Me and come and pray to Me,
>   I will listen to you.
> You will seek me and find Me
>   when you seek Me with all your heart. (Jer 29.11-14 NIV)

Hadassah's eyes flew open and the room was now dim with only the dawning sunlight filtering through her window.

What was that? What happened?

She pondered the dream, she remembered the faceless men, she remembered the shame and embarrassment of being naked and frightened; she remembered the cords of gold woven with thorns, she remembered the darkness—*the light! What was the light?* The horror of the dream was overshadowed by the awareness that something—*a light?*—had entered her. *What was it?*

She closed her eyes and waited for the presence of the light to return. The memory of it was strong, the brilliance of it unforgettable, it's feeling lingered. *What were the words?* Her mind could recall Mordecai reading similar—*no*—those same words. Words from the scroll of Jeremiah's prophecy.

And as she lay there, she repeated the words and felt the liquid light deep inside moving like a river.

———————— הַפְסָקָה ————————

> I prayed to Adonai, and He answered me. He freed me from all my fears.
> Those who look to Him for help will be radiant with joy; no shadow of shame will darken their faces.
> In my desperation I prayed, and Hashem listened; He saved me from all my troubles.
> For the angel of Hashem is a guard; He surrounds and defends all who fear Him. (Psa 34:4-7)

In the groves of pagan gods, worship was taking place in the early morning dimness. Young, hopeful maidens were gathering with baskets ladened with offerings and gifts to be presented to Mithra, protector of the faithful, and to Ahura Mazda, the god of wisdom, and to the other ten most popular gods of Persia. The hopeful girls placed food, candles, and coins with their prayers for favor; and personal items to remind the gods of the identity of the maiden who should be the chosen.

As the marketplace opened, the shoppes that catered to services for women were filled with these same young women purchasing oils, creams, tinkling anklets and bracelets, nose and ear jewelry, perfumes and the blackening they used to enhance their eyes. Women skilled in weaving gold and jewels into hair were suddenly overwhelmed by customers.

Friendships strained among the maidens as each one was suddenly in competition with the other to be more beautiful. Identifying and pointing out flaws and insufficiencies suddenly became the source of many broken relationships and loud, angry disputes. All modesty among them took a sudden decline with the knowledge that the king's men, who were already known to have eyes of lust, would have the job of selecting those most beautiful and desirable.

The mothers, grandmothers, aunts, and married sisters observed all this with mixed emotions. Many were seen with red, puffy eyes from the crying and pleading with daughters who were determined to be chosen; while some had the same look from the fear that their daughters would be taken.

In contrast, some of the older women were shamelessly encouraging their young girls to prepare themselves in any way possible to be one of the chosen. The hope that a daughter or granddaughter in the palace would bring wealth to the family was the motivation. Suddenly, on every side, there were strained and heightened emotions. Attempts by the wisest among them to warn the maidens of what life would be for them if they were taken, but not chosen as queen, was heeded by only a timid few, and totally disregarded by the arrogant. The timid few were suddenly fearful and anxious. For the others, only greater determination and confidence in themselves resulted.

The posted edict was a sudden storm any way it was being received.

✡

Chapter Ten

The Chosen

> *When the king's order and edict had been proclaimed, many young women were brought to the citadel of Susa and put under the care of Hegai. Esther also was taken to the king's palace and entrusted to Hegai, who had charge of the harem.* (Est 2.8 NIV)

Hadassah stood in a long line of girls and young women. She kept her head down and willed herself to stay as still and as calm as possible in spite of her terror and weariness. On either side of her were younger girls who looked to be no more than ten years old, yet, Hadassah knew every maiden was required to be at least thirteen. They were softly crying while the older, taller and more imposing girls used elbows and eyes to try to silence them. Throughout the day, it was obvious, at least to Hadassah, the emotional difference between the girls that were hopeful in the prospects of their outcome, and others who were terrified by the thoughts of it.

The day had been brutal. The men came in heavily armed squads into the village center. They announced—as if no one knew—why they were there, and warned parents and anyone connected to the maidens against trying to interfere with the process. For a number of the adults, a number larger than Hadassah could even comprehend, the warning not to protest was not necessary. Hadassah observed that many of girls were excited by the opportunity to be part of the palace. From their excited chatter and egotistical smugness, the majority of them were absolutely convinced of becoming the queen. Since it was obvious to the men that not every girl held that lofty hope, each household was carefully and thoroughly searched to be sure no one was hiding. The fear of the consequences had taken hold on most of the citizens, and only a few who were willing to lose life or limb had attempted it.

Images of the adults who had resisted or had tried to hide their daughters flashed into Hadassah's mind. Nausea overwhelmed her as she remembered. The royal troops held no restraint or hesitation to immediately deal with the rebellious. With brutal force of such degree that Hadassah and many of the maidens had never witnessed, it was soon evident to all, resistance was futile. Regardless, from the chaos surrounding the collection, it was clear that even against the warnings and witnessing failed attempts by others, many men were ready to face punishment or death in attempts to keep from sending their daughters into the hands of the king's men. Sadly, all efforts against the armed and trained men were useless, and many fathers, brothers, and betrothed were beaten, chained, and hauled away to an unknown but certain undesirable end.

Hadassah was much relieved that Mordecai had been right about the way the maidens were treated. Great care was taken not to hurt them in any way to leave visible marks. However, once the girls were taken into the tents surrounding the village for the purpose of the men to decide who would not meet the requirements, things changed.

Some of the girls most desperate to be among the taken had immodestly dressed and displayed behavior, tone, and speech which shocked Hadassah. Their seductive attempts quickly drew the ill-intended attentions of the men. These brazen-faced hopefuls were unaware that their behavior would prove fatal to their desired end. To their great dismay, the most outrageous behavior did not help any who were found to have features or issues that King Ahasuerus had defined as unacceptable. As the men performed their preliminary inspections, those girls were ordered to return to their homes. Unfortunately, some of the rejected girls were belittled and others were even beaten by parents who had pinned hopes of wealth on their daughters. The others who were received with joyful relief were wept upon and quickly rushed into homes lest the king's men should change their decision.

Surrounding the selected maidens in the great domed hall of The House of the Maidens, were cold, smooth, deathly white statues of gods and goddess. Some stood alone while others were entwined into what appeared to be impossible positions. Hanging over archways leading into other parts of the house were displays of mounted shields and weapons. Along the walls were tiled mosaics in muted colors of blues, greens and beige displaying rigid images of the Immortals complete with helmets, spears, and shields in perfect marching lines. Other larger and more brilliantly colored mosaics illustrated battles and historical events of victors on horseback, trampling on the defeated dead with spears protruding from their bleeding, deformed bodies. Commanders with open, silent mouths appeared to be shouting orders while holding up bloody swords and waving flags.

Couches in rich woven multicolored threads of vibrant colors intermingled with gold sat along walls underneath lovely, pastoral tapestries in strong contradiction to the violence and horror of the adjacent mosaic tiled walls. These couches stood on legs of gold with lion's paws for the base while the arms of the couches displayed the open roaring mouths of lions.

Bald-headed eunuchs of every age and size stood in one line facing the girls. They were dressed in dark tunics over full-legged pantaloons that covered everything down to their ankles. Their feet were shod with what appeared to be red, silk shoes with pointed toes that curled back over the tops of their feet. Each shoe was embroidered with the image of the king's signet. The girls were being divided by the eunuchs into groups of no more than twenty-five. Each group was assigned to one of the eunuchs who would serve as their supervisor.

When Hadassah glanced up to see the eunuch in charge of her group, she knew immediately that he was not Persian. He had the look of someone from the far northern regions. The hole in his ear revealed that he at one time had been a slave, possibly on a sea-faring vessel. The skin around his eyes and mouth indicated that he must be at least the age of Mordecai, but without hair or beard, it was difficult to tell. She wondered if he were Greek or if he might be from as far away as Germania. He was taller and lighter-skinned than the others, with muscled arms, a square jaw line, and eyes the color of a stormy sea. He wore a blank expression that considering his present position and location, she knew he could not be a contented, happy man. Obviously, he had managed over time to perfect his current facial expression—or more specifically—the lack of one. He introduced himself as Hegai, the king's chamberlain and keeper of the women.

Bright rays of sunlight suddenly flooded the hall when the huge outer door to the House of Maidens was thrown open. Hadassah kept her head down, but cut her eyes toward the open door and watched as the silouettes of a tall woman followed by two guards and some smaller women approached. The entourage was for the moment backlit by the blinding afternoon sun and made quite an impressive entrance. Once the doors were shut, Hadassah saw a regally dressed woman wearing a crown accompanied by two heavily armed guards and several slave girls. Three more guards waited just inside the hall entrance.

When the eunuchs saw the woman, they immediately moved slightly away from the girls, folded their hands together, and drew them to their waist. Only Hegai was approached, and the woman wearing the crown and he conversed in quiet, inaudible words.

Mordecai would tell Hadassah from time to time information he learned from the eunuchs and others around the palace. Hadassah knew that when Queen Mother Atossa visited, it was usually to be with her son when something of importance had occurred—as she did right after the failed battle in Greece. The village women who knew about palace climate from the reports of their children in palace service said Queen Atossa was not one to be patient. In that regard, her son obviously had his mother's temperament. Hadassah immediately realized she was looking at Queen Atossa, the daughter of King Cyrus, and the wife of the late King Darius. As she wondered why Atossa was in The House of Maidens, Hadassah recalled some of the history Mordecai had shared concerning how she came to live in Babylon and not Shushan.

When King Darius died, his son Ahasuerus who ruled as governor in Babylon for ten years took over his father's empire and moved into the king's summer palace in Shushan. Soon after arriving in Shushan and beginning his reign, Ahasuerus learned that an Egyptian, Psamtik IV, whom his father had left in charge of the southern province, decided to rebel against Persian rule. Ahasuerus gathered his forces and upon arriving in Egypt, decided they could easily put the Egyptian army into submission by using a different approach than combat. Hadassah and Mordecai once laughed about how the Persians gathered hundreds of cats, and as they approached the Egyptian army, they released the clowder to scatter between the Persian and Egyptian infantries. Since the Egyptians worshipped cats, they immediately laid their weapons down and surrendered.

As soon as Ahasuerus' retuned to Shushan, news arrived that a rebel uprising in Babylon required him to take his men there to remove Shamasheribat. Ahasuerus besieged the city, burned the temple of Mardok, the Babylonian god, then took the statue of Mardok to Shushan and had it destroyed. Queen Atossa with her attendants and eunuchs accompanied the forces, and after the insurrectionists were put down, she decided to stay in Babylon. Without a Persian in charge there, she took over the city as Queen of Babylon, and immediately ordered Shamasheribat to be hanged.

Mordecai had mentioned recently that Queen Mother Atossa returned to Shushan for another visit. Hadassah assumed by her appearance in The House of the Maidens, she intended to assist or take over the supervision of the girls.

Hadassah watched as Atossa ignored the eunuchs as she would a piece of worthless furniture. Proceeding toward one of the groups of girls, she spoke audibly for the first time by giving a command.

"Line up."

Wearily, the girls moved into a line to face her. The supervising eunuch moved to stand slightly behind the line.

Atossa started at one end of the line and slowly moved from one girl to the next. Stopping directly in front of each one, and without any expression, she looked each girl fully in the face.

With a voice cold and precise, she gave the same instructions to each girl as she proceeded down the line.

"Open your mouth."

"Now, pull your tunic away from your legs and arms."

After Atossa inspected the girl's teeth, arms, and legs, she yanked the neckline of the girl's tunic down to allow her to examine the girl's breasts. She continued this process until each girl in each group had been inspected.

At least three among the first group were approached by one of Atossa's guards, separated from the others and escorted from the house by one of the slaves. No words were spoken and Hadassah finally decided that the Queen Mother was giving some sort of signal to her guards as to which ones were to be taken away—to where exactly, Hadassah could only wonder.

When Queen Atossa approached Hadassah's group, Hadassah was so hungry, so exhausted, and so ready for it all to end, she did not even care what the Queen Mother did to her. Two girls from Hadassah's group were removed.

This tedious and mysterious process continued until at least ten to fifteen girls had been taken from the collection and escorted out of the house by a slave.

Finally, Queen Mother Atossa gave Hegai a nod of her head, turned and left the hall with her guards following on her heels. Hadassah gave a sigh of relief. Hope filled her that food and rest would soon be offered to the hungry and tired girls after such a long ordeal.

Instead of food and rest, however, Hegai, led them though an opening on the east wall and they found themselves in a long, arched hallway with five doors on each side.

Hegai led the lines of maidens with their attending eunuchs down the hall and stopped at the first two doors across from each another. He motioned for the eunuchs in charge of the first two groups to lead their girls inside. Once the girls were safely inside, the eunuch returned to stand post at the door should any of them try to leave. Hegai repeated this process until every room down the hall had a group of girls inside, and their eunuch waiting at the door.

Once inside the room, Hadassah and the other girls found themselves in a brightly lit, large room flooded with afternoon sunlight from windows that were as tall as the room itself and aligned on one entire wall. Tables with instrument, bowls, jugs of liquids, and what appeared to be medicinal herbs lined the opposite wall. Men, whom Hadassah assumed were royal physicians and assistants, were standing in front of those tables. They wore white tunics, baggy white pantaloons, and tall, stiff, white hats on their heads. One feature that caught Hadassah's attention were the moustaches. Each man in white had a clean shaven face except for a moustache that filled his upper lip, hung down on each side of his mouth, and ended at his chin.

In the middle of the room were tables, or perhaps beds, covered with white cloths. Thin veils of fabric draped from rods attached to the ceiling provided a partition between the beds. Parallel to the windows were several couches flanked by highly polished, marble-topped tables which held pitchers and goblets.

A tall blank-faced, obese eunuch directed the girls to the couches and gave them instructions.

"You are to wait here until directed. Flavored water is available to you while you wait, and you may drink from any of the pitchers. In fact, I suggest you try water from several of the pitchers. You will find it to be quite refreshing and delicious."

Obediently, the girls took goblets and poured themselves water. As they drank, they whispered among themselves.

"Try this one. It's flavored with peaches."

"Oh, I really like this! It seems to have several flavors in it."

Hadassah poured herself a goblet filled with water from one of the pitchers that had lemon slices. She gratefully enjoyed a second one.

The girls sat quietly, sipping water, and waiting to be called.

One by one the girls were being escorted to a smaller table in one of the corners of the room where a scribe with a scroll and pen and ink was waiting. Assisting the scribe was a short, thin and rather frail looking eunuch who had the responsibility of ushering the girls one at a time to the table.

"What do you suppose the scribe is doing?" whispered a tall, blonde, Persian maid to the girl sitting next to Hadassah.

"I'm not sure. I suppose we will learn that when our turn comes."

"I know what he's doing," said a round-faced, short girl with green eyes. "He's giving all of us new names. I've been named Leila."

"What? Why would they do that?" the blond asked.

"Quiet! He might hear you. Here he comes!" whispered the green-eyed girl.

They stopped whispering and watched the thin eunuch return the girl to her seat near them. As she took her seat, the eunuch spoke.

"Please, follow me."

Hadassah looked up and realized the eunuch was speaking to her. She followed him to the scribe's table.

To Hadassah's surprise, the scribe did not ask her to provide her name.

Checking his list of unused names, he looked up at her.

"From this point on your name will be Esther."

Hadassah recalled that Esther was another title of the Babylonian goddess Ishtar, the goddess of love. To a Persian, however, the name meant *star*. The most ironic fact of her new name was that in the language of the *Yeduhim* the name meant *to hide* or *to conceal, hidden*. She smiled at the scribe knowing that Mordecai's prayers were surely being answered, and in that moment, she inwardly gave thanks to El-Nissi (God is my banner) for His assurance to her.

The scribe's responsibility, Hadassah confirmed, was to give each maiden a new name. However, he also recorded her age and wrote a description of her complete with measurements taken by the frail eunuch. Later, Hadassah learned that these records of the names and descriptions of each girl were given to Hegai. Another copy was put into the royal records. By that action alone, it was made clear to Hadassah that her previous life was over.

Once renamed, she was submitted to one of the physicians.

"Remove all your clothes," he said flatly.

Even though she was feeling quite light-headed, shame and embarrassment overwhelmed her as she fought against tears and choking in her throat. Struggling against the dizziness, it was then she reasoned that the fruit-flavored water she and the girls drank was probably tainted with an herb to relax them. She regretted she had not drunk a lot more.

"Now stand still."

Esther stood completely exposed to the eyes of everyone in the room. She steeled herself to endure the probing hands that worked through her hair and scalp, and into her mouth to count her teeth. Once that was done, he directed her to one of the tables.

"Lie down."

She stepped onto a small platform which allowed her to get on the table. Cold, dry hands pressed, squeezed, and manipulated her body to check for any marks, disfigurement, scars, or rashes. She closed her eyes and endured man's hands on parts of her that only she had ever touched. The physician placed his hands under each knee.

"Raise your knees and spread your legs."

Without any regard for her modesty, protest or tears, she was checked to be sure she was a virgin.

"You may sit up now."

He handed her a white, shapeless tunic.

"Put this on and return to your seat."

Shivering and shamed, and feeling completely violated and exposed, she gratefully pulled the thin tunic over her head. She clamped her arms against her sides and wrapped them around her middle. She reasoned that the white tunic was to indicate she had been processed, renamed, recorded, examined, and found pure.

She rushed back to her seat, biting her lower lip to keep from crying. Those without white tunics were waiting for the same inspection, sitting with their heads bowed and eyes downcast.

From one of the examining tables, a physician was heard roughly ordering one of the girls.

"Get up! Put your clothes back on!"

He motioned to one of the eunuchs.

Gazar! Take her out of here! Tell her eunuch she is a filthy liar."

Wide-eyed, pale, and terrified, the girl quickly scrambled into her clothing. Gazar roughly grabbed her by the arm and walked quickly so that she was practically being dragged. Once they reached the door, he shoved her through and the two of them disappeared into the hall. For a brief moment, it was all Esther could do not to beg to go with her.

Feeling stripped of all modesty, the white-robed maidens were returned to Hegai who led them through more hallways and arches and into a completely different part of the house filled with mouth-watering aromas of food. There tables were prepared with white stiff linens, huge arrangements of flowers, and more food than Esther and the girls had ever seen. Servants with large pitchers of wine poured each girl's goblet full as often as she asked.

During this meal, Esther noticed women of every size and nationality quietly slipping in to observe the girls. Most of them were attired in revealing but elaborate attire. They whispered in small groups among themselves, then floated back out of the room. Esther realized that in The House of the Maidens, she and the other girls were losing all rights to privacy or personal ownership. They were no more than living replicas of the nude marble statues that filled the entrance hall of the house.

In spite of Esther's hunger, she found she could only force down a small amount of food. The humiliation, weariness of mind, and the violation of her body had taken her appetite. Even though the overall atmosphere of the room was of relief and hope that the worst was over, some congratulations were overheard among some small groups of girls. In others a slight air of celebration hovered. But what Esther noted most were those that were struggling with tears, their faces still showing signs of humiliation and shame, and she realized she was not alone in her emotional condition. Even now, everything was being supervised closely by the eunuchs and servants standing at each doorway and the occasional concubine or two that slipped in to view the competition.

Esther also suddenly realized with some confusion that she did not see any girls she recognized. Yet, there was a sense that most of the girls knew each other.

Where are the other girls from my village? Where are Ari's twins, and Samuel's beautiful daughter? Why were they not taken?

Then as realization came, she wrapped her arms around herself and silently moved her lips to pray in thanksgiving for what Hashem had done.

"O praises to Hashem! Sara and Ruth are married and safe, and the eyes of the men were blinded by Hashem to spare my *Yehudi* sisters."

———————— הַפְסָקָה ————————

Never had Esther seen a room like the one the women were escorted into after the meal. *It is like a sea surrounded by caves*, she thought. Three large pools of water connected by steps from one to the next filled the huge room. Around the pools were twelve half-circle openings into what seemed to Esther like caves with entrances draped by sheer, white fabric hangings with an opening in the middle to allow entrance. Inside, the caves appeared to be smaller, dome-topped rooms with tables and couches designed for reclining. On each wall, inside a dimly lit niche, a small golden image of a nude female woman was standing on a shelf inches above a grate covered with black rocks being heated by a slow burning fire. A small stream of water from a source inside the wall dripped onto the hot rocks which produced a misty steam that filled the room with a medicinal odor that opened their nostrils and filled their lungs. Once inside the rooms, the girls were told again to undress, and then they were directed to the steps providing entrance into the first pool.

Floor to ceiling gigantic marble columns were covered with engravings of nude men and women, various kinds of trees and fruits, and with what she assumed were images of gods and creatures, part man and part animal. These columns supported the dome-shaped ceiling which was painted with images of the sun, the moon, and stars. Lines connected the stars to indicate the Zodiac signs.

Esther was stunned to find the water in the first pool almost too warm to be comfortable. But in minutes her body adjusted, and she was drawn into the warmth and weightlessness, giving her some ease from the raw emotions of the day. Slave girls carrying large spouted urns entered the waters with the girls and surrounded them to pour scented oil from the urns; and then they took a plant-like brush to rub the oil into their skin.

Esther remembered a day in one of the shoppes in the marketplace when Jacob, the shoppe owner's son, had shown Sara and her a filmy, thin, slick fabric like none she had ever touched. Jacob told the girls the fabric came from the East and was made from the secretions from a worm making a cocoon. But even the smooth, luxurious feel of that fabric did not compare to the feel of that pool and the fragrant potions being poured over her skin.

By the time the water had heated her body until she was no longer comfortable, she and the girls in her group were instructed to enter one of the other two pools divided by the steps between them. As she stepped into the pool, she drew her breath at the cool temperature of the water. However, the slaves in unison, pushed the girls into the two pools, then laughed at them as they lost their breath and objected in squeals of shock. Gratefully, they were quickly called to the other end of the pools where they stepped out and were immediately wrapped in warmed towels and led into one of the small-domed rooms where they had undressed.

Esther's small group was told to lie face down on the beds. Deliciously hot, perfumed oil was poured onto their bodies and with strong, experienced hands, the slave girls rubbed the oils into their skin, causing them to sink into an other worldly-sensation they had never known.

When they left the domed, steamy rooms, they were heavily soothed and sleepy—the drama, chaos, and violation somewhat removed by the baths and oils. Hegai was waiting to show them to their quarters.

In multiple rooms, the girls found beds on foundations of silver and gold with sheets made from the silky, slick fabric from the East, and woven flax and linen coverlets filled with feathers. Around each bed were curtains that provided privacy that none of them had experienced since being taken from their homes.

Esther selected one of the beds and sank gratefully onto it and pulled the coverlet over her head. As images of the day that had been unbearably long and trying replayed in her head, she wept. She quietly whispered the *Shema* and with her eyes closed, she envisioned Mordecai holding the *tallit* over the two of them.

Exhausted and feeling completely lost and alone in a room occupied by girls she did not yet know, she wept again until there were no more tears. She begged sleep to come. She prayed for the river of light from her dream to return, and she hoped that when she opened her eyes, she would be in the sunlight of her own room in the house she shared with Mordecai; and all of the previous events were just a bad dream.

"Please, *Abba*, send the light to me again. I am afraid."

But when she opened her eyes, there was only the strange darkness of an unfamiliar and frightening place.

The quietness of the rooms was clearly evidence of the weariness in all of the girls, but also of the sheer awe for such elegance that none of them could have imagined. She would gladly give it all up to be back with Mordecai.

Just as she was sinking into the numbness of sleep, she heard some of the girls talking in whispers and occasionally giggling. Irritated, Esther hoped Shahin, the eunuch assigned to their room, would soon come in to stop them, but the noises did not last long and the room grew quiet again.

Through the darkness, she heard the whimpers of someone softly crying. When it became louder in the stillness of the room, there were multiple whispered instructions from some of the other girls telling whoever it was to stop, but that only made the poor girl begin to sob louder.

Creeping out of her bed, Esther followed the sounds. Girls around her peeped from their curtained beds.

"What are you doing? Get back in your bed! Do you want us all to be in trouble?" they muttered angrily.

Ignoring them, she made her way to the bed from where the pitiful sobs were now clearly coming as muffled sounds, and pulled back the curtains to reveal an alarmed, wide-eyed petite maid huddled in a fetal position with her mouth covered with pillows in an effort to stifle her sobs.

"Shhhhh . . ." she whispered to the girl. "Don't cry. What is the matter?"

Even as she asked the question, she realized the foolishness of it.

The poor maid did not answer. She drew further into her bed as if she feared Esther would hit her.

"I'm not going to hurt you. I'm Esther. I understand how you're feeling. This is all strange and new and scary. I feel that way, too. What if I stay with you until you're asleep?"

"I miss my mama" she sobbed, and fresh tears poured. "I want to go home!" she wailed.

"Stop the whining!" Someone hissed. "Go to sleep, you foolish girl!"

"Ignore them . . . I know how you feel. I do, too," Esther soothed, "but we cannot go home. We are here, and this is where we will be, so we must try to be strong. What is your name?"

"Roxanna," she replied.

Esther closed her eyes and dropped her head stunned. Raising her eyes she asked, "Do you know what your new name means, Roxanna?"

"No . . . I don't care what it means! I hate it! I liked my real name!"

"It means *light*, Roxanna. And you may not believe this, but I was just praying for God to send me light—and here you are!"

Roxanna sniffed, and pulled herself closer to Hadassah's face and whispered.

"Do you think the gods hear us here? Do they know we're here?"

"I know He knows. He sees everything. Don't be scared. He is with us."

Roxanna peered into the darkness as if she might see Him.

"What does your new name mean?"

"It means *hidden* and, in some languages, it means *star*."

"Oh . . . Hidden Star and Light!" She smiled weakly. "We are both named for things that are bright! I am Light and you are Star! That's funny!" Her smile faded. "Will you stay with me for a while, Star?"

"Of course, I will, Light! I was feeling very alone, too. Move over a bit so I can lie down."

Roxanna rolled over to allow Esther to lie down, and as Esther lay there she thought, *How strange that her name is Roxanna! Oh, Abba, you do know where I am!*

When Roxanna was finally making soft sleeping sounds, Esther crept back to her own bed with a satisfaction that although she did not feel better about where she was, at least she had been able to help Roxanna.

"Now to sleep and rest," she whispered.

———————— הַפְסָקָה ————————

Instead, rest and sleep were filled with images of the day: scenes of massive walls surrounding exterior gardens and entrance ways covered with carvings of the Immortals in long rigid lines. Interior vast rooms with immense, high ceilings painted with winged children, clouds, celestial bodies and astral mappings. Everywhere white marble statues of kings, queens, gods and goddesses stood with cold, blank eyes that stared into nothingness. Palace walls were covered with carved images of ferocious warriors on horseback in hand-to-hand combat surrounded by winged creatures casting fire and weapons down upon cringing people with mouths opened in horror in silent screams. Esther ran through the halls and doorways and into dark passageways searching for the light that had given her such strength and peace. But instead, she was pursued by men on foot and on wild-eyed horses that chased her into a tower of narrow, steep stairs and only small crevices that were not large enough to hide her and to keep herself from being captured.

Covered in sweat but freezing cold, Esther awoke with her heart pounding and her mouth open in a silent scream. Sitting up, for a moment she did not know where she was. Then realization came, and drawing her cover around herself, she did what Mordecai had in wisdom told her to do. She pulled from her memory a scripture and prayed it with all her heart.

> *"May those who seek my life be disgraced and put to shame;*
> *may those who plot my ruin be turned back in dismay.*
> *May they be like chaff before the wind,*
> *with the angel of Hashem driving them away;*
> *May their path be dark and slippery,*
> *with the angel of Hashem pursuing them."* (Psa 35. 4-6)

——————— הַפְסָקָה ———————

Every day he [Mordecai] walked back and forth near the courtyard of the harem to find out how Esther was and what was happening to her. (Est 2:11 NIV)

Mordecai sat at his table with his fingers on his head holding his hair in his fists. He had followed the carriages and wagons that the king's men had used to take the girls to the palace. Once they reached the gate, the sentries opened for the wagons and carriages to enter, but no one else was allowed. Men, brothers, uncles, cousins and friends stood outside the closed gates with ashen faces and feelings of helplessness. Their girls had disappeared into the royal abyss of loss.

Mordecai stayed outside the gates until the sun set, waiting for something that was not going to happen. Finally, in twilight he trudged with feet of lead back to his village quarters and went into the house that had completely lost its life and light. He could not eat; he could not read; he could not pray. Instead, he sat in the dark and cried.

During the next few days in the homes of the *Yeduhim* whose daughters were not taken, caution and fear kept the girls inside lest the king's men should change their minds and return. The scenes from the chaos were all too fresh in the minds of the villagers. Parents of daughters rejected were relieved, but more, they were astounded.

What no one could explain was what happened on the morning of the collection. Girls with beautiful skin awoke with rashes, outbreaks on their faces, some awoke to find growths and marks and even scars that had appeared for no known reason. Because of these easily visible imperfections, they were rejected. Now that the threat was over, the blemishes and flaws had faded.

Mordecai remembered Hadassah's face in the moonlight after the meeting in the temple. When she awoke the next day, she looked to him more beautiful than he had ever seen her. The *Yeduhi* women were thankful that their daughters had been saved by El-Nissi (God our Banner), but they could not understand why Hadassah had not been saved. They remembered how Mordecai had encouraged all of them to hope in *Melek* who was mighty to save. Still, Mordecai's reputation as a respected and holy man among them was suddenly tarnished because it certainly was true—El-Nissi (God my banner) had saved others, but He had not saved Hadassah.

When Sara heard the news, she stayed in her bed, weak with grief and overwhelmed with horrible thoughts of Hadassah's losses and future. For days she could not eat until Nathan was fearful that she might get sick from her misery.

Knowing how much Hadassah loved Sara and how close the two girls were, Mordecai went to see her three days after Hadassah was taken. He reminded her that Hashem is sovereign, and he comforted her that El-Rohi (the God who sees) was with her. The sorrow did not leave, the hurt was not gone, but now Sara could find hope that Hashem Elohim had purpose in all that He had allowed to happen. From that day on, Sara prayed for her *achot*.

Every day Mordecai went to the gate of The House of the Maidens to learn what he could about Hadassah. He soon befriended a eunuch named Shahin, who was a helper to Hegai in charge over the rooms of five of the girls in Hegai's care. Mordecai was careful to hide his own identity, and told Shahin that he was a friend of the maiden's family. He begged information about the one named Hadassah.

It took three days for Shahin to identify the maiden in his assigned area as the one Mordecai referred to as Hadassah. Shahin explained to Mordecai that she was now called by another name, and he was forbidden to reveal that name to the girl's family or friends. However, other than the secrecy of her name, Shahin did tell him some of what was happening with Hadassah: her studies, her ability to assist the younger and more homesick girls, and her favor with all who knew her. By these reports, Mordecai knew that Hadassah was being faithful to Hashem, as he knew she would be.

A few men, especially some of the younger men who had lost their betrotheds, went to the gates for a few weeks, but gradually the realization of the maidens' future became accepted, and they stopped going to the palace. Among some who continued to come with Mordecai, there was an air of hope that a queen would be chosen quickly, and those who were still maidens would be sent back to families.

But no girls were released.

✡

Chapter Eleven

Gaining Favor

> *She pleased him and won his favor. Immediately he provided her with her beauty treatments and special food. He assigned to her seven female attendants selected from the king's palace and moved her and her attendants into the best place in the harem.* (Est 2.9 NIV)

In the following weeks Esther learned that when she and the other maidens had been brought into the palace, Queen Mother Atossa had chosen some of the girls to return with her to Babylon. Although Esther was not happy that she was in the palace, with her knowledge of the prophecies against Babylon, she was thankful to Hashem that she was not selected to be among those taken with Queen Mother Atossa.

Almost daily, the king's men arrived with more and more virgins from villages and distant farms until the number was considered sufficient to find a queen to replace Vashti. The House of the Maidens was filled. Hegai, diligent to learn about each girl, was intent on making sure each one was made ready before being called to the king's quarters.

Those most favored by Hegai because of demeanor, beauty, and grace were favored and given better accommodations in rooms of the palace that the maidens had not seen. It became obvious that Hegai favored Esther most when he moved her into a suite of rooms on the upper floor of The House of Maidens where Esther had access to a private roof garden, a portico, and access to her own pool. Hegai also allowed her to help him select seven personal attendants from the king's court. They soon became fiercely loyal to her. Although some of the other maidens privately resented Esther's position with Hegai, they refused to make their feelings known. By gaining favor with Esther, they hoped to gain greater opportunity for themselves. It soon became apparent that Esther had great favor with all who knew her.

Hegai noted that Esther's beauty radiated with an inner glow that he found unique from the others. Esther did not need the special adornment others were given to enhance her beauty. Still, Hegai quickly and generously provided her attendants the oil of myrrh, sweet perfumes, and other needs in unlimited amounts for Esther's year of purification.

Each day the maidens' hours were measured into slots of time for meals, treatments, and training in the ways of the palace. They were also instructed in math, languages, Persian law, dancing, and etiquette. Some of the willing concubines and wives of the king were assigned to instruct the maidens in manners of presentation, response, and the preferences of the king. The staff of the palace were assigned to instruct the maidens in the management and the operations of the palace. The maidens not chosen to be the wife or one of the concubines of the king would perhaps be required to assist in those staff duties.

One area of instruction that was most difficult for Esther was in the worship and reverence expected to be given to the gods of Persia and Media. Esther knew there were more than ninety gods, goddesses, and demons in Persian mythology and traditional tales and folklore. She had received some understanding of the most popular of the gods through shopping in the village booths. Multiple items of idolatry were sold in the marketplace along with instructions dedicated to their proper worship and acceptable sacrifices. Having to endure the history of their origins, their fearful powers, abilities, and reasons to be worshipped and given sacrifices was especially grievous and troubling to her. Although the maids were being instructed to fear them, Esther knew she never would.

Many believed and worshipped Mithra, the best known and most powerful warrior against the forces of darkness, the protector of the faithful, and the guide toward *asha* (truth). The poorest of the Persians spent time and resources worshipping Baga, the god of wealth and good fortune, hoping for a sudden turn in their finances. Ahura Mazda, the "Lord of Wisdom" was known as the king of the gods, the supreme creator, maker of heaven, earth, animals, humans, and the sacred elements of air, water, earth, and fire. Ardvi Sura Anahita, the goddess of fertility, health, water, wisdom, and war was especially worshipped by barren women or the sick and handicapped. Āz, the demon god of greed for wealth or material gain, lust and envy for position and power was one that Hadassah was most confused about.

Why would anyone worship a demon god?

The origins of the gods and the way some rose from humanity to deity were not only new to Esther, but she was also alarmed that anyone would believe such ridiculous ideas. She gave herself to the instruction of these origins in the same manner she listened to the fables and legends of the wars, the rise and fall of legendary kingdoms, and the imaginations of pagans. She heard tales about creation, the mystic powers of astrology, and messages by false prophets; but she did not accept any of it as *asha*. Through a multitude of ways, she managed to avoid the required worship of them with the assistance from Hegai, her devoted attendants, and in many cases, the miraculous intervention of El-Mitkadesh (the God who Sanctifies). Mordecai's faithful teachings about Daniel, Hananiah, Mishael and Azariah being commanded to worship the golden image of Nebuchadnezzar gave her courage. When the men refused the command, they were thrown into a fiery furnace. When the fire did not burn them, the king looked into the furnace and saw one like the son of God with them. Their deliverance by Hashem gave her courage and determination that although her body may belong to the Persian empire, her worship would not.

The other class that Esther hated with a righteous hatred was dance. The instructor was a tall, beautiful, dark-skinned woman with markings on her forehead which indicated she was a princess from one of the southern provinces. Princess Elaheh always wore the customary clothing of the royal dancers: a tasseled top that revealed most of her breasts, and pantaloons of an extremely thin material that barely hung on her hips and ended at her feet. Her feet were bare except for some golden chains on which bells and trinkets were hanging. Her lower abdomen revealed a pierced naval which had a jewel imbedded. On her wrists were bands of gold, and on her arms were multiple trinkets which provided sounds like small melodious bells. Small thin metal attachments on her already long fingers provided hypnotizing movements, and along with multiple scarves, were used in a most seductive mesmerizing way in her performance.

The first time Esther saw Elaheh she felt blood rush to her face in embarrassment that any woman would allow herself to be so immodestly dressed. Remarkably, Elaheh drew more attention to herself by her costume than if she were completely nude.

"Ladies," Elaheh said in her heavy accent, "each of you need to understand that if you are chosen to be in my performing dance troupe, you will be attired in clothing similar to what I am wearing. Yes?"

Esther glanced at the other maidens to see if they were as panicked by the idea as she. There were giggles and a few showed a bit of surprise by the idea, but for the most part, many of the girls seemed excited by the prospect.

"Today and the next three days of meeting, you will dance a prepared dance of your own. That will allow me to see your level of previous instruction you may have received, if any.

"It will also allow me to see how comfortable you are to perform. You will dance in front of the class, and you may choose whatever you want to include in your dance. After I have seen each of you dance, and I have determined your comfort and expertise, I will instruct you in the kind of dancing that is required to entertain the guests of the palace. Yes?"

Dance class immediately became the favorite among the maidens.

When Esther's turn came three days later, she skillfully used a tambourine to dance one of the familiar *Yehudi* dances she and other *Yehudi* girls danced for celebrations in her quarter. During her performance, she closed her eyes and remembered the music, fun, and joy everyone shared at Sara's wedding. Breathless when she finished, her joy was instantly quashed by Elaheh's laughter and the giggles of the other maiden's joining into the instructor's reaction.

"Ah, Esther . . . that is your name, no? That was a sweet attempt to do something like a dance, but what I will teach you will not only move you, my dear, but you will cause men to desire you above all others."

Red-faced and humiliated, Esther took her place with the other girls hoping that her *sweet attempt to do something like a dance* would keep her from Elaheh's selection for further, more intimate instruction.

After the individual dances of the girls were performed and evaluated, Elaheh started her instruction.

"Today I will teach you the art of alluring and sensuous moves. You will learn the steps and techniques necessary to hold your audience spell-bound. This will include using your eyes to make eye-to-eye contact with members of the audience to arouse and perhaps put them under your spell."

The girls giggled covering their mouths with their hands and their eyes looking from one to the other to see their reactions. Esther was stunned and wondered how a worshipper of Hashem would survive the class.

"Also, my dears, I will show you specific movements of your body, so that the tinkling of the metal bands and the bells will provide a rhythm to hold attention. You will soon master these movements. Our metal workers will fit each of you with the extensions like the ones on my fingers. You will be provided with scarves like the ones I use. The extension and the scarves will serve to hypnotize and mesmerize men that will not be able to take their eyes off of you. Yes?"

Elaheh grinned a toothy smile and winked her eyes.

The girls were already mesmerized.

Esther prayed to Hashem that she would never be called upon to use her body for such as what she was watching and hearing. She knew it was not what she had been created by Hashem Elohim to do. Her disdain for it all filled her to such a degree that as the instruction continued, Elaheh rarely used her as a dancing partner in practice. Privately, Elaheh regarded Esther as a hopeless case, and soon Esther became the one in the group that was referred to as *the goat with five legs*.

When the first dance class ended, Esther made her way to the purification pool on the rooftop where she stayed until her skin was wrinkled and her mind could focus on more than what Elaheh was attempting to teach a virtuous *Yehudi* maiden.

───────── הַפְסָקָה ─────────

Every morning and evening, Esther faithfully prayed the *Shema* and as often as her mind was given the freedom, she would rehearse the prayers, songs and scriptures she had learned under the teaching of Mordecai.

Faithful to Mordecai's warnings she did not reveal her faith or heritage. During times when the maidens were given freedom, one of the favorite activities among them was to share stories. Since Esther had many from the scriptures, she entertained them with what they considered fables of an unknown god that surpassed all gods, and one that uniquely created woman as his highest achievement. She used her sharp mind to weave her stories without the possibility they would associate her with the *Yehudim*. This not only fascinated the women, but also intrigued them that a god who could cause a bush to be on fire but not burn, who could part a sea to provide a dry path of escape, who could send fire and brimstone on a city filled with acts considered unnatural and abominable, who could make a shepherd a king—a single, all knowing, all present god who far surpassed the images made of clay, stone and wood—was a god worthy of worship.

As she told them story after story, they came to desire a god who not only held supreme power, but was a god of love, and one who treasured and honored his creation. Although she did not know if any of the other maidens were *Yehudi* who knew the source of her stories, she was confident that they would not make themselves known either.

───────── הַפְסָקָה ─────────

For twelve months Esther applied herself faithfully to her studies, patiently accepted her hours of purification, attended instruction, and endured the dreaded dance classes. As the months passed, the routines and the palace atmosphere gradually became customary. The relationships among the maidens gradually separated them into distinct groups by their preferences, skills, personalities, and most importantly, their level of determination to become the chosen one. The older maidens seemed most convinced of their chances to become Ahasuerus' Queen due to their bodies being more developed. Also, due to age differences, their experiences with men were more advanced, at least to a degree. These facts alone caused those not in that elite group to despise and avoid them at all costs. This resulted in frequent catfights, arguments, and schemes to dash the hopes of other equally ambitious girls who were deficient in male exposure other than family time with close male relatives. The elites plotted, schemed, practiced, and mastered their abilities to manipulate the eunuchs, flirt with the guards, and of course, undermine the confidence of the younger maidens, all to ensure their advantage.

In the group of the younger maidens Roxanna was often chosen as the object of berating, teasing, and domination by the older girls. Roxanna was small-built with a slim, athletic body. Roxanna was also extremely beautiful with a radiant smile and a wide-eyed innocence and purity the older girls hated. Esther considered it ironic that sweet and gentle Roxanna excelled in dance class. From conversations with her, Esther knew Roxanna did not grasp the seductive purpose of such dancing—she loved it because it came easy to her. Esther suspected Roxanna's preference for dance was also because Elaheh showered her with favor and praise—something Roxanna had never been given. She poured her efforts into the mastery of it like an addiction, and Esther knew the jealousy of the older girls was the source of their negative treatment since Roxanna proved, at least in dance, that she surpassed them.

Besides trying to support and comfort those who were still homesick, depressed, and dominated, Esther spent her energy and free time to learn more about the history and people of the Persian Empire. Due to her favor with Hegai and the eunuchs with access to the records, she spent as much time as possible in the library reading about the other provinces, the war efforts, and especially any records related to her own people's history in Babylon before the empire was overthrown by the Persians. These historical records, which she suspected were written with intent to overly favor the Persians, were also shared in stories with the groups of girls who spent time with Esther and her attendants. Most of the maids had no idea of their history.

It did not take long for Esther's ability to entertain and teach through story-telling to be, not only encouragement for herself, but also the beginning of a revelation to the maidens that there might be an unseen, loving and powerful God, who was always present and all knowing.

> *I will bless Adonai at all times:*
> *His praise shall continually be in my mouth.*
> *My soul shall make her boast in Adonai:*
> *the humble shall hear thereof, and be glad.*
> *O magnify Adonai with me, and let us exalt His name together.* (Psa 34.1-3)

✡

Chapter Twelve

The Tenth of Tebeth

Now when the turn came for each young woman to go in to King Ahasuerus, after being twelve months under the regulations for the women, since this was the regular period of their beautifying, six months with oil of myrrh and six months with spices and ointments for women— (Est 2.12 ESV)

When the year of the six months of myrrh, the six months of perfumed oils, and the year of training and purification ended for Esther's group of maidens, Hegai began to send them to the king's house evening by evening. He told Esther that her appointment would be on the tenth of Tebeth. Esther was relieved that there were many who would go before her, and she honestly wished each maid success with all her heart that she would be chosen to be the next queen.

During the days before her appointment, Esther silently witnessed the changes that came over each maid as she neared her appointed day. Esther felt a deep, connected concern for each one, especially on the day of her final preparation when Hagai gave his last instructions. Each maiden experienced extreme tension due to the unknown expectations she would face. Also, with the possible result of rejection, came the insecure feelings and mental struggle of why she might not be acceptable. The most obvious concern was where she would spend the rest of her days.

As the numbers dwindled Esther grieved that no one had been chosen. Many of the maidens that she had grown to know and love and had shared so much with were now in The House of the Women. Perhaps it was a foolish thought of her own making, but she had convinced herself that if a queen were chosen, she and the remaining virgins would be allowed to return to their families.

Esther's anxiety grew as she neared the event for which she had been brought to the palace. She concluded that being the queen of a vast empire built by the overthrow of small, peaceful cities, the indiscriminate slaughter, and the forced slavery of those who were spared had no appeal for her—in fact, it was a thing to be despised. The knowledge of why Vashti was removed was foremost as she hoped she would not please the man who would place such a shameful requirement on a woman, much less his wife.

She tried to mentally select some song or poem from Mordecai's scrolls to bring a word of comfort to her soul. She remembered a favorite writing from the beloved King David and meditated on the words that had once given her much joy and hope.

Praise Hashem.

Blessed are those who fear Hashem Elohim,
    who find great delight in His commands.
Their children will be mighty in the land;
    the generation of the upright will be blessed.

As she allowed the words to come into her spirit, Esther knew that she would not be blessed with children who would be mighty in the land since she lived in the palace of an idolatrous king. How could her generation possibly be blessed? Perhaps the promises of Hashem concerning blessings and children were not for her.

Wealth and riches are in their houses,
    and their righteousness endures forever.

"O, Hashem," she groaned, "I am surrounded by wealth and riches, but I seek righteousness above all that this palace can give! But how can a *Yehudi* maiden be righteous when the very reason for her existence is to be used for the pleasure of an unrighteous, pagan king?"

Even in darkness light dawns for the upright,
    for those who are gracious and compassionate and righteous.
Good will come to those who are generous and lend freely,
    who conduct their affairs with justice.

Had she not tried to be gracious? Had she not shown compassion? Did she not desire to be among the righteous? When would Hashem come with justice for her?

She remembered her dream on the last night before she was taken. She closed her eyes and tried to find again the river of light that had filled her, but all she found was a dry desert. She had made every effort with everyone in the palace to conduct herself with truth and fairness. *Perhaps Hashem will indeed come to me!*

Even in darkness light dawns for the upright.

"Abba, please let light dawn for me! I feel I am swallowed in darkness and my path is a way that leads to isolation, uselessness, and death. When my time comes to go to the king, give me the power to be gracious, compassionate, and above all may I not come away counted among the unrighteous."

The words continued . . .

> *Surely the righteous will never be shaken;*
> *they will be remembered forever.*
> *They will have no fear of bad news;*
> *their hearts are steadfast, trusting in the Lord.*
> *Their hearts are secure, they will have no fear;*
> *in the end they will look in triumph on their foes.*
> *They have freely scattered their gifts to the poor,*
> *their righteousness endures forever;*
> *their horn will be lifted high in honor.*
> *The wicked will see and be vexed,*
> *they will gnash their teeth and waste away;*
> *the longings of the wicked will come to nothing.* (Psa 112.1-10 NIV)

As Esther considered the promises that the righteous would never be shaken, she thought of the nights when she had covered her head in despair and hopelessness. She had even wished her life would end. Guilt and shame flooded through her being. Every day she had lived in the knowledge that she was permanently separated from Mordecai and Sara and the community of *Yehudim*. Never would she be married in a *Yehudi* ceremony to a *Yehudi* husband. Never again would she have the hope to be the maiden whom Hashem would use to bring forth *Mashiyach Melek*! Her heart often shattered, and her faith wavered as she considered her future compared to the promises of Hashem to those who lived for Him. Her future promised that she would be locked in a house for concubines, unworthy to be a wife or queen, or to ever hold a child of her own. Her future was to be used and thrown away. How was she to believe she could ever know honor? How could she ever hope to see the wickedness of her present existence come to an end?

She covered her face with her hands. Esther could not remember a previous time when she had doubted the writings on Mordecai's scrolls. They had always comforted her and given her faith in Hashem Elohim.

But as the days drew closer to her appointment with the king, she realized she was overwhelmed with uncertainty and fear that El-Shammah (the God who is present) had left her in this palace that was to her a gilded, vile prison.

Without knowing why it entered her mind, she suddenly remembered the day she stood with her beloved Sara and watched Uriel at his pottery wheel. For a few moments she laid her head back, closed her eyes, and relaxed in the still vivid memories of that day.

Then her mind connected the passage in the scrolls from Jeremiah's writings with her mental images of Uriel working:

> *So I went down to the potter's house, and I saw him working at the wheel. But the pot he was shaping from the clay was marred in his hands; so the potter formed it into another pot, shaping it as seemed best to him.*
>
> *Then the word of Hashem came to me. He said, "Can I not do with you, Yisrael, as this potter does?" declares Adonai. "Like clay in the hand of the potter, so are you in My hand, Yisrael."* (Jer 18:3-6)

Esther raised her hands in surrender, felt a rising presence in her being, closed her eyes, and allowed the hot tears to pour and a prayer from her heart.

"I am in Your hand, *Abba*. Hashem Elohim, My Creator, direct my path and my destiny; mold me as You see fit, and if necessary crush my will and my desire that I may be used by You. Make me a vessel fit for Your use."

———————— הַפְסָקָה ————————

In the next few days, Esther marveled that among the maidens still in her group, some were actually looking forward to their evening with the king even though already more than half of them had been sent to his house and were now living in The House of the Women.

Of the maidens in Esther's group that were preparing to go into his house, there arose questions about the king's temperament, his character, and the requirements that would please him. They had no opportunity to ask for answers to those concerns from the concubines or the girls who had recently been with him because they were locked away in The House of the Women. The most disturbing information they had was the fact that each maiden was being compared to Vashti's statuette that was located just outside his bed chambers. The idea of being compared to a woman of white, cold marble, caused anxiety to some, and gave others confidence—since flesh was far superior to stone, or so they reasoned.

THE TENTH OF TEBETH

The maidens had many questions.
The king did not find any of the previous beautiful maidens desirable?
Why were they not called again?
Why is it rumored some returned in tears from their night with the king?
Why were some sent to The House of the Women still virgins?
But to the dismay of the maidens, no replies were sent back to them. Esther observed, listened, and dreaded her upcoming evening with the king.
I am clay in Your hands, Hashem. Use me for good and not for evil.

──────── הפסָקה ────────

She was taken to King Ahasuerus in the palace in the tenth month, the month Tebeth, in the seventh year of his reign. (Est 2.16 CSB)

On the ninth of Tebeth, the tenth month of the Persian calendar, Hegai reminded Esther about her appointment the following evening with the king.

"Is there anything you would like to take with you, Esther?" asked Hegai.

"No, Hegai, I know of nothing I need to take with me. I put my trust in you to determine what I should take. I have watched as the maidens before me collected items to take, and not one of them apparently helped. I will present myself, and nothing more than what you suggest."

Hegai looked at the most beautiful, gentle and kind woman he had ever met. He still could not quite decide what it was about her that made her far superior than any of the others. They were all beautiful, but all were quite different. They had all gone through the year of treatments to make themselves more beautiful, but the beauty that Hegai saw in Esther was beyond natural beauty. She had about her a fragrance—*yes . . . it is like a fragrance*— that did not come from a plant or an oil. He could not define it.

"Will my clothes and personal items be moved for me from The House of the Maidens to The House of the Women, or should I move them tomorrow?"

"Your place in The House of the Women is already determined and prepared for you. Tomorrow evening, I will oversee the movement of your items. You do not need to be concerned about them. I will see that nothing is taken or damaged."

"Thank you, Hegai. I am sorrowful that I will not be under your protection and watchful eyes any more. You have been very kind to me and have given me peace of mind."

Never had anyone spoken with such gentleness and gratitude to him. Realizing that his time with her was ending, he stood looking at her with pity that one such as she should be in such a situation. *He does not deserve this one,* the eunuch thought.

"I have spoken with Shaashgaz, the king's chamberlain over The House of the Women, and informed him of your integrity, excellent character, and favor among the women who have come to know you and respect you. Rest well, tonight, Esther. May the gods to whom you pray and honor give you favor with the king and may you be chosen as Queen of Persia."

―――――― הַפְסָקָה ――――――

That evening after the girls in The House of the Maidens had gathered around Esther for possibly her last night with them as maidens, they asked her to tell them one more story about the unknown god.

"You must not leave us, Esther," said Farah, a girl as happy as her name, "until you tell us more about the mysterious and wonderful god!"

"Yes," they all chorused. "You must!"

"Tell us one of romance!" giggled Roxanna.

Esther closed her eyes to decide which of her favorite stories she should share with these maidens who she had come to love so dearly. She suddenly remembered a story that every *Yehudi* girl hoped would one day be her own, the story of Avraham, Sarah, Yitzchak, and Rebecca. Smiling, she began.

> There was once a very wealthy man named Father who was married to a beautiful woman named Princess. For many years Father and Princess longed for a child, but soon they were both very old and past the time of bearing children. Many times Father had asked God to give them a child.

"How strange that his name was Father, and yet he did not have children!" interrupted Roxanna.

"Sometimes a name is given to a child with the hope that the child will fulfill the meaning of his name!" replied Esther. "Shall I continue?"

"Yes. We will not interrupt you again!" said Yasmin with a threat in her tone and an eye turned to Roxanna.

"Sorry, Esther," Roxanna said meekly.

> One day God spoke to Father in a vision and said, "Don't be afraid. I am your shield and your very great reward."

Father said, "What will you give me since I have no children? You have not given me any seed and only my servant born in my house is my heir."

God promised, "Father, you will have a son."

One day Father was sitting outside his tent when he saw three strangers approaching. He immediately jumped up and ran to meet them and invited them to stay for a while and eat with him.

He ran into the tent where Princess was sitting and said to her, "Make three cakes on the hearth!"

He ran to the herd, caught a calf and gave it to a young man and said, "Prepare this calf!"

He took butter and milk and the calf which had been prepared, and spread it on a cloth under a tree so the three strangers could sit and eat.

After they had eaten, one of the men told Father that he and his wife would have a son by that same time the next year.

The old woman named Princess was listening behind the tent wall and when she heard the stranger's words, she laughed.

"How ridiculous! I am too old now to have a child!"

You see, Princess was now 89-years old and Father was 99-years old. But she did not know that the one speaking to her husband was the Mighty God.

Suddenly she heard Him say, "Your wife laughed, but you will have a child."

Princess drew back from the tent's wall in shame that she had been overheard. She wondered what kind of man would say such a thing about her.

"What kind of man can hear me from inside this tent?"

The next year at the same time the men had eaten with the old man, Princess—who now was now 90 and her husband Father was 100—gave birth to a little boy. She remembered the promise of the stranger and her reaction, so she named the baby *Laughter*.

The girls burst into a hysterical laughter that echoed in the room.

"That is impossible! No woman that old can have a baby!" screamed Ariana in a high pitched voice. "Even prayers to Ardvi Sura Anahita would be pointless if one were that old!"

The girls nodded and agreed.

"Oh, by the gods! I hope that isn't possible! Can you imagine?" Daria added with tears running down her face. "What would you do?"

By now Daria was so tickled she got the hiccups.

The girls were so loud, Esther wondered if Hegai would come running.

"Oh, but you forget my friends. This God is a God of miracles. Even two of His names are *Creator* and *Provider*. He can do anything!"

With eyebrows raised Esther looked at the girls as their laughter slowly changed to a more serious tone.

"But . . . but . . . why didn't he let them have the baby when they were young?" asked Nima who was known to have elderly parents.

"Nima, women have children when they are young, but God wanted them to know, and everyone who would know about Laughter, that only God can make it possible for a 90-year-old woman and a 100-year-old man to have a baby!"

"I have never heard of a god like that! Even Ahura Mazda has never done such a thing!" answered Leila.

And the others in the room agreed.

"What happened next, Esther?" Roxanna asked.

> When Laughter became a young man, Princess died. Of course, Laughter was very sad. He grieved for his mother, so Father decided that it was time for Laughter to have a wife of his own. He called his oldest and most trustworthy servant to help.
>
> "Go to the land where my relatives live and from my brother's children choose a wife for Laughter. Promise me that you will not choose a wife from another tribe, only my relatives. Do not take Laughter with you. And if the maiden that you find will not come with you, I will release you from your promise."
>
> The servant started his journey with other servants of his master and ten camels heavily ladened with gifts. After days of travel, he reached his destination. He stood near the well where the maidens came to draw water, but he was such a good and faithful servant, he suddenly feared he would not please his master so he prayed.
>
> "Oh, Lord God of my master, please prosper me and show kindness to my master. I stand here at the well with my camels, and the daughters of the men of the city are coming to get water. When I ask the maiden to let down her pitcher to give me drink, she will say, 'Drink, and I will water your camels also.' Then I will

know she is the one you have chosen for my master's son, and that you have shown kindness to my master."

"What?" Yasmin's eyes were wide and incredulous. "Water ten camels? Esther, he is making this too hard! What kind of girl would do that? What kind of girl could do it?"

"I could do it!" boasted Nima.

"So could I!" exclaimed Roxanna.

"No! No, you couldn't!" replied Yasmin.

"Y-e-s-s-s-s, I could!" argued Nima, and Roxana nodded.

By now the girls were all involved in whether any of them would attempt it.

"Don't you understand? The servant asked for something impossible! He knew if it happened, it was proof that God was with him! If one has a real God, a request for something only He could do is proof that He is really God when it happens! If prayers are always restricted to only what can happen naturally, how would one know that God answered? Why would one even pray? Now, shall I continue, or shall we continue to argue?"

Esther crossed her arms, and with her eyebrows raised again, she waited.

"Oh, please, I can't wait to hear about the servant that went home without a girl!" said Roya sarcastically; and this remark brought more laughter.

When they quieted, Esther continued.

> So even before the servant had finished praying, he saw a young maiden coming to the well with a pitcher on her shoulder. She went to the well and filled her pitcher. The servant saw that she was very beautiful.
>
> The good servant ran to her and said, "Please, give me a drink of water from your pitcher."
>
> So the young woman lowered her pitcher and gave him a drink.
>
> "I will also water your camels," she said.
>
> She ran back to the well, filled her pitcher, emptied it into the trough, and did this repeatedly until she had watered all the camels.

Esther looked at their skeptical faces with pity. They worshipped gods of wood, stone, and clay who had never answered even an easy request. The concept of a god who hears and answers, well, no wonder they could not believe there was such a god.

She continued . . .

The servant watched her and silently wondered about her. He wondered if God had prospered his journey.

When the maiden had watered all ten camels, the servant gave her two gold bands to wear on her wrists, and a gold ring for her nose.

"Whose daughter are you?" he asked. "Does your father have a place where we can stay tonight?"

"I am the daughter of Bethuel, the son of Nahor," she said, "and we have plenty of straw and feed for your camels, and a place where you can rest."

At the words of the girl, the servant knew Nahor was the brother of Father.

He bowed his head and prayed, "Blessed be the Lord God of Father, who has not forsaken His mercy and truth toward my master. As for me, He has led me to the house of my master's brethren."

The young maiden ran to her house and told her mother, brother, and father these things.

When her brother saw the golden nose ring, and the gold wrist bands, and heard all that his sister had to say, he ran to the well and found the servant standing there.

"Come in, blessed of the Lord! Why are you standing here? I have prepared the house for you, and a place for your camels!" he said.

The girls started laughing.

"What is so funny?" asked Esther.

"The brother!" they replied in chorus.

"He's a man that can see where the gold comes from!" said Roxanna. "He wants to make sure he and the family get all they can from this man with servants and ten ladened camels with him!"

"Ah, you think you know this man?" smiled Esther. And the girls all started giggling and nodding.

"I will continue."

After arriving in the home and being made comfortable, the servant was offered food.

"I will not eat until I have told you why I'm here."

The family said, "Please, go on."

"I am the servant of Father, your brother. He is very rich in flocks and herds, silver and gold, servants, camels and donkeys. He has a son that was born when he and his wife were very old, and he has given all that he has to his son."

"Ah, ha!" interrupted Nima. "I'm sure the brother was all ears to hear that!"

"Shush, Nima! Don't interrupt the story!" chided Ariana.

The servant continued. "My master sent me to his brethren to find a wife for his son who is grieving over the death of his mother. My master said to me, 'The Lord will send his angel before you on your journey, and you shall take a wife from my brethren.'"

Then the servant told how he came to the well, what he had prayed, and how the maid had done everything that he had asked.

"When I asked her who she was, she told me you are the brethren of my master.

"When I asked her name, she said, "My name is Captivating."

"Captivating?" asked Leila. "Her name should be Astounding!"

The others broke out in stifled giggles.

Quickly Leila responded, "Shhhhh...Let Esther finish!"

Captivating's father said, "It is the work of our God."

He looked at his daughter and asked, "Captivating, what do you want to do?"

She said, "I will go and be the wife of Laughter."

The servant gave the family many gifts and gave Captivating gold and silver and many beautiful garments.

Captivating's mother knew she would miss her only daughter. She begged the servant for more time.

"Please, give us more time to say goodbye to our daughter. It is too soon for you to leave with her. Just wait a few days."

But the good servant said, "I cannot wait. My master is old and Laughter's mother is dead, and he grieves over his loss. I must not delay but leave immediately."

The father and brother of Captivating loaded the servants' camels with Captivating's belongings and the servant started home with her and her maids.

As they neared the end of the journey, the servant saw Laughter in the fields meditating. When Laughter looked up, he saw

Father's servants, the ten camels, and with them a young woman accompanied by maids.

When Captivating saw Laughter she asked the servant, "Who is that man walking in the field to meet us?"

And the servant said, "That is Laughter, my master's son."

So Captivating immediately got off her camel and put a veil over her face.

The servant told Laughter everything about his trip and how he found Captivating. When Laughter heard all that God had done, he took Captivating into his mother's tent. She became his wife, and he loved her and was comforted after his mother's death.

The room was silent. Some of the girls looked at Esther with soft expressions. Some had tears, and some had closed their eyes. Others, started mumbling among themselves, and agreed the story was just too hard to believe.

"Oh, Esther, that is the best story yet," said Yasmin dreamily. "I wish a god would do that for me."

"Not me!" said Leila. "Who wants to go live in a tent when you can live in a palace and be the queen of the empire!"

"You are not the queen, Leila!" piped up Nima. "Maybe none of us will be! I would be happy if god would find me a man that would marry me and take me home!"

"Too, bad, Nima! The only thing the gods of Persia are giving us is a chance to be rejected and then to live the rest of our lives locked up in a harem with a bunch of old women!" said Zahra bitterly.

As Esther listened to their chatter, she felt deep sadness that she could not tell them that the stories were true, and that Hashem loved them. If they knew, and could believe, and would give Him their worship, He would rescue their spirits and give them joy that no palace or king or empire could give or take away. The room was silent.

Instead, she said, "It is late, my friends, and as you know, tomorrow will be busy for me. I will no longer be here with you; but when one is chosen as queen, may you remember the love that we had for each other."

Esther kissed each one.

Even before they had reached their own quarters, the spirit of competition and self-promotion took over most of them again. Esther knew they would later pray to their pagan gods that she would not be found pleasing to King Ahasuerus. That was one prayer she hoped would be answered.

Later as Esther lay in her own bed behind the privacy of the curtains, she whispered the *Shema*. Then as she thought about the evening with the girls, she remembered a prayer that Mordecai had taught her:

Trust in Adonai and do good.
   Then you will live safely in the land and prosper.
Take delight in Adonai,
   and He will give you your heart's desires.
Commit everything you do to Adonai.
   Trust Him, and He will help you.
He will make your innocence radiate like the dawn,
   and the justice of your cause will shine like the noonday sun.
Be still in the presence of Adonai,
   and wait patiently for Him to act.
Don't worry about evil people who prosper
   or fret about their wicked schemes. (Psa 37.3-7)

As the familiar words resounded in her spirit, she felt the inner moving of the light returning.

She grabbed onto the words, and she knew what she must do.

   Trust. Delight. Commit. Radiate. Be Still. Wait.

She clung to the promises that would follow her obedience to Hashem's words...

Safety. Prosperity. Heart's Desire. Help. Justice. Presence. Action.

She repeated the prayer again, focusing on each word and felt energy like a breath of air entering into her. She prayed it again, and tears—not of sadness or despair—but for the first-time tears of joy ran down her face. A courage entered her that cleansed away fear and doubt from her spirit that even pools of purification could not achieve. A presence she could not understand replaced the grieving, the dread, and the worry. She drank it in and allowed it to remove the darkness in her mind and soul, and the heavy weight that had lingered in her body, lifted like a sparrow set free from a cage.

✡

Chapter Thirteen

The Image in the Mirror

Now the king was attracted to Esther more than to any of the other women, and she won his favor and approval more than any of the other virgins. So he set a royal crown on her head and made her queen instead of Vashti. (Est 2.17 NIV)

It was early morning when Mordecai left worship and the *Torah* reading and started on his way as usual to check on Hadassah and to sit in the city gate with the other elders that heard disputes needing to be settled. Coming toward him, with the bright morning sun behind his back, a palace courier on a black steed almost ran him down. After he passed, Mordecai turned to watch him fade into the distance until only a cloud of dust was visible. Mordecai wondered what news he was carrying. As he pondered on the many possibilities. He came to suspect a queen had been selected. *It's been almost two years.* The thought brought a bad taste into Mordecai's mouth. Although Shahin had not reported to him in several days, he believed Hadassah had not been called to the king's chamber as yet. He held on to a thin hope he would hear news that Hadassah and the other virgins would be returned to their families and not kept as property of the king. He quickened his pace to reach the gates.

When the walls and the entrance gates were in view, Mordecai saw on the tallest palace turret, the king's flag. It was the same flag used to announce major events. This time, however, another flag was under the king's. It was the flag of the queen. Mordecai felt his heartbeat quicken.

Maybe today. Maybe today she will be allowed to come home.

As he neared the gates, it was evident the news was of great impact by the size of the crowd. Men whom Mordecai assumed were fathers, brothers, and the betrothed of the maidens filled the area.

Their frenzied chants, "Long live the great King, Ahasuerus! Long live his Queen!" caused a strange fear to overtake Mordecai, and at the same time a wrestling hope as the crowds repeated "Long live the great King, Ahasuerus! Long live his Queen!"

As the chant continued, the crowd watched the platformed balcony where the king or one of his attendants sometimes appeared to make announcements. The crowd was hungry to see the king—but even more to see the queen.

"Is the king expected to make himself seen? Will the queen be seen? Does anyone know where the queen is from?"

Mordecai went from man to man asking these questions. No one seemed to know any more than what was being chanted. So in frustration, Mordecai searched the crowd for other men he knew, then without seeing any friends, he took his customary place of waiting to hear the announcement.

———————— הַפְסָקָה ————————

Esther stood in front of a mirror looking into the eyes of a woman she did not know.

Who are you? How did you get here? What are you doing here? How did this happen? What will you do now? Where is Hashem?

The image in the mirror looked back with dark, sad eyes, and no answer came. She bent over a golden bowl filled with water and splashed her face with the cool liquid. On the other side of the door to the private chamber she was in, she could hear Ahasuerus giving orders and instructions to his attendants. She could hear men coming and going from his room where she had—in an unforgettable and surreal night—allowed him to take possession of her body.

Unfamiliar sounds and images flashed through her mind. She shook her head hoping to be rid of them but they were there, in permanent residence. She clenched her hands on the bowl then leaned over it and vomited until nothing was left but heaves. Once the heaving stopped, the pounding in her head was relieved. She straightened herself, poured fresh water from a pitcher to rinse her mouth, and eventually she felt the sickness within her lessen.

With another look in the mirror just to be sure she was not someone else, she opened an adjoining door and stepped into the steamy room that was a slightly smaller spa than the one she had visited on her first day at the palace. Her seven faithful attendants stood waiting with guarded eyes. With silent motions they welcomed her toward the bath they had prepared. They silently watched as she loosened her robe and allowed it to slide to the floor.

Looking up at them to see if they still recognized her, she waited to see if they would seem alarmed that a stranger had replaced her.

She stepped into the warm bath as one of the attendants collected her robe and Soraya, her most trusted attendant, stepped into the pool to bathe her. A drop of blood floated upward in the waters from between her legs like a red, swirling teardrop slowly dissipating into the foam of the water. Esther watched it as one might watch a strange, newly formed creature. Then loosing all strength, she laid herself backward against her attendant Soraya who allowed herself to be used as a pillow. Soraya wrapped her arms around Esther and held her head against her own while tears flowed from Esther's face and dripped into the pool. From deep inside she heard a whisper . . .

> *Fear not, for you will not be put to shame;*
> *And do not feel humiliated,*
> *for you will not be disgraced;*
> *But you will forget the shame of your youth,*
> *And the reproach . . . you will remember no more.* (Isa 54.4 ESV)

———————— הפָסָקה ————————

By noon everyone in the palace had received the news. Reactions were as different as their reasons for being there. Many of the residents received the news as they might a weather report. *Oh, good today, but who knows about tomorrow?*

The eunuchs took the news as fresh hope that the activity around choosing a queen would now be less demanding. Hegai felt somewhat relieved that his responsibility to ensure the maidens were prepared for their evening with the king was now, mostly, reduced. Of course, he knew maidens would still be requested by the king from time to time, but the expectation of their visit had taken a whole different perspective and purpose. The worst duty Hegai had was to inform those still in The House of the Maidens that Esther had won the crown since he had no idea how most would react. Just answering their questions took way more time than he had imagined. After leaving them, he congratulated himself for recognizing a winning choice based on more than a one night experience.

Hegai's most pressing and urgent duty after the announcement was to make arrangements for Esther's things to be moved from The House of the Women into the Queen's House, primarily to the rooms that once housed

Vashti, although Hegai knew Esther would probably never use most of those items again. Also pressing, by order of the king, he directed several of the king's most able-bodied servants to bring a cart into the hall outside Ahasuerus' chambers, load up the image of Vashti, and move it outside the palace walls to the place where other worthless items were discarded, crushed or burned.

At one o'clock the palace trumpeters took their positions on the rooftop overlooking the city of Shushan and blew their trumpets to indicate an announcement was to be made. Couriers on horseback had delivered the news, and the villagers had responded. Chants from the crowds below resounded and echoed off the massive walls of the palace. Then, to the delight of those in the courtyard and to those outside the gates that could see, the balcony trumpets sounded as Ahasuerus dressed in his finest robe and with his gold crown on his head appeared with Esther on his left arm. Esther was without full regalia since she had not yet been coronated Queen, but she was wearing the jewel-studded gold crown that once sat on the head of Vashti. A veil covered her face. A hush settled over the palace as eyes looked upon the woman who by declaration and extensive search had won the crown.

A royal crier stepped forward on the balcony to the king's right and ceremoniously unrolled a scroll. The crowd immediately hushed, and as breaths were held, the crier announced:

"BY THE DECREE FROM THE KING OF KINGS, THE EMPEROR OF THE PERSIAN EMPIRE, THE GOD KING AHASUERUS OF THE SHUSHAN PALACE; MAY ALL MEN TODAY, ON THE ELEVENTH DAY OF TEBETH, KNOW A QUEEN FOR KING AHASUERUS HAS BEEN CHOSEN AND IS THIS DAY DECLARED AS QUEEN ESTHER, QUEEN OF THE PERSIAN EMPIRE!"

Ahasuerus turned to Esther and removed her veil. Then the trumpeters sounded, and the crowd of people that had not had daughters taken, roared their approval, and started their chants again, "Long live the great King Ahasuerus! Long live Queen Esther."

Standing near the city gate, among excited and anxious family members who had been awaiting the reveal of the new queen, Mordecai felt his heart grip with the announcement.

He has chosen! It is done!

Pushing his way through the crowd of disappointed and grumbling family members, Mordecai shielded his eyes from the sunlight to get a better look. Once inside the gate, the glare of the sun was shadowed by the palace, so he glued his eyes on the couple above the crowd. He desperately tried to see the new queen's face. Fighting against the exuberant, yelling crowd, finally he was able to get his first clear look at her.

Regal, stoic and pale, Hadassah stood by the king, crowned and wearing a simple but elegant purple robe with a white fur collar. Shock overtook him; confusion filled him. He fought against the sudden weakness and his pounding heart as he realized it was she.

Hadassah. He chose my Hadassah. I must see her, he thought.

He dropped his head and closed his eyes.

"She is devastated," he whispered.

"O, Hashem, what have You done?"

As they cheered and celebrated, the crowd jostled and shoved against him. Family members of maidens not chosen continued to express disappointment and anger. Mordecai stood still, suddenly alone in his loss, and pondered in his heart how Hashem could have let this happen.

✡

Chapter Fourteen

Accepting the Crown

And the king gave a great banquet, Esther's banquet, for all his nobles and officials. He proclaimed a holiday throughout the provinces and distributed gifts with royal liberality. (Est 2.18 NIV)

Two months after the king's announcement princes, servants, military commanders, satraps, nobles and wives were coming by invitation to the palace for Esther's Banquet and Coronation.

Unlike King Ahasuerus' previous banquets, and to Esther's great relief, the feast and the coronation were to be held with great decorum and dignity. Through her attendants, the queen requested the palace be filled with flowers, candlelight, and incense. Food, wine, and the finest of all that the palace had to offer was in abundance.

As customary, the regents had planned the entertainment for the feast. Palace musicians practiced daily for the big event. Orders were sent to Elaheh to appear with her very best dancers. Although not especially looking forward to these performances, Esther was curious to see if Roxanna had been selected to be one of the performers.

In response to the king's pleasure in his queen, decrees had been made to the provinces announcing six months of release from taxes. Monetary gifts and wagons of food were sent into the villages so public celebrations in Esther's honor could be held. Never had the kingdom enjoyed such a celebration.

During the hours before the banquet, Esther received a secret, hand-written message delivered by the hand of Soraya.

"My Queen," she whispered, "a message from the eunuch Shahin who works with Hegai has been passed to me. I was told it must be delivered to you."

Esther looked at the script on the message and knew immediately it had come from the hand of Mordecai. Fighting to control her emotions at the thought of hearing from him, she hurried into her private quarters and read the message.

You are My servant,
I have chosen you and not cast you off;

Fear not, for I am with you;
  be not dismayed, for I am your Elohim;
I will strengthen you, I will help you,
I will uphold you with My righteous right hand. (Isa. 41.9b-10)

"Oh, *Dod!* What does this mean? I recognize it as from the scroll of Isaiah, but why do you send it to me? My life as a servant of Hashem is taken from me. Now I am the servant of King Ahasuerus. I have no power of my own. Do you send me the word of Elohim telling me I am chosen by Him? Why? Why would Hashem choose me? I am chosen by a king, yes, but not by my *melek*! I am chosen by this king, this Persian pagan, king! Ahasuerus!"

Her throat tightened, her eyes burned and she was filled with despair as never before.

She had spoken aloud as though he were there, and the memory of Mordecai that she had tried so hard to push out of her mind with the rest of her former life flooded over her. The loss of him pressed down on her, weakened her, and forced her to her knees. She wrapped her arms around herself, rocked back and forth and silently wept while she longed for him, his comfort, and his words of assurance.

Then she heard a familiar whispering wind, and dared not move lest she lose it. She held her breath and waited with her face wet and her heart broken. Then she heard the words as from deep inside her:

Esther, Esther, I took you from the ends of the earth,
  from its farthest corners I called you.
I said, "You are My servant";
I have chosen you and have not rejected you.
So do not fear, for I am with you;
  do not be dismayed, for I am your God.
I will strengthen you and help you;
I will uphold you with My righteous right hand. (Isa 41:9)

"O My *Melek*," she whispered back to Him, "I hear You again and I desperately want to believe You are with me, but I feel so far from You! I long to be without the fear that comes upon me at all times saying I am lost from You. It tries to strip from me Your words, and I wrestle at the thought that You chose me to be here in this place, in this marriage! And I can't understand why! I already feel cast off from my friends, *Dod*, my people."

ACCEPTING THE CROWN

She prostrated herself on the carpets, wrestling with hope against the doubt—trying to understand the why, yet, wanting desperately to believe. In her mind she envisioned Mordecai with his *tallit*. She felt it as he spread it over her, and remembering his voice, she tried to hear it again.

Then a feeling like warmth started on her face, down her neck, over her shoulders and spread slowly over her entire body like the warm oil in the palace spa. Every muscle relaxed, every fear vanished, and with her eyes closed, she realized with astonishment every thought of despair, shame and hopelessness was gone.

"I believe!" she said with surprise. "I do! I don't know why; I don't understand any of this, but I believe what Hashem says."

Then she pulled herself up, stood looking at the royal attire laid out for her to wear for her coronation, and raised her face upward. Calmly and with the voice of a queen she spoke.

"You are still my Elohim! You are still my strength. I wait to know why You have chosen me. I rest in Your hand."

The soft raps on her door and the sounds of her attendants excited voices, told her the time had arrived.

✡

Chapter Fifteen

The Day of Small Things

> When the virgins were assembled a second time, Mordecai was sitting at the king's gate. (Est 2.19 NIV)

Esther awoke, opened her eyes, and the room seemed to be spinning. She quickly shut them again and took a deep breath letting it out slowly. Opening one eye at a time, another issue began to arise. Alarmed, she slid from under the covers on the bed, fought her way through the veils, planted her bare feet on the cool, tiled floor, staggered to her private chamber, bent over the basin and vomited.

When she raised her head to the mirror, her dark eyes were the biggest part of her pale face. Another wave hit her, and she gripped the stand that supported the basin. Her mind flashed back to the first time she had ever looked in that same mirror and had a similar morning almost a year earlier for a very different reason. She pressed a cloth over her mouth and feared she might have awakened the king.

When the nausea passed, she peeked out the door. Satisfied the king was undisturbed, she tiptoed back through the darkness to the bed, and easily slipped back into her spot that was still warm. She breathed a sigh of relief that she had not awakened him. At that moment, it occurred to her that since her first time in that bed, Ahasuerus had never awakened during the night. Storms, sudden noises—nothing bothered the man. When he went to sleep, it was as if he gave a command and sleep obeyed; and sleep did not dare retreat until he decided.

Like sleep, she also was not to come into the bed until he gave her permission, and Esther was expected to stay there until he was gone. She really did not know why and had never dared to ask him. She reasoned it was just the way he ordered everything around his life. Like the throne, the bed was a place for taking care of his business, and sleep and having a woman in his bed were part of the business.

The bed was not for conversation, that was for sure. Conversation, when it happened was limited to the few minutes before he got into the bed. Usually, he gave instructions and asked questions, and she answered and obeyed. Esther had accepted the fact that she was his chosen possession, a comfortable convenience—at least until he decided otherwise.

Waking up was the same. Not one to spend time in the bed once awake, he immediately went to his spa, bathed, had a massage, dressed, called his eunuchs, and started giving orders which Esther imagined was his normal communication with almost everyone he encountered. Remarkably, once he finally left, one freedom she enjoyed was to stay in bed as long as she liked. And this morning, she planned to do just that.

She lay there in the semi-darkness and thought about possible reasons for the spinning room and the nausea. Mentally counting days, she adjusted her head deeper into her pillow, and stared upward. Seeing nothing clearly, she wondered.

Slowly the darkness was being overcome by a few small rays of early morning light piercing an entrance through the small openings in the curtains. As she watched it, she wondered how something so small could completely change everything. Laying her hand on her abdomen, she thought of another small thing she now knew was changing everything.

How do I feel about this? How will it change my life? Will I be allowed to hold him? Or her? Will my time be measured, or will I have freedom?

She turned her head to study the king in the soft, warm glow of light now taking over the room without permission. He was lying flat on his back with his head on the silken pillows, his beard on top of the coverlet, and a strange strangling sound was coming from his slightly open mouth. It was a sound that she had finally learned to sleep through.

She wondered if he would care. She realized with some discomfort in her acknowledgement that she had never known the king to visit any of his children in the harem. It was as if they did not exist.

I'll never understand this man. How very little I know about him, and yet, now I have his seed growing in me.

The thought sent a shiver through her as she fought in her mind against the memories of her past life and the loss of what might have been.

"*I called you.*

I chose you."

She closed her eyes and shook her head at the memory of the words. She remembered her promise to Him, then she remembered His promise to her.

Is this part of the promise? What of my child? Will he belong to You, or will he belong to the king who owns my body?

Suddenly her mind saw Jochebed, the *eema* of Moses. For the first time in her life she understood how hard it had been for Jochebed to leave her baby. She felt some of the desperation Jochebed must have felt.

Hashem protected him. Hashem used him. Will Hashem use my son? Will Hashem protect him? In that moment she knew she would not let the gods of Persia have her sons or daughters. She would trust Hashem to allow her to be the *eema* of her generation.

With that, she closed her eyes and waited for him to leave so she could request Saroya to bring her a dry piece of bread and a cup of watered wine so the early morning event would not repeat itself.

✡

Chapter Sixteen

The Plot

During those days while Mordecai was sitting at the King's Gate, Bigthan and Teresh, two of the king's eunuchs who guarded the entrance, became infuriated and planned to assassinate King Ahasuerus. (Est. 2.21 CSB)

When the people realized the king had ordered a second collection of maidens—those who were too young during the first collection— anger and outrage arose surpassing the first time it happened. From his usual post outside the palace gates, Mordecai noted on this particular morning, unlike recent days, an atmosphere of chaos as business as usual was now being pushed aside; venting and rebellion filled the air.

Two days earlier, Mordecai had received a message by the hand of Shahin from Hadassah announcing her condition. When he heard the king's plan to collect more maidens, he knew the reason behind it; but he also understood the outcry among the citizens. He wondered what the king's plan for Hadassah would be in light of this unexpected action.

On certain days Mordecai and Uriel conducted business for citizens needing help with producing written documents concerning legal matters. But on this morning, Mordecai was alone in his booth and was observing two men who were not taking any notice of the angry citizens involved in the loud, irate discussions. Instead, these two chamberlains of the king seemed to be arguing near the palace gate and were now fully engaged in what looked to Mordecai as a heated discussion of their own. Mordecai recognized the two as the well-known eunuchs, Bigthana and Teresh.

During the last collection of maidens taken by King Darius, these same two men jointly owned a business in the village. They had tried to stop the king's men from taking their daughters by barring themselves with their families inside their business. They hid their two daughters in empty crates. Denying they had daughters eligible for the selection, the suspicious guards had made a search through the business which resulted in destruction of goods, furniture, and shelves. When the guards raised their hatchets to crush open the crates, the two frightened owners had intervened by throwing themselves upon the crates to save their daughter's lives. As the girls were being dragged from the building, the two men were dragged to the prison.

Two days later, they were sentenced by Darius to be made eunuchs in service of the king, or to be put to death. The two men had chosen to become eunuchs. As public examples for disobedience to the king's collection, Farzad the military commander announced in the public square that the two men would be made eunuchs and placed into the king's service. To Mordecai's knowledge, they were the two most famous eunuchs in Shushan, as they were also the only two eunuchs with wives and children. However, they were not permitted to see them.

As two guards moved toward the gate where the two eunuchs were arguing, Bigthana and Teresh stopped their conversation and turned their attention in the direction of the guards. Instead of entering the gate and returning to the palace, Teresh and Bigthana moved themselves away from the gate and Bigthana signaled for Teresh to follow him into what he intended to be a place for a private meeting behind Mordecai's booth.

Once believing it was safe to talk, Teresh turned himself to face Bigthana. He was red in the face, his neck veins were bulging, and his eyes were flashing with unrestrained fury. He spat out his words through clenched teeth.

"What are you saying? Have you lost your mind as well as your manhood?"

"Oh, that's a low blow, Teresh. Didn't you hear what I said? I have a plan. Do you want to hear it?"

"I doubt it. The last time I listened to one of your plans, I lost my business, my family, and my . . . well, you know. But I know you're not going to let me leave until you tell me. So tell me."

"We lost our first daughters to Darius', and in King Ahasuerus' first collection we had daughters taken. Now our younger daughters are of age to be taken this time. I won't let that happen if I can find any way to stop it. They are still my daughters. And yours are too, even if we can't see them. In fact, no one's daughter should be ripped from their home to become a number in a harem. Do you want to save your life or your daughter's?"

"Well, if I have a choice, I'd prefer to save both! How do you plan to do that?"

"I have been asking Savara, the eunuch over the palace herbs and potions, to give me the potion that the king demands from time to time when he gets a hangover. It causes one to go to sleep. As of yet, I do not have enough for what I plan to do, and since the men are already assembling to start taking maidens, I need you to go to Savara and get some of the potion."

"What? And what reason do I give Savara so he will give me potion?"

"As the king's chamberlains, we can ask for the same potion as the king

THE PLOT

by simply saying we have a pain or a body ache, or just need it to sleep. It's a simple potion, Teresh, and should not raise any alarm from Savara. He dispenses potions to all the palace servants, and since you have never asked him for it, he will not suspect you of any evil plan."

Teresh considered the plan. He stood so still contemplating it for so long that Bigthana said, "Teresh, do you understand? What's wrong with you?"

"Nothing. Just let me think this through. So say I get the potion. Then what is your plan? We help him what . . . sleep?"

"Right. We help him sleep. Every night Hargazah gives the king wine after the woman comes to his room. I've watched Hargazah for several weeks now. He has a special hiding place where he puts the king's wine so he can get it quickly for the most impatient man on earth. All we have to do is put the potion in the wine and when Hargazah gives the king the wine, it will cause him and the woman to go to sleep . . . a sleep that will be so deep neither of them will wake up when one of us goes into the room to kill the king."

"How do we know which bottle to put the wine in? And how will we do it without Hargazah seeing us do it?"

"Hargazah only keeps one bottle each day. With the amount of potion that I have, added to what you can get, we should have enough to make sure the wine will achieve our goal. We simply wait until Hargazah goes to relieve himself."

"I can get the potion. I can go along with putting the potion in the wine, but Bigthana, I cannot kill the king. I'm a simple man, a eunuch with a family, and I will do almost anything to save them. But I don't think I can kill a man—even one I hate. Besides, Hargazah sleeps on the couch outside the king's door. How will one of us go into the king's room to kill him without Hargazah knowing? It seems too risky. Or do you plan to kill him, too?"

"Think man! What is required of the eunuch that gives food or drink to the king or queen?"

Bigthana watched his face until he saw it register.

"Right! He must taste the food, and he must taste the wine. I've noted that the reason Hargazah had a bottle of wine hidden close to his couch is so he can taste the wine before the king gets the urn he puts it in. And, Teresh, Hargazah is a faithful eunuch; he takes big, big tastes."

"Enough to make him sleep that soundly? Are you sure?"

"Do you remember the day you had to wake me?"

Teresh nodded.

"I had tested a small amount of the powder. So yes, Hargazah will sleep. Since he is much heavier than I, with the amount of wine he will test, he will sleep until morning; I'm sure of it. Once Hargazah delivers the wine to the king, we will wait until he is soundly asleep, then I will go into the king's room and slash his throat. When the woman wakes up in the morning, she will not remember a thing."

"It seems a plan that will work, Bigthana, but if my Juliana—or now she is called Roxanna—is the maiden in the bed with him, the plan must not happen, for it is certain the maid will be blamed for murdering the king."

Bigthana beamed at Teresh. He had it all worked out.

"So can you get the potion?"

"First, promise me. If it's Juliana . . ."

"All right. All right!" interrupted Bigthana.

Teresh added, "You've convinced me. And if Hargazah doesn't go to sleep, we can always try again."

"Maybe, but I have been saving potion since I heard the queen was with child. I had surmised what the king would do even through there are still virgins in The House of the Maidens."

Teresh looked at him with great sadness and whispered, "Roxanna, . . . my sweet Juliana is there."

"We don't have much time," Bigthana urged. "Go to Savara, get the potion, and I will try again to get more, too."

With their plan made, the two men looked to be sure no one had noticed them, then started for the palace gate and their mission.

What neither of them realized, although they were using lowered voices, they were still within hearing range of Mordecai who was suddenly startled to hear their angry voices through the thin back wall of his booth, and even more alarmed at what he had heard.

Mordecai had not missed a word. Although he sympathized with the men's frustration and anger, he could not agree with a conspiracy to commit murder of the man married to his daughter. When a king was murdered, Mordecai knew wives and children were also murdered. Knowing their plan was to take immediate action, Mordecai wasted no time.

✡

Chapter Seventeen

Messages

> So the matter became known to Mordecai, who told Queen Esther, and Esther informed the king in Mordecai's name. And when an inquiry was made into the matter, it was confirmed, and both were hanged on a gallows; and it was written in the book of the chronicles in the presence of the king. (Est 2.22-23 NIV)

Shahin took the sealed message from Mordecai and immediately headed into the Queen's Palace and toward the south wing of the queen's quarters. Queen Esther and her attendants spent most of their afternoon time there. Hadarah, one of the queen's attendants, was sitting comfortably on a silk couch in the corridor outside Esther's private suite. She was working her needle through a fabric with a partially finished floral image she was embroidering with an array of colorful threads. Instead of handing the message to the door chamberlain, Shahin handed the message to Hadarah and spoke quietly.

"This is of urgent business. Please see that the queen gets it right away." Shahin startled her by his urgent tone.

Hadarah took the message, and without hesitation rapped on the queen's door. Shahin stood watching to be sure it was delivered. He quietly waited in case there should be a forthcoming reply.

At the sound, Leeza, the most curious of the seven maiden attendants, jumped up from her seat in the garden and ran to the door. She and the other attendants were there with Esther for one of her stories. As Leeza admitted Hadarah, she noted that Shahin was waiting which made her even more curious about the message. Hadarah made her way into the garden and handed the message to Esther. Esther glanced down at it and saw that the message was in Mordecai's distinctive script. Trying to mask her alarm, she stepped away from the circle of maidens, turned her back toward them, and opened it.

Why is Mordecai sending me a message during the day instead of the usual evening time when I am alone?

Unrolling the paper, her face paled. She read it again. Her mind immediately grabbed the urgency and the importance of the message.

How do I let him know? He's in a meeting with his regents. What do I do?

"Ladies, I must ask you to leave me. I have to attend to this message. Hadarah, please stay."

She dismissed the wide-eyed, curious maidens with a promise that she would send for them later to finish the story. Waiting until she was alone with Hadarah, Esther moved across the room to her writing desk, and with trembling hands, picked up her quill and copied the message from Mordecai.

> *My King, I have overheard this day two chamberlains, Bigthana and Teresh, plotting to take your life.*
> *Your humble servant,*
> *Mordecai.*

Turning toward Hadarah still standing at the door to the garden, Esther motioned for her to approach.

"Hadarah, I have an urgent message for the king who is meeting now with his regents. However, I cannot interrupt him, and I dare not present myself. I have written a note to him, and you must see that it is delivered to Hathach, the king's most trusted chamberlain. See that he deliver it to the king's hand without delay."

She read over the note again, closed her eyes and silently prayed.

"Hashem, protect Mordecai and me, Your servant, in this action to reveal an evil plot against the king."

Her heart started pounding as she suddenly realized the potential outcome. *If the king is killed, my child will also be killed!*

Oh, Adonai! Let this message get to the king!

Hadarah watched as she picked up a candle, lit the wick, and allowed the wax to drip along the edges of the message. She noticed with confusion that the queen did not seal it with her ring and wondered just what kind of note she was sending. She turned away lest the queen see her watching.

It must be a secret message! *The seal of her ring would reveal that it came from her,* thought Hadarah; suddenly she realized that it was no ordinary message.

With her hands still trembling, and her heart pounding, Esther turned to Hadarah.

"Hand this off to Hathach, if possible, or one of the other king's trusted chamberlains. Do not reveal its origin, or your life and mine may be endangered. Tell him to pass it through to the king only. Be sure he understands it is of upmost urgency."

Hadarah listened to her queen with wide eyes and her own heart pounding. She had no idea of the message contents, but she knew by the queen's face and her trembling hands that it was of dire importance. Realizing the danger of the mysterious message and her mission, she took it in her own trembling hand, and pressed it into her garment's folds.

"Yes, My Queen," she quietly whispered.

"Hadarah, you must not show any fear or intimidation. You are simply delivering a message. You have no idea of its source since it was handed off to you. So be careful that you are of a calm spirit, countenance, and innocence. I am confident in your ability to do that."

Esther smiled at her and took her hand.

"It will be fine, Hadarah. I am sure of it. You are fully capable to do this without incident."

Understanding the instructions, and slightly comforted by the queen's words and touch, Hadarah took a deep breath, smiled feebly at Esther, turned and headed to fulfill her mission. Once outside the queen's quarters, she dismissed Shahin, took a deep breath, straightened her shoulders, and headed toward the palace to find Hathach.

After Esther watched her retreat, she hurried to her private quarters, fell on her knees and poured out her requests to the king she knew would hear her—to El-Elohe-Yisrael (the God of Israel).

———————— הַפְסָקָה ————————

Haman held the note in his hand with a burning desire to open it. He was standing outside the hall where the king was meeting with the regents for the purpose of solidifying the order to take more maidens. When he left the meeting to attend to personal needs, he found Hathach standing at the doors to the throne room.

"I have a message for the king. It is urgent."

Haman noticed the paper in his hand, but he did not see a seal on the wax. "Who sent the message?"

"I do not know, Sir. It has passed through the hands of several servants," Hathach lied. "I am to give it directly to the king."

"Well, unfortunately, that is not possible. The king is in a business meeting with the regents. However, it is your lucky day. I can deliver the message."

Hathach eyed the vice-regent.

"Come on, man. I'm the vice-regent. If you cannot trust me, who can you trust?"

Now, with the message in his possession, he examinined it for a clue as to what it held, and who sent it. He considered how he might gain advantage by what he held.

I must be cautious. I do not know what this contains, but I am sure it must be of great importance.

With his mind made up to take a risk, Haman entered the hall and without any hesitation, approached Ahasuerus dramatically without waiting for the king to raise his scepter. The regents in the room watched in shocked silence. Ahasuerus eyed the foolhardy regent in the same manner a crouching cat watches an oblivious mouse in imminent danger.

Obviously Haman has lost his mind, since death is the result of such a reckless action, King Ahasuerus thought.

Holding the message with an outstretched arm and bowing with a flourish, Haman took his opportunity.

"King Ahasuerus, a most urgent message."

Ahasuerus nodded to one of the elite guards to take the message from Haman. Silence reigned in the hall as the king studied it, ripped it open, and with a clear expression of irritation began to read what he considered an impertinent interruption.

To the surprise of everyone, and without a word, Ahasuerus stood up as if propelled and handed the message to the scribe, Sergazi. Without even a nod to his protective military presence, and without waiting for them to assemble in their usual formation for procession, he left the hall with long, heavy strides, leaving the elite forces scrambling behind him to catch up.

An hour later, commanders and fifty of the fiercest selected Immortals in full armor gathered in the king's war room under the orders that the mission they were being given was only for the ears in the closed room.

"Find them. Bring them to the prison. Search them. Torture them to tell if others are involved. Then take them into the prison yard and impale them by sharp implement. I want their death to be slow and painful. After they die, leave their dead bodies hanging in the courtyard of the guards as a reminder to any and all who would attempt treason against the king."

Ahasuerus spoke the words in a flat voice as if he ordered impalements and hangings on an hourly basis. Although this was not the case, it was true that killing a man came easily for the Persian king.

Waiting in her quarters for confirmation that the king had indeed received the note, Esther heard a soft rap on her door.

"Enter," she said turning to see who she had just given permission.

"It is done, My Queen," said Hadarah.

———————— הַפְסָקָה ————————

Three weeks later, the king received another message: Vice-Regent Memucan had suddenly died. As the news of his death spread through the palace, every regent began to hope he might replace the king's number one advisor. Whoever received the position would be ranked above every other regent. Memucan had been second to the king.

Not satisfied with the slim hope of the promotion, and certainly not leaving it to chance simply due to the death of Memucan, Haman, using clever devices, initiated gossip that he would be promoted to Vice-Regent. He spread the rumor that due to his brave and quick action to reveal the identity of the two guards who plotted the death of the king, he would be promoted. Since no other regent had ever saved the king's life, soon everyone believed that Haman would soon replace Memucan.

Esther heard the palace gossip from her attendants. When she knew the reason Haman was to become the vice-regent, she wondered how Haman had managed to take the credit.

I know I put Mordecai's name on the message. So, how did the king think Haman was reporting the plot?

She had never privately met with Haman, but she did remember him standing before the throne when the crier announced each man's name and rank at her coronation. There had been something about him that made her uncomfortable. The same sensation returned now as she heard the news. Since she really had no reason for the feeling, she tried to push it aside and to forget about him. However, Esther knew Haman had access to the king due to his reputation as a seer. She also knew that seers, mediums, witches, and false prophets held power she did not trust. Hashem forbade the *Yehudim* from seeking help from those using mediums and witchcraft, or from making sacrifices to idols as a means to gain information or to see the future. As a shiver went through her, she eased her mind that maybe it was best that Mordecai had been saved from being remembered as the one who reported the plan of treason, especially one of such magnitude that resulted in the gruesome and slow death of two men.

———————— הַפְסָקָה ————————

Two weeks after Haman planted the report of his pending promotion, Ahasuerus, unaware of the gossip, but slightly aware of Haman's sudden popularity, entered his throne room for a called meeting with the regents and the royal guard.

Sergazi, the royal scribe stood and read aloud in the presence of the king and the regents the notes the king had dictated earlier that day.

To all in attendance:

This meeting of King Ahasuerus, King of the Empire, and God of Persia is for the following matters of importance to be determined and reported:

The top priority is to hear the report concerning the treason which was the plot of murder against the king, and the fulfillment of the king's decree to put to death the two door keepers, Bigthana and Teresh.

The second most urgent matter is the announcement of the promotion and appointment of a regent to replace the deceased Vice-Regent Memucan.

Finally, the receipt of the report from Farzad and the royal guards on the progress of the gathering of maidens.

Finished with his report, Sergazi returned to his desk to write the minutes of the on-going meeting.

From his throne, Ahasuerus noted the empty chair of Memucan. With a frown and obvious irritation, he noted one other empty chair. He was glancing quickly around the room to see who was missing when the doors opened. Every eye turned to see Haman standing in the entrance waiting for the king to raise his staff to give him permission to enter.

Scowling that anyone would dare to come in after he was seated, Ahasuerus hesitated, then with impatience and with an action much like the thrust of a sword, he held his staff out at arm's length to permit Haman's entrance.

He better have a good reason for entering late.

Ahasuerus with a steely stare noted that every eye watched Haman stroll toward his chair. Eyes watched as he bowed to the throne, took his place, and with a confident air bordering on arrogance, made a slow and intentional nod toward the other regents. Ahasuerus did not miss that every regent's head nodded in return.

"You may give reason for yourself, Haman," Ahasuerus said icily.

"My King, I was delayed by my visit to the prison yard to determine if your orders had been fulfilled. I was detained by the foreman of the prison who reported to me the many requests made by the men's families as to when the bodies would be removed from the stakes. I beg your forgiveness for my late appearance."

With his black eyes still on him, Ahasuerus suddenly remembered that previously Haman had interrupted a meeting. Scowling so that his eyes became slits, the king cleared his throat and spoke.

"That report is the duty of Farzad, Haman. See that you do not take on the responsibilities of others in the future. This is twice now you have interrupted by being late. Don't let it happen again."

Haman made an oily slide to the floor and bowed his head to the tiles. On his knees he begged with forced humility.

"My King, forgive me. I find myself loyal to oversee matters and to report them to you without delay. I meant no harm to the king or his regents. It is a fault of mine to be concerned about all matters relating to your safety."

Haman's remarks reminded Ahasuerus the reason for his first interruption. The scowl disappeared and suddenly he contemplated his decision about who would replace Memucan.

"I suppose a king should be grateful for such a one as involved as you, Haman," he said dryly.

Ahasuerus noted that every regent was regarding the kneeling Haman with what could only be described as great respect.

What's the reason for this? Do they expect Haman to replace Memucan? Haman? To become Memucan's replacement? He isn't even of noble background!

Ahasuerus glanced toward Admatha, the man he had intended to promote then back at Haman.

He is obviously honored by the regents, and I suppose he is also due a royal reward and proclamation for his part in the discovery of the traitors.

"You are forgiven, Haman. Please take your seat."

With a slight move of his hand, Ahasuerus motioned to Farzad to approach him.

"Now, Farzad, report on the matter of the two traitors. They have been gored and hung?"

"Yes, My King!" Farzad replied slightly louder than necessary.

"And the bodies . . . do they need to be removed? Haman reports that the families of the men are requesting it."

"Yes, My King, they are badly decomposed; in fact, they are barely on the stakes."

"See to it," he ordered. "Take the bodies to the heap and burn them."

"Immediately, My King."

Farzad bowed his head and turned to leave.

"Just a moment, Farzad. Are the men still dispersed and collecting maidens?"

"Yes, My King. I expect The House of the Maidens to soon be filled again."

"Good. You are dismissed."

After Farzad left the room, Ahasuerus turned toward the regents and looked each one in the face leaving Haman last. When their eyes met, Haman with an expression of confidence edging toward smugness, nodded toward the king.

Haman? I had not considered Haman. But he is a man of great insight and wisdom. I do count on his advice and predictions quite often. He glanced again toward Admatha. *Why did I pick Admatha?* He tried to remember his reasons for selecting him, but now could not remember any reason that outweighed Haman, or any of the others, in fact.

Ahasuerus nodded a signal to Sergazi who was already busy recording every word. He knew now that the king's next announcement was of most importance. Because Sergazi was more informed due to the rumors and gossip in the palace than the king, he turned his head slightly to hide his grimace.

The king has no idea that what he is about to announce will not be a surprise to anyone in this room, or even the palace—except perhaps to the king himself, he thought. *I have to hand it to Haman, he knows just how to manipulate the king to get what he wants.*

Ahasuerus cleared his throat and began.

"Today it shall be written and recorded that King Ahasuerus of Persia decrees that due to the death of Vice-Regent Memucan, the high office shall be filled by the promotion of Regent Haman, the son of Hammedatha the Agagite, to Vice-Regent.

"Furthermore, because Haman revealed the plot to take the life of the king, he is to be rewarded and recognized by the use of one of the best horses from the king's stables. A parade of full display, including royal trumpets, banners, criers, and dancers shall proceed through Shushan. May it also be decreed and published throughout the palace and to the palace gate vendors that all palace residents, and the village residents that are permitted to do business outside the palace gates are to bow in honor of Vice-Regent Haman just as they would in my presence."

To Ahasuerus' surprise, the room exploded in applause as Haman slid from his seat again and humbly bowed before the king.

"I am highly honored, My King. My life for your service."

"Now, let all the regents and the new vice-regent gather with me and the queen in the dining hall."

Ahasuerus, satisfied with the finishing of necessary duties of the meeting, arose and was escorted by his guards, chamberlains, and attendants in procession toward the dining hall where Esther and her attendants were waiting to join him for the noon meal.

After the king and his entourage left the meeting hall, the regents bowed one by one before Haman and congratulated him on his promotion. However, many of them were still wondering how Haman had managed to rise to such prominence within such a short time.

With no further delay, and with Vice-Regent Haman proudly leading, they proceeded toward the banquet hall.

———————— הפסָקה ————————

Escorted by Saroya, her six other attendants, and the eunuch Hathach, Esther arrived at the banquet hall. Once there, she was surprised to see the table set for more than the usual number. She had no idea who may be attending, but before Ahasuerus left his quarters earlier that morning, he had simply given orders to his chamberlain to inform Hathach and Saroya to have the queen in the banquet hall for the noon meal. In his usual manner, he gave no explanation.

"My Queen, do you think the promotion has been given?" whispered Saroya. "Although for weeks it has been rumored that Haman is to be promoted, according to one of the king's most trusted attendants, Admatha is the king's choice to be promoted."

"The king does not discuss his decisions with me, Saroya. I know about the rumor concerning Haman, but I have not had opportunity to ask the king about it."

Truth was Esther had never, and intended to never ask the king about any of his decisions.

At that moment Ahasuerus, the guards, and Sergazi entered the dining hall. Ahasuerus took his place at the head of the table and nodded to Esther at the other end where she and her attendants took their seats. From the distance, the sound of footsteps and men's voices gradually grew louder as the regents approached from the corridor. Esther noted that Haman was leading with an obvious strut, and from his glowing appearance—and the fact that he was in lead—she deduced that Haman had indeed received the rumored promotion.

At the sight of him, the familiar uneasy feeling moved through her.

✡

Chapter Eighteen

Rescued

"My heart rejoices in the LORD! The LORD has made me strong. Now I have an answer for my enemies; I rejoice because you rescued me. No one is holy like the LORD! There is no one besides you; there is no Rock like our God." (1 Sam 1.1-2 NLB)

When Esther's pregnancy became obvious to everyone in the palace, Ahasuerus stopped asking for her to attend him at night. Esther acknowledged with sorrow that maidens were going to be taking her place. They would be used without any hope of any real long-lasting reward.

She was grateful that she would no longer be spending time near Ahasuerus' rooms to know which maidens were coming and going. She suspected he did not want her to know. Since the girls in The House of Maidens were those collected when she came to the palace, she knew them and loved them. As she thought back to her days in The House of the Maidens, Esther wondered if one of her most beloved friends might still be there waiting her turn to be called, but now without the possibility of a crown.

With that in mind, Esther sent for Hathach.

"Yes, My Queen. You sent for me?"

"Hathach, I am concerned for one of the maidens I spent a lot of time with when I was in The House of Maidens. I have written a note to Hegai, and I want you to deliver it."

"Yes, My Queen."

"Hathach, I do not want my actions to be hidden from the king. So in your reports to him today, know that it is pleasing to me that the king knows of my inquiry."

He looked at her with a face that as usual showed no indication of his thoughts.

She handed him the note sealed with her signet.

"Since it is an easy to answer inquiry, please wait for a reply."

"I will, My Queen."

"You may go. Thank you, Hathach."

She watched as Hathach left and felt gratitude toward Ahasuerus for assigning his most trusted chamberlain to her. He became her attending eunuch after Ahasuerus learned she was pregnant. Also, the king instructed her to stay in the Queen's Palace until the child was born.

When she asked Hathach what the king had defined as his duties toward her, he was open and honest.

"I am to see that you are safe and contented. Also, I am to report daily to the king any visitors or communication with you. The king also instructed me to attend you to the library, outside gardens, or any other place you may go in the palace. He is concerned that you are well-protected."

Esther believed Hathach. She had been careful that none of her activities would displease her husband. In her heart, she was thankful for Hathach, and he served her faithfully.

Hegai met Hathach at the door of The House of the Maidens. Because Hegai felt pleased that Esther had become Queen, he often inquired after her welfare. He and Hathach agreed that she was extraordinary and the king was lucky to have her.

"I have a message from the queen for you, Hegai."

Hegai took the note, rubbed his finger over the seal and broke it.

Hegai,

If the maiden Roxanna is still in your excellent care, please send the maiden to me as soon as you can gather her things, and move her into the quarters with my other attendants. Remove her from the list of maidens and add her name in the palace records as one of my attendants.

Queen Esther

"I am instructed to wait for your reply."

"Yes, well, it will be more than words. Come with me and you can help me prepare the answer."

Hegai grinned at Hathach as he tried to make the assignment mysterious.

Within an hour, a rap on the door of Esther's quarters stopped her pacing. She quickly opened the door herself. Surprised to see not only Hathach, but also Hegai personally delivering the maid, she smiled at him.

"My friend, thank you."

"My Queen," Hegai replied with a smile, and bowed deeply before her.

Walking away, he smiled and whispered to himself, "You never disappoint me, My Queen."

One of Esther's eunuchs had told her that the recently killed eunuch Teresh was Roxanna's *abba*. Her heart had broken for her friend.

Standing like a small child with the look of expectancy on her face, Roxanna looked into Esther's eyes. When she saw the queen smile and open her arms, Roxanna threw herself into Esther's arms and began to weep.

———————— הַפְסָקָה ————————

An unused suite in the queen's palace was being renovated into a nursery for the coming prince or princess. By decree, the king had placed the full decision-making power and budget into Esther's hands. When she received, his permission through Hathach, she went into her quarters and in private worship, wept with joy and thanksgiving.

For the first time since coming to the palace, Esther had personal freedom and an opportunity to make decisions about a part of the palace that in the future would be especially important to her—her baby's quarters. Her mind began to envision how she wanted it. The designs of the nursery, sitting room, play area, and classroom were completely hers to decide. She felt purpose, independence, and happiness that had been missing in her life since she had been taken from Mordecai. With added excitement from her attendants, she planned, drew plans, and discussed the layout. At times joy overcame her, and she could do nothing but laugh and sing.

One day while she was selecting fabrics, Sergazi interrupted with a message from the king. Actually, it was a message to the king from his mother.

My son,

I will be arriving shortly to Shushan to help with the preparation for the arrival of the royal prince or princess . Although my duties here are many, and I am pressed for time, I feel it is important that I attend to the preparation of the child's quarters. I will also personally handle the selection of the wet-nurses, teachers, and physicians.

Please have my quarters prepared for my arrival.

Your mother,
Queen Atossa

Taking a deep inhale, and letting it out slowly. Esther sat down.

"Thank you, Sergazi. Please let the king know that I have received the message."

Watching Sergazi leave, Esther suddenly felt weary and overwhelmed. Flashes of images from the first time she met Atossa flooded her memories.

RESCUED

The image of her entering The House of the Maidens, and the humiliation she felt while Atossa was examining her swept through her again.

During Esther's coronation, Queen Atossa had barely spoken to her and when she did, it was with coldness and disdain as though Esther was a filthy woman off the street. For days afterward and until she finally went back to Babylon, her expressions and her words had continually been aimed toward demoralizing Esther. Now Esther realized that when Atossa received the news of the pregnancy, she was responding as if Ahasuerus were solely responsible for it. The child had no mother. She knew she had favor among the residents of the palace, and the thought that Atossa would humiliate her again in front of everyone, made Esther grieve.

For days Esther's joy and happiness waned as she anticipated Atossa's arrival. She forsook the nursery and the plans. Everything the king's decision had given to her by his permission to make the quarters to her own taste was suddenly gone.

Finally, she accepted the news and the position of Queen Atossa. Regardless of how Atossa acted toward her, she was Ahasuerus' mother and a queen. Esther decided to take her disappointment to Hashem.

On her knees, she waited as her mind searched for just the right words to pray, then from her memory came the words of the psalmist.

> *Hashem Elohim,*
> *You are my portion,*
> *And my cup of blessing*
> *You hold my future.*
> *The boundary lines have fallen for me*
>   *in pleasant places;*
>   *indeed, I have a beautiful inheritance.*
> *I will bless Hashem who counsels me—*
>   *even at night when my thoughts trouble me.*
> *I always let Hashem guide me.*
> *Because He is at my right hand,*
> *I will not be shaken.*
> *Therefore my heart is glad*
>   *and my whole being rejoices;*
>   *my body also rests securely.*
> *For You will not abandon me to Sheol;*
>   *You will not allow Your faithful one to see decay.*

> *You reveal the path of life to me;*
> *in Your presence is abundant joy;*
> *at Your right hand are eternal pleasures.* (Psalm 16.5-11)

Rising from her prayer, she washed her face, left the sadness and disappointment, and joined her attendants for a time of sharing a story.

———————— הפסָקה ————————

Two weeks later, Sergazi returned.

"My Queen, the king has sent you another message."

Esther was not sure, but it seemed Sergazi had a very pleased look about him.

She took it in her hand and immediately recognized the same script.

My Son,

With a broken heart, I must report that I will not be coming anytime soon to Shushan. Another uprising here in Babylon is taking my full attention and time. However, I have written my own personal suggestions and ideas for you to use in the preparation of the birth of your child.

Your mother,
Queen Atossa

Esther, now confident and filled with peace that she would not be hindered, spent hours continuing her designs, choosing fabrics, and selecting furnishing. Everything she requested of the king was granted, and joy returned and was as evident to everyone as her growing abdomen.

In her flurry to prepare for the birth, Esther's messages to Mordecai reporting on her condition and activities gradually declined, as did her inquiries concerning news from her friends, his health and business, and the reports from Jerusalem. Her sadness and loneliness over the loss of her past life with him, her former social life, her friends and relatives were slowly being replaced by the joy of her pregnancy. The close friendship with her attendants, the business of palace life, her time spent with her maiden attendants, and the duties related to the wives and children of the regents became her focus. The responsibilities to oversee the welfare of family members of the servants in the royal household kept her life filled with activity and distractions.

Known for her gentle, understanding and compassionate nature, she was held in high regard and esteem and often sought out for her company. She was famous for her stories, and anyone who had the opportunity to hear one of them was delighted by her.

With her new life taking on purpose and joy, gradually Esther lost knowledge of what was happening in Mordecai's life.

✡

Chapter Nineteen

The Parade

> . . . King Ahasuerus honored Haman, son of Hammedatha the Agagite. He promoted him in rank and gave him a higher position than all the other officials. (Est 3.1 CSB)

The day after the king's announcement of Haman's promotion, Mordecai was in his booth near the palace gate working with a couple of citizens in dispute over a land transaction. While the three of them were engrossed in their discussion, they were suddenly distracted by trumpet blasts and a great commotion outside. They left their work and moved into the street that led to the palace gate to see the source of the commotion.

In stunned amazement, what Mordecai saw was a procession much like one for the king. Dancers leaped, twirled, and beat tambourines while those blowing trumpets led a man on horseback coming from the direction of the palace toward the gates. Quite an impressive number of attendants who followed him were carrying banners to indicate the man was of high importance. The reaction of the guards and palace servants, confirmed that this was indeed a person of high esteem—they were all bowing to the ground before him.

As the procession reached the gates, the servants and visitors coming and going through the gates stopped where they were and also bowed in homage. When the merchants and market shoppers around Mordecai also began to bow, he realized that while he was away for the Sabbath, something of great importance must have transpired without his knowledge.

"What is going on?" he mumbled to himself.

The man beside him turned and with an expression of surprise explained.

"Oh, didn't you hear? Haman, the son of Hammedatha, was promoted to replace Memucan. The king has ordered that all servants of the palace, the guards, nobles, regents and those with permission to do business at the palace gates must bow before Haman whenever he is present."

Stunned, Mordecai jerked his head toward his customer.

"Haman? Haman, the Agagite? But why? That was never done for Memucan."

"It seems Vice-Regent Haman saved the king's life by reporting two eunuch door keepers who were planning to kill him. He is a seer, you know. So, of course, Ahasuerus trusted him."

"Haman? Haman reported?"

Mordecai placed his hand to shade his eyes to get a better look at the man coming toward him on horseback.

Is that really you, Haman?

As the horseback rider grew nearer, all doubt as to who was on the horse was removed when Mordecai saw clearly the same black eyes under the heavy, bushy brows, a long pointed nose protruding above a black moustache that framed his mouth and his long, sharp chin. It was the man he knew.

Although Haman was older now, Mordecai stared in silence at the same man who as a youth had been so poor and indebted, he had been forced to sell himself to Mordecai as an indentured servant. That same young man later became involved in idolatry to the point of having the image of his god Āz embroidered on all of his garments. Unsuccessfully, he had made attempts to become a priest of that same idol after Mordecai released him from his indentured position. But instead of becoming a priest as he had desired, the desperate Haman found work as a barber and for the next twenty-five years promoted himself as an astrologer and a fortune teller.

Mordecai had lost track of him. In recent years he heard the rumor that Haman had been invited by Darius, and later his son Ahasuerus, into a position as a royal seer and political advisor. More recently he heard that he had been appointed the position as a regent.

Seeing Haman now on horseback being bowed to as if he were a god was so shocking that Mordecai was speechless. Apparently, Haman had been given an even greater promotion.

Mordecai felt a coldness enter his soul at the sight of the man whose ancestors, the Amalekites, in the most treacherous and dastardly manner attacked the Israelites' camp in Rephidim when the people were desperately crying for water. Perhaps the goal of the attack was to claim the possessions and items of value from the Israelites. However, when the Amalekites realized the women, children, aged and infirmed persons were in the rear of the camp behind with the baggage, they smote them with a deadly blow and took their spoils. Hashem had given the order to wipe the Amalekites out when they were defeated, but because of King Saul's greed and disobedience, God's instructions had not been carried out.

Haman! How did this descendant of Agag whom Hashem has cursed rise to this high position? How is it that this man who is a known worshipper and seer of an idolatrous god ascend to such a position of power? And how did a message from me to Hadassah get passed to the king as though from Haman?

"Yes, he reported it!" the client said interrupting Mordecai's thoughts.

"I heard he walked boldly into the chamber of the king and without waiting to be admitted, approached him with the message! So naturally one so brave, one so respected was promoted by the king to the office of Vice-Regent in thanks for saving his life! His reward as the king's closest advisor and even possible successor to the throne says a lot about a man who rose up from the ranks of the common man!" he exclaimed.

As Haman came nearer to the booths of the men and women of business outside the city gates, the two men with Mordecai fell on their knees and lowered their heads to the ground along with every man and woman—every man and woman that is except one—and that man dared to stand with his eyes locked boldly on him.

From his high perch, Haman swept his eyes over the bodies of the men and women bowing before him. Pride surged through him. Suddenly, he caught sight of one, middle-aged man still standing. Even the horse seemed to stumble in response to the sudden yank on the rein.

Is he blind? Is he demented? Does he desire to be hanged? How dare he remain standing! Who is this fool?

He did not recognize the man, but something about his stance and bearing brought a distant memory of a *Yehud* he had once known. To this very day Haman still hated him with every fiber of his being. He remembered his voice from so long ago giving him a ridiculous choice that had something to do with the *Yehudim Shemittah*. The *Yehud* spoke of the festival of *Sukkoth* that included the remission of debts every seven years among the *Yehudi*. He told Haman he could be set free from his debt, but only if he would forsake his own god and choose to worship and serve the invisible god of the *Yehudim*.

Haman snorted as he remembered his quick decision.

What? Serve the same god that long ago had ordered the annihilation of his own people—the god of the Yehudim who had cast his so-called chosen people into slavery and caused their glorious city to be burned? Never! He would not be where he was now if he had made that decision!

The memory brought a fresh rush of disgust and hatred for the *Yehud*. In anger he clenched his teeth, locked his jaw and made a determination to investigate who this man was that refused to honor him. Maybe this is one of them. *How dare you disobey the command of the king? I will see you hanged, you filthy Yehud!*

Mordecai remained in his position until after Haman's troupe was out of sight. As the servants of the palace and the vendors began to stand, some noted that Mordecai had refused to bow. Whispers of shock and confusion mixed with fear came from the crowd. Soon several of those closest to Mordecai's booth surrounded him and his two clients and began to question his actions.

"Why did you refuse to bow, Mordecai? Did you not know it was a command of the king?" asked Chavezi, the baker.

"You bring shame on us, Mordecai! You will bring the guards to our businesses! What were you thinking?" yelled Zebudiah, the seller of oil. "All you had to do was bow!"

As the crowd around him grew, the questions laced with fear and insults continued until Mordecai felt overwhelmed.

Finally, Mordecai raised his hands in an effort to stop them.

"My friends, I am a *Yehud*, a follower of Hashem, my God; and by the law of Hashem I am commanded not to bow to another god."

Zebudiah moved his face close to Mordecai's.

"He's not a god, Mordecai! He has been promoted to Vice-Regent."

The tone Zebudia used indicated that he thought he was speaking to someone with none or little intelligence.

"Zebudiah, to a *Yehud* any image of a god is as much an idol as one of wood or stone. Haman's clothing is embroidered with his god's image and name. If I bow to Haman, I also bow to his god. If I bow, I disobey Hashem's command, and bring dishonor to Him and on myself."

"You know you will be reported! You disobeyed a command made by the king!" said Chavezi.

"Rest assured, if it is reported to the king, I will make it clear that I am the one that refused to bow. Do not be afraid or worried for yourself. I will stand for myself when the time comes."

Zebudiah shook his head and gave Mordecai a look of disgust. Men and women not fully convinced that somehow Mordecai's refusal would not become a problem for them slowly moved away. A few continued to loudly hurl insults and anger toward him. Small groups huddled casting looks of irritation and even hatred in Mordecai's direction.

Mordecai sadly noted this and returned to his own shoppe realizing that in a moment he had lost favor with his neighbors and fellow shoppe owners. The two new clients had retreated in fear, as well.

As Haman continued his parade through the streets and crowds, his day had gone from sunny, bright and glorious to dark, gloomy and stormy. Even as he waved to the people who cheered and chanted, the image of the standing man was burned into his vision and mind. Gone was the satisfaction of reward from years of effort to gain a position in the empire. Gone was the elation that had carried him from the palace to the gate. All he had now were dark images and imaginations of various and multiple ways to murder the *Yehud*, as he strongly suspected the lone, standing man was one.

Still muttering under his breath at the edge of the city, as the other participants of the parade headed to homes or palace, Haman reigned his horse into the passageway that led toward the massive house and grounds that he and Zeresh, his sons and their wives and their children had lived in since he became a regent and was given the home by the king. Just the sight of it usually thrilled him every time he turned toward it, but today those feelings of appreciation for what he had achieved and been given were crushed. Even now realizing that he would also have his own office and suite of rooms in the palace did not change his sour mood. He fought against the bitter taste in his mouth even while he waved and forced himself to nod and smile at his neighbors and the tradesmen who had been waiting in the alleys and open doorways. Some were even hanging from windows to congratulate him on his arrival.

In anticipation of his arrival for the evening meal, Haman knew Zeresh was preparing the very best they had to offer for the large family gathering. Seeing his wife and family, friends, and business associates bowing on the pavement as he and his procession had passed, brought tears to his eyes. He had never felt such joy and pride. The standing man faded from his thoughts.

When Zeresh had received the news of her husband's promotion, a flurry of activity to prepare for a celebration in their home had begun and was now being finished up as the sounds of the crowd chanting Haman's name, and the clip-clop of horses' hooves on the tiled entrance to their home became audible. Zeresh grabbed a towel and wiped her hands. She knew by the joyous noise that Haman had indeed finally realized his dream and it had been royally made known—*the Vice-Regent to Ahasuerus*!

She rushed toward the door calling for the servants, grandchildren, and her son's wives to join her in the courtyard for his welcome. Beaming with pride and with her head held high to see the reactions of the jealous neighbors, she clasped her hands to the center of her chest and felt her pounding heart. Tears streamed down her face and into her wide, grinning mouth.

Seeing his wife, grandchildren, and daughters-in-law clapping and rejoicing in sheer joyful pride, Haman felt some of the darkness in his soul fade. He could hardly wait until his ten sons arrived and all of the family would be present to celebrate with good food, wine, and congratulations on a long-awaited achievement. The parade had finalized the promotion.

Once he dismounted, just getting to the door of his home proved a task. Men with agendas and motives of self-promotion fought their way through the throngs to slap Haman on the back. Their wives ladened him with gifts of food, wine, jewels, and coins wrapped in expensive fabrics in woven baskets. Haman's servants moved toward him to help receive the gifts and adulation and to keep him from being smothered by the crowd.

As the throng was thinning, Haman's sons began to arrive. Surrounding him, they ushered Haman into the house that soon filled, not only by Haman's immediate family of his sons and their wives, but also by Haman's brothers and sisters, and the closest friends of the family. Everyone was eager to hear Haman's retelling of the day's grandeur, and he had practiced his presentation throughout the afternoon just for this moment.

As he savored the noisy and joyous reception, the image of the one lone man standing tried to recapture his mind. With determination he gave a jerk to his head, and thought, *Maybe another day. This one is for celebration.*

✡

Chapter Twenty

The Meeting

[Samuel to Saul] "This is what the LORD Almighty says: 'I will punish the Amalekites for what they did to Israel when they waylaid them as they came up from Egypt. Now go, attack the Amalekites and totally destroy all that belongs to them. Do not spare them; put to death men and women, children and infants, cattle and sheep, camels and donkeys.'"

Saul went to the city of Amalek and set an ambush in the ravine. But Saul and the army spared Agag and the best of the sheep and cattle, the fat calves and lambs— everything that was good. These they were unwilling to destroy completely, but everything that was despised and weak they totally destroyed.

"Enough!" Samuel said to Saul. "Let me tell you what the LORD said to me last night."

"Tell me," Saul replied.

Samuel said to him, "The LORD has torn the kingdom of Israel from you today and has given it to one of your neighbors—to one better than you."

But Samuel said [to Agag], "As your sword has made women childless, so will your mother be childless among women." And Samuel put Agag to death before the LORD at Gilgal. (I Samuel 15 NIV)

The entire royal staff at the King's Gate bowed down and paid homage to Haman, because the king had commanded this to be done for him. But Mordecai would not bow down or pay homage. (Est 3.2 CBS)

Before Mordecai reached his home that evening, he also had someone waiting for him. He slipped out of the shadows near the area where Mordecai had prayed the night before Hadassah was taken, and met him near his door.

"Please excuse me, Master Mordecai, I have an urgent request, Sir."

It was one of the servants of Simeon, a *hazan* elder of the *Yehudim*.

"Very well, Rahm. What can I do for you?"

He kept his voice level, but he felt sure he already knew what request was coming.

"Oh, it is not for me, Master Mordecai, but for the elders of the village. They sent me to ask you to meet with them in the worship hall. They are waiting for your arrival."

"Very well. Please return and let them know I will attend shortly. I just need to place my tools and materials in my office and I will be on my way."

THE MEETING

Rahm gave him a slight bow and quickly headed toward the village.

Once in his office, Mordecai stood in the dimly lit room, took a deep breath and let it out slowly. So much had happened; so much had changed. Weariness seemed to suddenly overtake him. He stepped into his closet, poured water into a basin, wet a cloth, and held it over his face until the coolness of it was gone. Turning toward the window that faced the East, he closed his eyes and lifted his face and hands toward the sky and quoted in the same prayerful tones that Hadassah had loved so much, an encouragement that Joshua had given to Israel after Moses died.

> *"Have I not commanded you? Be strong and of good courage; do not be afraid, nor be dismayed, for Hashem Elohim is with you wherever you go."* (Joshua 1.9 NKJV)

He remained still until the words sank into his heart and refreshed his spirit. Filled with renewed assurance that he had obeyed the command of Hashem no matter what should come next, he finished by saying, "Amen," then turned and headed for the worship hall.

Even before he entered the door, he heard the raised and angry voices. As he stepped into the room, every head turned and silence fell like a rain-filled cloud; the atmosphere was saturated with discontent. Mordecai walked toward the front, turned and calmly said, "*Shalom, achim.*"

It was like fire to kindling. Immediately everyone began with raised, angry voices.

———————— הַפְסָקָה ————————

Mordecai sat slumped in the dark under the olive tree in his garden. All of his community was outraged. The evening had completely exhausted him. He could not stop the sound of their words bouncing in a jumble of voices inside his brain. A headache that started over his eyes and wound around to the back of his head was like a tight band. He thought if it grew any tighter surely his head would explode. The questions and irate comments were connected like a string of beads about to break and scatter.

You will see us all killed, Mordecai! We've managed to live in peace, run our businesses, build a place of worship! We've established a community with the pagans and guards!

Now with one act of disobedience to the king's command to honor this promoted regent we are all in danger! How are we to proceed? Do you expect us to also refuse to honor him? We'll lose everything! It's bad enough the guards are gathering our daughters again!

Where is Hashem? Why doesn't He see what is happening? Why doesn't He deliver?

You have sentenced us all to disaster, Mordecai!"

He could still hear the women sobbing behind the screen. Nothing he said calmed the congregation but rather seemed to only cause greater outrage. If defending his actions based on the commandment of Hashem was not enough, what else was there to say? Even when he tried to call for prayer, they would not allow it. They were inconsolable.

What really caused the greatest sorrow, and drained all strength from him was the realization that his *Yehudim* community were making a declaration that their worship, customs, traditions and faith were important and would be followed only as long as they did not contradict the laws or expectations of Persia. As a scribe of the scriptures, he knew all too well the consequences and judgment that would come upon them if they failed to love and obey Hashem.

He bowed to the ground until his pounding head was pressing into the dirt. Tears poured from his eyes which caused the pain in his head to intensify due to his swollen nasal passages. For several moments all he could do was moan and sob.

Finally, he whispered a prayer.

"Hashem Elohim, forgive me for my sorrow and my complaint at this unexpected trouble. Bless me, O Hashem, because I love your words, and I desire to obey You. By my obedience, may your promises be fulfilled in my life."

He quoted the promises of Hashem from the *Torah as a prayer*:

> "I will send rain at the proper time from My rich treasury
> > in the heavens,
> > and will bless all the work you do.
> You will lend to many nations,
> > but you will never need to borrow from them.
> If you listen to these commands that I am giving you today,
> > and if you carefully obey them,
> I will make you the head and not the tail,
> > and you will always be on top
> > and never at the bottom." (Deut 28.13-19 NIV)

He made his vow in response.

THE MEETING

"I also remember Your words when I may be tempted to disobey You. Your word reminds me..."

He quoted more.

> *"You must not turn away from any of the commands I am giving you today,*
> *nor follow after other gods and worship them.*
> *But if you refuse to listen to Hashem Elohim*
> *and do not obey all the commands and decrees I am giving you today,*
> *all these curses will come and overwhelm you:*
> *Your towns and your fields will be cursed.*
> *Your fruit baskets and breadboards will be cursed.*
> *Your children and your crops will be cursed.*
> *The offspring of your herds and flocks will be cursed.*
> *Wherever you go and whatever you do, you will be cursed."*
> (Deut 28.14-19)

Remembering the words, he understood that Hashem gave commands for the blessing and good will to His children. His blessings required one to obey or the blessing would not be given. Praying them to Hashem now caused Mordecai to dry his tears and resolve to remind his *Yehudi achim* the words of Hashem.

From his heart, he poured out his prayer for his people.

"*Abba*, I beg for mercy for my community. They are frightened. They have seen and borne such great suffering and mistreatment. The results of our forefathers sins against You for idolatry, rebellion, and refusing to hear Your prophets and Your many calls to repentance brought us into our present circumstances.

"Help us, *Abba*, with courage to resist the fear and walk obediently before You that we will be delivered from all these curses and rise to the top. Strengthen me, and give me voice to encourage them into Your promises. Amen."

When he arose, he turned to see Ari standing quietly, close enough to hear his prayers.

"Ari..."

"My friend, you have prayed for us and even before the words reached the throne of Elohim, they have been answered—at least somewhat."

"What do you mean, Ari? Answered? Explain."

"After you left, Rabbi Joseph ben-Gideon quieted the men. He began to read from the book of D'varim.

> 'Now these are the commandments, the statutes, and the judgments, which Hashem Elohim commanded to teach you, that ye might do them in the land whither ye go to possess it . . .' (Deut 6.1 KJV)

"Suddenly, a voice in the back began to quote the next words aloud and in unison with the rabbi as he read. With each verse more of the men joined in. Some began to weep, some fell on their faces, and by the end of the reading everyone said together,

> 'And it shall be our righteousness, if we observe to do all these commandments before Hashem Elohim, as He hath commanded us.' (Deut 6.25)

"Mordecai, *achi*, we are *Yehudi* and El-Elohe-Yisrael is our God. We are with you. We are ashamed of our anger, our words, and our fear. But Hashem has moved our hearts to Him, and we have asked for His forgiveness and now we ask for yours.

"We remember how you spoke before the taking of our daughters, how you helped us to trust in Hashem and expect Hashem to deliver. It was miraculous what happened. Our daughters were spared . . ."

He stopped suddenly.

"Ari," Mordecai whispered, "Hadassah is in His hands as well. Do not feel ashamed to mention her name. She is the queen, and who knows what Hashem has placed her there to do."

Avi moved toward his friend, kissed him on each cheek, and placed his hands on the chest of the man whom he loved above all the men of his community.

Mordecai stood with swollen eyes, stuffy nose, dirt on his forehead and hands, and his face still wet and streaked from his tears, but his heart was suddenly melted with the peace and joy that only comes when one knows his prayer is not only heard, but answered by El-Elohe-Yisrael.

✡

Chapter Twenty-One

The Report

When they had warned him day after day and he still would not listen to them, they told Haman in order to see if Mordecai's actions would be tolerated, since he had told them he was a Jew. (Est 3.4 CSB)

In the coming days and weeks, when Haman entered or left the gates of the palace, now without the parade and fanfare, the people bowed in honor. Most of the times when Haman was passing, Mordecai would stay in his booth to avoid another upset from the tradesmen. However, during those times when Mordecai was going to and from the business and Haman should appear, Mordecai was the one remaining upright man in the crowd or on the road alone.

Every day that Mordecai refused to bow, the servants of the king would ask him the same question.

"Why do you break the king's command?"

And each time Mordecai would explain.

"I am a *Yehud* and I cannot bow to another god, and Haman has his god embroidered on his garments."

The community, market tradesmen, and especially the servants of the palace noted Mordecai's refusal and also clearly saw its effects upon Haman. His irritation had now turned from irritation to anger, and from anger to rage.

Finally, three hired palace servants saw in the situation a way to possibly improve their lives.

"I wonder what Haman would do if we told him about that man."

Behzad stopped pulling weeds to look at Javad.

"What man?

"The one that refuses to bow when Haman goes by. I mean, look at him. Everyone has noticed that he stands when everyone else bows! I think Haman needs to know who he is. Do you?"

"I will only go to Haman if there's a reward in it for me," said Masoud. "I have watched the man enough to know that there is something about him to beware!"

"I think we should do it. We know this man; we know where he works; and we know he's a *Yehudi* captive," Behzad said decisively.

Masoud rolled his eyes at Behzad.

"You do know we are captives, too. Why is it important for Haman to know he is *Yehudi*?

"Because I think the more information we give, the more reward we may achieve."

Masoud nodded. It made sense, and suddenly he felt confident.

"Let's do it," said Javad.

They had watched Mordecai standing when everyone else bowed before Haman. They also were aware of Haman's rage about it. The hope of gaining favor with Haman, and the possibility of monetary reward or maybe even a promotion from their low-paying jobs, gave them the courage to make an effort to meet with him through his eunuch assistant, Keyvan.

First, their biggest problem was gaining access to Keyvan. Secondly, they would have to convince Keyvan to allow them access to Haman. These problems were the subject of many discussions over multiple bottles of wine they shared after their workdays. These discussions resulted in outrageous suggestions while they were under the influence of drink. Finally, their wives became aware of their reason for meeting every evening, and they decided to give the three some unsolicited advice.

"Have you ever been in the palace?" asked Marible. "Are you allowed into the palace?"

"Well, no," replied Masoud to his wife. "We were hired by commander Farzad's order. We have been in the prison yard from time to time to construct gallows and such, but never in the palace."

"Why don't you ask a guard to help you get admittance to Haman?" asked Paraia with her arms crossed over her ample bosom.

Behzad looked at her with a look she had seen many times from her husband.

"What? Woman, why would a guard help us? They don't even see Haman unless they are ordered to appear! You speak like a fool."

Marible placed the palm of her hand on the table and leaned in to put her face in Behzad's.

"Then maybe you should get a woman to do it for you, Little Mousy. Anyone with a brain knows that if a guard, eunuch, or kitchen maid knew there was information of importance to be passed along, they would give aid in hopes of a reward for themselves."

Watching Marible get into Behzad's face caused Masoud and Javad to burst into laughter. When she twisted herself around to glare at the two of them, they quickly sobered.

THE REPORT

"Uh . . . maybe she's right," said Javad.

Paria, Marible, and Helezai gave each other knowing looks.

"All right. So here's what we'll do . . ."

──────── הפסקה ────────

"Haman is very busy. What possible business would you have with a man of such importance?"

Keyvan looked down his nose at them.

Masoud knew Keyvan was always looking for information to pass on to Haman. In fact, that was how he got his position as Haman's assistant. There was no way Masoud, Javad, or Behzad were going to give him anything to pass along.

"It's urgent. We need to speak to him directly."

"If you don't help us get to him, we'll find another way, and we'll be sure to tell him you wouldn't help us."

Behzad had a threat in his tone and Keyvan knew it.

"I can't just send three yardmen into the presence of the man second to the king without letting him know the urgency."

Keyvan gave it one last attempt, but he could tell by the look of these hardened men's faces, he was not going to get far.

"Fine," spat Javad. "Let's go. I have an idea of how to get word to him without the aid of this hungry jackal."

The three turned to leave, but Keyvan's desire for favor and possible pay-off was defeated by his curiosity.

"Wait! Stay here. I'll see if I can persuade him to see you."

Masoud gave Behzad and Javad a crooked smile. Getting Keyvan to cooperate had seemed the biggest hurdle to get to Haman.

Masoud whispered to his two friends.

"Now we must approach Haman like we planned. We don't just throw the news at him, we give him bits of it at a time."

"Sure, sure," snarled Javad.

The confidence of the three waned a little more minute-by-minute when Keyvan didn't return.

"Do you think he's just trying to torment us?" asked Masoud.

"Of course, he is! He wants to make sure we know how unimportant we are!"

Javad jumped to his feet. His face was red and his eyes bloodshot. This was just one more irritation in a long day.

"Let's go. We can get to Haman without Keyvan! Even if we have to go to his house."

"Fool! He would have our heads if we dared to show up at his home! What are we going to do next? Scale the palace wall, burst through the window and fight off several of the Immortals?"

Behzad shoved Javad back into his seat.

Finally, they heard the heavy footsteps of Keyvan who was almost as round as he was tall, and tall he was. In fact, his height was the second reason Haman had picked him as his closest assistant. Having an assistant that towered over others gave him an advantage—at least, that was the idea.

"Follow me. It took some persuading, but I finally got him to agree to give you a few minutes. I warn you, though, if you come with a message he deems a waste of time, you may get thrown into the prison."

Javad's step faltered, but Behzad put his hand in the middle of his back and forced him to keep up. Javad gave him a dark look and used his elbow to jab him.

These three men whose work was to clean and groom the area around the palace walls had never dreamed of being this deep into the palace. Behzad felt his mouth go dry as he looked at the carvings of the gods of Persia glaring down at them from the columns, and the tiled murals of the Immortals in fierce battle made his stomach tighten.

"Hey, hey . . . Masoud! Javad! Maybe we need to rethink this pl . . ."

His voice trailed off as Keyvan suddenly stopped outside double doors which were at least three men tall.

"He's in here. Give me a moment to announce you."

Keyvan disappeared through the heavy wooden doors that opened like walls.

The three stood in the cavernous hallway listening to their own hearts pound in their ears. Suddenly someone's stomach made a loud growl and Javad snickered.

"How hard can it be?" he whispered. "I heard someone say he was a barber for over twenty years! He's one of us!"

The other two gave him completely deadpan expressions.

Double doors swung open to reveal a floor padded with a thick elaborate Persian rug woven in deep blues, reds, and highlighted with yellow-to-gold tones. Massive dark, red-toned cabinets covered with carved fruit and flowers filled one entire wall adjacent to the heavily drape-framed, floor-to-ceiling windows filled with inlaid, colored glass that made images of Persian hillsides filled with brilliant sunlight.

Sitting behind a desk the size of a chariot was a dark-haired man with black eyes under heavy brows divided by a sharp, long, pointed nose over an invisible mouth hidden behind a black, fuzzy mustache. They immediately recognized Haman who seemed surprisingly much smaller now behind the huge desk than he appeared sitting astride the king's gigantic steed.

"Well?" bellowed the esteemed Haman. "Are you going to just stand there?"

The question jolted them from their trance-like states and instinctively the three of them fell to the floor on folded knees with heads touching the thick carpet.

Rising to a crouched position Masoud stuttered, "We beg your patience, Sire. We have an important message for you."

"From whom?" asked Haman.

Not expecting the question, Javad looked at Masoud and Behzad with wide eyes and saw four wide eyes looking back at him.

"Uh . . . well . . . *us*, Sire," croaked Javad. "Masoud, Behzad, and me, Javad."

"What kind of message would three such as you have? You have interrupted my work, so this message had better be worth taking my valuable time!"

"Yes, Sire."

Javad turned to Masoud to continue, but he gave an almost indiscernible shake of his head. So much for their well-planned presentation. Javad, realizing the two cowards with him were completely mute, swallowed hard, tried to imagine Haman as a mere barber, and lunged forward with the message.

"We have news, Sire, of a *Yehud* that refuses to bow to you, thus, disobeying the king's command. We have asked him multiple times why he will not bow and . . ."

"Wait!" Haman stood up and placing both palms on his desk, leaned forward. "A *Yehud*? You're sure?"

"Yes, yes, Sire. We are sure. He has repeated that each time we . . ."

Haman interrupted Javad again.

"I knew it! What is his name?" Haman demanded.

"His name? Sire? His name is Mordecai."

For a moment Haman seemed frozen except for his black eyes. The left one started twitching.

That filthy Yehud, he thought. *It is him!*

Then glaring at the three men in front of him he said, "I knew he was a Yehud! I've seen him myself! He refuses to bow! The gall! Where does he work? I know it's somewhere near the gate."

"He's a scribe, Sire. He has a booth on the left of the city gate. He's there ..."

"The audacity! The brazen audacity!"

Neither of the three men trembling on the Persian rug had expected the degree of anger they were witnessing. For a moment, sweat broke out under collars and on foreheads and in palms as they realized a man in power this angry may suddenly decide to order a hanging—or worse an impaling.

They stood silent and pale and actually slightly began to feel sorry for the man Mordecai, although it was clear he had brought whatever might be the results upon himself.

"Tell me," Haman spoke through gritted teeth, "did this man, this *Yehud* tell you why he would not bow to me?"

When the three stood speechless and obviously afraid, Haman jabbed his pointed finger at Masoud.

"You," Haman said. "You answer me! Or are you suddenly mute?"

"He did, Sire," Masoud said weakly.

Behzad frowned at him and Masoud knew immediately weakness would push the man further into anger. He straightened his back, raised his chin and with more force spoke again.

"He said he could not bow to ... bow to ..." Masoud froze. He was about to tell Haman that Mordecai was not rejecting him, but Haman's god!

"He could not bow to ... to ..."

"To what?" Haman completely out of patience screamed. "A vice-regent? A king's second? A man of high honor? What, man? What did he say?"

Haman's face was red, his eyes were glaring. He was livid. When he started around the desk to approach the men, Behzad suddenly finished Masoud's answer in a rush of words.

"He cannot bow to another god!"

There! It was said. The three waited.

Haman stopped as if he had hit a wall. His impatience suddenly turned into stunned confusion.

"Another *god*?"

"Yes, Sire. The one ... the one embroidered on your cloak," finished Behzad.

"That's ridiculous! That's not the reason! It can't be. That's absolute insanity!"

"But it is, Sire. The *Yehudim* only bow to their god, the one they call Hashem Elohim. If they bow to another god, even an image of one, they disobey Hashem Elohim and lose favor with Him. At least that is what Mordecai said."

At the sound of the name, Haman reared back.

"Mordecai," he hissed.

Haman turned back to his chair and fell into it. Frowning so that his eyes almost disappeared, he began to wring his hands as he watched them. His mind was in a whirlwind of anger, confusion, pride, and shock. He needed time to think this through.

"What did you hope to get for delivering this news to me? Money? Position? What?"

He yelled and stared at the three of them as they seemed to shrivel in shame.

"Tell me, what are your jobs?"

"We are the royal yard sweeps, Sire. We clean and sweep and on occasion we plant flowers and trim the bushes."

Javan realized how unimportant they must seem and blushed, even to a man who had cut hair for over twenty years.

"Sometimes we also build gallows, . . . uh . . . when they are needed," he said with his voice trailing off. He certainly did not want to give this angry man any ideas.

Haman laid his head on the back of his chair and rolled his eyes upward. When he sat forward again, he spoke with a completely calm voice.

"You may go now, but when you get outside, tell Keyvan to enter."

Bowing again to Haman, the three men stood, bowed again just from the waist, then turned to leave. Once outside, they knew Keyvan had been pressing his ear to the door to hear what occurred inside the room.

"Vice-Regent Haman wants you to attend to him. We will show ourselves out."

And they did. Without a word they walked again down the halls, through the arches, and past the columns that had held their attention earlier. But this time they didn't notice anything around them. They only walked in silence back to the gate with the words, questions, and anger they had just witnessed being relived in their minds. One thing each of them knew:

Mordecai's life was about to change, and not for the better. Another thing they agreed on: they would not tell their wives about the meeting.

"Well, that didn't go well!" Javad finally said.

✡

Chapter Twenty-Two

The Prince

O that there were such an heart in them, that they would fear me, and keep all my commandments always, that it might be well with them, and with their children for ever! (Deu 5.29 KJV)

Near the end of Ahasuerus' eleventh year as king, Queen Esther gave birth to her black haired, olive skinned, chubby baby boy. For the first time in her life, Esther had a love so profound, so deeply felt that she was obsessed with love for him.

Ahasuerus made a visit to her quarters when the birth was completed to look into the wrinkled and red face of his son. He kissed Esther's hand, nodded to the physicians and promptly left.

He immediately sent couriers throughout the empire announcing the birth of Prince Darius II. Trumpets and bells sounded the news, and a new flag from the palace spires announced the birth of a prince. Those closest to him knew King Ahasuerus was delirious with pride and joy. He showered Esther with gifts, and so did the satraps and governors from every province in the empire. At last, there was an heir to the Persian Empire.

In the *Yehudim* homes, prayers were offered for the young prince and his beautiful *eema*. Also, along with gifts from the Persians, *Yehudi* made blankets, trinkets, carvings, baskets, and urns to be delivered to the palace gates to be given to the queen who was one of their own. Careful attention was given to hide their connection to her due to Mordecai's instructions not to reveal her *Yehudim* heritage.

Any concerns that Esther had carried in her heart that she had been disavowed by the *Yehudim* community were dispelled when she recognized and cherished the handiwork of many of her *Yehudi* friends. By their workmanship, identifying markings and the words written in the language of her people on the gifts, she easily identified them. Seeing their outpouring of love crushed her heart in longing to show the prince to them, but especially to Mordecai. As she wondered if that day would ever present itself, she determined in her heart that somehow, it would happen.

In the queen's palace, guards were posted in the halls and at the doorways, for suddenly servants, regents and their wives, eunuchs, and even kitchen staff had urgent business in the wing where Esther and the prince were housed. Esther's private suite of rooms would have been invaded if not for Saroya's and Hathach's protective measures that even the fiercest lioness could not have matched.

In addition to guarding her and her son bodily, royal physicians and wet nurses were housed in the rooms near them to be available at any time. The most trusted servants were assigned to test every morsel of food and every drop of liquid that was to be consumed by Esther. Specially assigned eunuchs and house maids were trained to daily check her quarters for scorpions, spiders, or any other harmful intruder. Esther herself selected additional attendants to sleep in the nursery on rotating shifts to watch over the prince.

After the required time of rest and isolation, Ahasuerus announced the day that he, Esther, and Prince Darius would appear on the king's balcony to allow the public to see the newborn heir.

Esther secretly dispatched Hathach to Mordecai's business to deliver the announcement.

> Dod,
> I have a son, and he is beautiful! Prince Darius. I am filled with joy.
> In one week from today the king, the prince, and I will be on the balcony to allow all of Shushan to see him. I have instructed Hathach to designate a private position for you, so you will have the best opportunity to see him. I hope you will attend.
>
> Baht

The only part of the palace that did not rejoice in the birth of the prince was in The House of the Women. Several of the concubines had sons and daughters conceived by the king, but those children would never be recognized as heirs or as princes. The regents and the court of magistrates saw to the education and well-being of the children, but Ahasuerus never visited them nor acknowledged their existence. The birth was a source of bitter grief to the mothers. However, the birth of Darius did quell any arguments among them concerning which son among them might one day reach the throne. Esther's son had ended that hope.

Also, unhappy about the birth of a prince was Haman. As second in authority in the empire, should Ahasuerus have died, or been killed, Haman would have been in line to take the throne. On the day of the prince's birth, Haman was so irritable until even Keyvan avoided him at all costs.

THE PRINCE

Ahasuerus' brother was reigning in Egypt and his mother in Babylon. Now that a prince was born, Haman also knew that his motives and actions could very easily be mistrusted. Betrayal was always a suspicion.

Quite unaware of all the different opinions, attitudes, threats, or even possible plots to harm the prince, Esther was enraptured by her son and totally consumed by his every sound, expression, wrinkle, smell, and touch. In her mind, her world had suddenly opened into a happiness and fulfillment she had never known could exist.

The attendants were as enamored over the newborn as Esther. Suddenly, the prince was the center of the world in the Queen's Palace.

Little did she know during those first three months, that all too soon Ahasuerus would have her moved back into the adjoining suite. She would then be required to submit the care of her son to the palace nurses.

When that time arrived all too soon, her heart was ripped open, and her duties to her husband and king once again became her priority and duty.

✡

Chapter Twenty-Three

Setting the Date

> *In the first month, that is, the month Nisan, in the twelfth year of king Ahasuerus, they cast Pur, that is, the lot, before Haman from day to day, and from month to month, to the twelfth month, that is, the month Adar.* (Est 3.7 KJV)

In the month of Nisan, the first month of the twelfth year of Ahasuerus' reign, Haman had had enough.

After months of losing sleep, neglecting profitable duties, and growing in his hatred for Mordecai's continued refusal to honor him—and the growing awareness of it—Haman was constantly conceiving ways and means to destroy Mordecai. After several months of his obsession, he finally realized it was not enough to do away with only Mordecai. He came to the brilliant deduction that the entire captive *Yehudim* nation, in his opinion, was overpopulating the empire, and needed to be eradicated.

In order to make a solid plan, and determined to see it happen without an accusation of murder on his part, Haman decided the 365 counselors assigned to him by the king were not to be included in the planning to be rid of Mordecai. Instead, he consulted Zeresh. She had heard the name and the infuriating actions of the despicable man from day one. Together, they decided Haman should organize a small committee of eleven men. Upon consideration, he chose men he most trusted and had known since his youth. He knew they were men who had attached themselves to him for their own personal gain and reputations, but they shared his religious views.

Without revealing the true basis of his idea to cleanse the empire of the *Yehudim*, he followed the plan made with his wife and convinced the eleven men that *Yehudim* were rebels against the empire and haters of anyone who did not worship Āz. On those two points, the eleven were all in.

Further, to assist in his plans, he summoned Keyvan to bring in Masoud, Behzad, and Javad.

Keyvan did not like the idea, but he found the men outside the gates pulling weeds and cleaning the area of debris. They were filthy with dirt.

"Haman wants you to come back to his office."

He hoped his tone and voice sounded like Haman was out to punish them.

"What for?" asked Javad, his eyes wide with fear.

"That is not my job to tell you."

Keyvan was pleased that his efforts were paying off.

"When?"

Masoud looked at his companions and hoped it was not immediately.

"Now, Fool! If you do not know how impatient the vice-regent is, you were not paying attention the last time you met him!"

"Oh, we know!" interjected Behzad. "But meeting him like this would not be appropriate." He waved his hands over himself.

"All right. Here's what I'll do for you. I'll stay away from the palace long enough for you to get cleaned up, then we'll all return together."

Keyvan, always the shrew negotiator was a man with plans to insure future events.

Thirty minutes later, Keyvan and the three men approached Haman's office. Keyvan went in to let Haman know what a hard time he had finding them. Shortly he returned with a flushed face.

"He is ready to see you. Do not do anything to irritate him further."

The three looked at each other and considered leaving, but Keyvan opened the door and Haman bellowed.

"Get in here! Where have you been? This time of day you should have been working and easy to find."

Without knowing what Keyvan had told him, they had no idea how to respond, so they just hit the floor on their knees and their heads on the carpet.

"Get up. Keyvan, you may leave."

When the door shut behind Keyvan and his ear was pressed against it on the other side, Haman continued.

"I am prepared to hire the three of you as my personal spies. I will pay you double what you are presently making and at least you will stay clean."

He ran his eyes up and down the men and by that action proved, that in his opinion, all their efforts to be clean before meeting him had obviously failed.

"Spies, Sir?" croaked out Masoud.

"Did I stutter? Yes, man! Spies. I am looking for men to infiltrate a certain section of the village and identify rebels. I specifically mean those who are *Yehudim*. Of course, I am prepared to also provide funds for any recruits you find among the *Yehudim* to help you identify the rebels, where they are located, and what businesses they own."

They stood mutely before him unsure how to respond. Their dreams of promotion and more income seemed to be before them.

"Well, don't take all day!"

In unison the three began nodding and grinning.

"Good. Consider yourselves my employees. Mind that you understand you are not the king's men! You are mine."

"Yes, Sir."

Haman had a chorus of three ready and willing agents to help him with his plan.

Once outside the palace gates, the three broke into a run to tell their wives they were not idiots, afterall. They had a bag of gold to prove it.

Shortly after the assignment, the mission was underway. It did not take long before they engaged a disgruntled man named Anwir who was married to a *Yehudi* woman. He was presently under judgment by the rabbi and the *Yehudi* counsel for an adulterous affair with his neighbor's wife. He was all too happy to point out the members of the community who were *Yehudi*, even without the bag of gold.

Haman, his eleven men, the adulterer, and the three spies conceived a plan for the destruction of the entire race. However, due to their trust in astrology as the foundation of their faith, all things related to decisions and outcomes must be according to the movement of the stars, moon, and tides. They agreed the best way to know when to initiate the plan was to cast lots so Āz could reveal the date.

"We must first decide what day of the week," Haman said. "The day must not be a day that is favorable to the *Yehudim*. So let us cast pur (*lots*) to determine the day."

Using the stars and the lot as the determining factor, it was soon made clear, much to Haman's distress, no day the lot landed on was unfavorable for the *Yehudim*. Finally, after many casts of the lot, the date of the thirteenth was approved.

Exasperated and impatient, Haman asked, "What about the thirteenth of this month? What about this month?"

"No," said Anwir. "*Passover* is in this month on the thirteenth. It will not work for your favor. It is a Sabbath—a holy day of the *Yehudim*."

Haman signaled and the lot was cast again, this time landing on the month Iyyar. Haman looked at Anwir.

"No, Iyyar is the month of the small passover."

"I think you are trying to deceive us!" Haman's eyes were black and threatening.

"No . . . I am not! Keep casting. These people have many days of acknowledgement to their god!"

Continuing to cast the lot to select the month, every month was refused because it favored the *Yehudim*. Finally, the lot fell on Adar, the twelfth month. No reason to reject it could be determined.

"No! That is eleven months away!" Haman impatiently exclaimed.

"It is the month selected by the lot, Haman. It is the month of the fish," Anwir said flatly.

"Adar? Adar is the sign of Pisces! Wait! Ah ha! Yes, that is the right month! Now I shall be able to swallow them as fish swallow one another!"

Haman grinned so broadly he showed almost all of his big teeth.

The conniving group laughed and congratulated themselves on the favor of the stars and especially Āz in selecting the perfect day and month.

Haman was ready for his meeting with Ahasuerus, but he realized that for the desired decree to be approved by the thirteenth—less than a week away—he had no time to waste. He and his men met the next morning in the room connected to his office that he had designated for the worship of the demon god of greed, lust, avarice, avidity, and concupiscence, Āz.

The room was painted in black and dark blues with the constellations and Zodiac in whites and yellows covering the walls and ceiling. To the left of the room's entrance, a pedestal held a basin for burning incense. Center stage was a stone image representing Āz. Under the image was a hollow oven for burning sacrifices.

As Haman and his men entered, each one in turn made several cuts on his arms to allow blood to mix with the incense. Haman threw in a powder which mixed into the incense and when ignited filled the room with a cloud of smoke. Soon the smoke filled room brought with it a feeling of euphoria. They lay prostrate with arms spread out to either side, fingers touching to fingers in a circle around the idol as they called on the demon god to hear their requests.

Rising and standing in a circle around the image, Haman prayed to the carved image of Āz and the men repeated after him in quiet monotones.

"Āz, great and powerful god of desire and unlimited wealth and energy, arise and hear the petition of your faithful followers. Go before us into the chamber of King Ahasuerus and place within his mind the desire to bring about our petition to destroy, annihilate, and erase the *Yehudim* and to take their wealth and possessions."

Satisfied by their prayers and with worship finished, they were confident of success. Still feeling the effects of the smoke and the prayers, the men returned to Haman's office to review the messages received from the closest attendants to Sergazi regarding the king's appointments.

From the information in the king's schedule, Haman was beyond delighted to see that a date on the ninth had been set to receive the satraps and governors of the 127 provinces. They were coming to bring gifts in honor of the new prince. Knowing that such a royal visit would result in too much food and an overabundance of wine and late hours of continued drinking—well into the early morning—Haman found the tenth to be the perfect day to approach the king. He knew Ahasuerus would still be under the influence of celebrating and wine, and that was what Haman needed.

Haman's plans were coming together better than he had hoped. He sent Keyvan to Sergazi to request an appointment with the king the morning of the tenth. Keyvan was instructed to inform Sergazi that the purpose of the meeting would be to inform the king on a matter of dire importance. If these planned steps succeeded, and if he convinced King Ahasuerus to make the decree, he would have three days after the meeting to write a decree to match the designated date selected by the lot.

Later that afternoon, after Haman had paced the floor impatiently, Keyvan received word from Sergazi that the king had approved the date and time of the meeting. After Haman heard the news, he returned to Āz to offer thanks for his success.

Too proud to reveal his plans to his family lest he fail, Haman had restless days until the tenth. His dark moods and sharp responses caused his wife to ask him too many times what was troubling him. To escape her nagging, he finally started staying overnight at the palace. Zeresh came to the conclusion he was having an affair. It was common knowledge that regents were not faithful in marriage.

By the time the tenth approached, Haman went to his home to dress in his best. His mood was so much improved, poor Zeresh comforted herself that perhaps the affair was over. When he grabbed her and kissed her like the days before their marriage, Zeresh immediately began preparations for his favorite meal when he returned in the evening. She also made a trip to the market to buy a new supply of perfumes and oils. The day had taken an upturn and a promise of an even better evening.

✡

Chapter 24

A Momentous Day

And Haman said unto king Ahasuerus, There is a certain people scattered abroad and dispersed among the people in all the provinces of thy kingdom; and their laws are diverse from all people; neither keep they the king's laws: therefore it is not for the king's profit to suffer them. (Est 3.8 KJV)

Ahasuerus awoke with a blinding headache. He stretched his left arm across the massive bed to see if Esther was there. Feeling her warmth still on the coverings, he opened his left eye to find her. The light filtering through the crack in the drapes caused him to quickly shut it again, and he moaned.

In her closet, Esther heard him and quickly finished attending to her needs, tip-toed back to the bed and slipped in beside him. It soon became obvious that he had not recovered from the celebration of the previous night. She closed her eyes feeling irritation and impatience that his condition would require her to lie still in the bed until he was able to arise, dress and dismiss her. She ached to see Darius.

A rap on the door caused Ahasuerus to try again to slightly open his eyes and then to roll himself into a semi-upright position.

"What?" he bellowed.

Immediately the explosion in his head made him regret it.

Through the door Sergazi's voice was muffled but distinctly his.

"Sire, you have an appointment this morning. Shall I cancel it?"

"No. But come in."

He turned to Esther and signaled his permission for her to leave the room, which she happily did.

Sergazi opened the door and without looking toward the bed, he entered the dim room and stood waiting.

"What appointment? What time?" he mumbled.

"Sire, you have an appointment with Vice-Regent Haman. Keyvan said the appointment was to discuss an issue of grave importance with dire consequences."

"What time is it now?"

"Sire, it is the ninth hour of the day. The appointment is in two hours."

Another moan.

"Tell Zethar to attend me immediately and to bring me something to eat. Call a physician!"

"Yes, Sire. Immediately!" Sergazi closed the door quietly behind him. Grinning at the two eunuchs who had been waiting for hours to be called, he gave Zethar the king's request, and sent Harbona scurrying to find a royal physician.

"It's going to be a momentous day," Sergazi said to the other three eunuchs. He had no idea how true that statement was.

———————— הַפָּסְקָה ————————

Haman's happy morning had faded into a knotted stomach, sweaty palms, and pacing outside in the garden where Sergazi had instructed him to wait for the king. Glancing at the sundial near the garden entrance, he noted that the king was late. *I hope he hasn't changed his mind and wants to put this off for another day!*

His mind was a wad of worry and fear of failure. Success surprised Haman, for he was well accustomed to years of feeling like a failure. Thus, the refusal of Mordecai to honor him rose into such importance. His insecurity drove him to humiliate and retaliate when anyone made him feel small.

Just when he was almost sick with worry, he heard the footsteps of approaching men. He stood and with great effort, hoped he was displaying an air of confidence, and a mission of importance. He took a deep breath.

Sergazi, Zethar, and Harbona appeared first followed by the king. Behind the king were two burly guards. Haman happily noted the king's red eyes and pale skin.

He's got a hangover! Good!

Haman was counting on the king not thinking with his usual sharpness. He was nervous about his ability to convince him to annihilate an entire race of people. He had practiced his speech in front of a mirror to be as convincing and sincere as possible. This was the moment for which he had been waiting for months.

Ahasuerus took a seat on an elevated throne under an elaborate fabric tent. Harbona and Zethar stood on each side and waved huge woven fans back and forth.

Haman stood like a statue until the king wearily raised his scepter then let it drop. Moving toward the king, he bowed until his forehead was on the ground. Ahasuerus tapped his shoulder with the scepter and Haman stood.

"All right, Haman, what is this dire situation you need to report? Sergazi, record everything." The king's voice was one of irritation.

"My King, live forever. There is a certain group scattered and dispersed among the people in all the provinces of your kingdom; their customs and laws are different from all other people's. They do not keep the king's laws."

"What? Well, rebellion is not tolerated in my empire!"

Haman noted that Ahasuerus was speaking in a lower volume than usual, and although his words were strong, he did not seem as upset as Haman expected. He guessed it must be due to the effects of the previous night.

"It is not fitting for the king to let them remain," Haman stately flatly.

"What, Haman? Are you chiding me? Are you insinuating I'm incompetent?"

Haman's heart lurched into his throat.

"No, My King, I'm saying they are unprofitable to the empire, and it's not in your best interest to tolerate them. They are disrespectful to our people, their customs are strange, they refuse to follow our laws and instead live by their own. This causes much confusion, and unrest in the city, the villages, and in your other provinces."

"Humm . . . I guess I've been too occupied with all the activity around the birth of my son to notice. It certainly seems it cannot continue."

Looking at Haman with drooping eyelids, he continued.

"Since you are the one reporting to me, you have obviously been diligent enough to investigate these rebels. I'm sure a man such as you is on top of the situation. I am guessing you have also come up with how to deal with this problem?"

Haman felt a wave of heat through his entire body. The king's words were like food to a starving man, and now he was asking for a plan.

"Well . . . Sire, I strive to be the kind of man, who when a problem is evident—before I present it to anyone—I put effort into finding a working solution."

Haman hoped his bragging did not come off too strongly. He did not want to injure his obvious advantage in the situation.

"It seems I chose the right man! So Haman, tell me your solution."

"After much consideration and evaluation of the issue, I think a sound and reasonable solution would be to rid our empire of these rebellious, disrespectful, and law-breaking vermin."

"Rid . . .? Are you suggesting we move them from the empire?"

"It would be advantageous to be completely rid of them, Sire. If we merely move them, they will return. So I am suggesting a decree be written to give permission to the people in the 127 provinces to destroy these rebels on a designated day. Further, if it pleases the king, I personally will pay ten thousand talents of silver into the hands of those that have the charge of the business, to bring it into the king's treasury . . . if it pleases the king."

Ahasuerus closed his eyes and pressed his fingers to his temples. All this talk of rebels and killing made his head pound.

"You take charge of it, Haman. I give you charge over these rebels. Do whatever seems good to you; . . . and keep the money. Here, take my ring. Take Sergazi with you and make the proclamation. Sign it with my signet, and let the post of the messengers go throughout all the provinces."

Frowning and rolling his head, Haman heard several cracks from the king's neck. Obviously done with his meeting with Haman, and confident the problem was in capable hands, the king was done.

"Harbona! Tell the guards I'm ready to return to my quarters. And Zethar, tell Savara to make me another potion for my headache. Guards!"

As Haman bowed, he turned his head just enough to watch the king with his escorts, leave the garden. Knowing that the king had no idea the number of lives he had just given permission to be destroyed, Haman closed his eyes, grinned, and had never felt as much elation in his life. He could hardly wait to tell Zeresh.

> *Then were the king's scribes called on the thirteenth day of the first month, and there was written according to all that Haman had commanded unto the king's lieutenants, and to the governors that were over every province, and to the rulers of every people of every province according to the writing thereof, and to every people after their language; in the name of king Ahasuerus was it written, and sealed with the king's ring.* (Est 3.12 KJV)

✡

Chapter Twenty-Five

The Decree

And the letters were sent by posts into all the king's provinces, to destroy, to kill, and to cause to perish, all Jews, both young and old, little children and women, in one day, even upon the thirteenth day of the twelfth month, which is the month Adar, and to take the spoil of them for a prey. (Est 3.13 KJV)

Mordecai suddenly awoke in a cold sweat; his heart was rapidly pounding in his chest. The dream seemed real: the violence, the cries, the gruesome images were still there in the darkness. He squeezed his eyes and felt sickness like an overwhelming wave engulfing him.

Sitting up on the side of his bed, he leaned forward, his elbows on his knees, and put his head in his hands.

"It wasn't real. It was a dream. It didn't happen," he mumbled, willing his mind to accept the truth.

But a spirit of heaviness settled over him, pouring into his chest. Weariness was causing him to feel older than his years.

"There is nothing worse than a problem announced but unveiled."

He walked out into the darkness to his garden and sat under the olive tree. The events of the night when Ari had arrived to tell him about the maidens being taken came into his mind. The weight lay heavier.

"Oh, Hadassah, my girl, I have lost you, and now, also, your son. What will become of you both? Will I ever hold you in my arms again? Is this burden in me connected to you?"

A gentle breeze passed over him and his mind suddenly remembered words of the psalmist.

> *Evening, and morning, and at noon, will I pray, and cry aloud: and He shall hear my voice. Cast thy burden upon Hashem, and He shall sustain thee: He shall never suffer the righteous to be moved.*
> (Psalm 55.17, 22)

Ever listening deep in his spirit, Mordecai received the words, straightened his shoulders, took a deep breath, and repeated them.

"Evening and morning and at noon I will pray and cry aloud. He shall hear my voice. I will cast my burden upon Hashem, and He will support and strengthen me."

With that said, he lifted his hands and turned toward the East, and as the sun was rising, he cried aloud.

"O Hashem, You know the future. You have awakened me with visions that are disturbing and too heavy for me. I know you hear my voice, and I know you will send wisdom and guidance for whatever is before me. Show me the way that you would have me to take."

During the day's work, he continued to wrestle against the lingering, nagging feeling of dread and weariness. Often he stopped, went deep into the back corner of his booth, fell on his knees and called on Hashem to calm his spirit and give him strength. By mid-afternoon, he wearily stuffed his papers into his bag, closed the door to his booth and headed home. He had a pounding headache and wondered if he were taking ill. On the walk to his part of the city, men on horseback charged past him leaving clouds of choking dust in their wake.

When he finally reached his small house and had drawn water to clean and cool his face, loud pounding and voices were coming from his entrance. He rushed to the door and threw it open to find Ari, Uriel, Samson, Caleb, Rabbi Joseph ben-Gideon, the men from the *Yehudim* council, business men, and many others pressing their way toward his door. Ari and Uriel were struggling to bar the men from rushing headlong onto Mordecai. Faces were pale with fear and rage was evident in their eyes and in the angry flood of words. As he tried to speak, he was immediately shouted over by the mob. Some were threats, some broke into tears, while others stood as if in shock. Holding his hands open before him, he tried to speak over them to learn the reason for their appearance, their fear, and obvious anger toward him.

"It's the news from the palace, Mordecai! The decree! The whole village is enraged. The people want to stone you!" yelled Ari over the noise.

"News? What news? I've heard nothing."

Mordecai felt his stomach knot and the darkness of the early morning suddenly came to mind and caused weakness in his legs.

Yelling over the angry words of the men, Jonas announced the news.

"Soldiers from the palace just came through the villages scattering posts of a decree with the seal of the king! The post is to all the provinces, Mordecai, all 127!"

Turning to the men, Jonas began yelling for them to get quiet. Mordecai drew slightly back from the crowd trying to calm himself from the contagion of fear among the men. Whatever the problem, it was greater than he could imagine.

Finally realizing that Mordecai did not understand their reason for being there, the men began slowly to allow him to exit his house. As Mordecai came from his doorway into the garden, they formed a tight circle around him. The demands, accusations and questions rose again in waves of incomprehensible sounds overwhelming him.

"Please, *Achim*, calm yourselves. Tell me what has happened?" he pleaded.

Rabbi Joseph ben-Gideon moved closer to him and handed him the copy he had received. His eyes were pools of fear. With a trembling voice he answered Mordecai.

"We are all to be killed, Mordecai. It is indeed signed by the seal of King Ahasuerus that in eleven months the men who are not *Yehudi* are to take up arms and kill all *Yehudim* in the provinces!"

"But why? Does the decree say why? What reason is given?"

Caleb, red-faced in anger pushed forward.

"You brought this to us, Mordecai! This is your doing! Our lives are threatened! They want to wipe us out because of your doing! What's your response now to your decision to declare yourself a *Yehudi* so righteous that you refuse to bow to a man in high position? You have made us the enemy to the people of the provinces!"

Caleb's question was followed by another round of rapid-fire comments and questions as the men pushed forward.

"We don't know that is the reason, Caleb!" Rabbi Joseph ben-Gideon raised both hands still trembling. "Hold your anger."

He turned to face Mordecai.

"Do you know any other reason for this, Mordecai?"

"I have heard nothing from the palace, but to address Caleb's question, it is not a refusal to bow to a person in a position, Caleb. It's a matter of personal and spiritual integrity. Haman is not a man of honor. In fact, he's a descendant of Agag. Hashem has cursed the entire line of Agagite due to the attack made on our people. You all know very well the history.

"Haman is a seer, a false prophet, a medium of evil spirits. His idol is embroidered on his garments. To bow to him would be to spit in the face of Hashem. If that is the reason behind this decree, don't you understand it is not so much against us as it is against Hashem. Any one of us, that are as you say 'righteous' should refuse to bow to a man such as he and to disobey Hashem."

"So you will see us destroyed from the face of the earth?" Samson yelled.

"Samson, this is not my doing! Remember our history," Mordecai said.

"Remember the words of Elohim through His prophets. This is not the first time our enemies have made designs to destroy us! It is the promise of the *mashiyach melek* that is the target! If we are the people chosen by Elohim to bring forth *Mashiyach Melek*, of course, our lives are endangered. Of course, Lucifer has moved this Agagite to convince Ahasuerus to commit a mass slaughter. Do we panic? Do we rage *ach* against *ach*?"

The din quieted to a dull roar of mumbling under the seething anger and fear.

"My son who makes deliveries of vegetables to the palace was told by one of the kitchen servants that Haman is offering large amounts of silver to those who kill us. But the money won't come from Haman! His intent is to take all we have—our land, our livestock, our businesses, our homes—and use our own wealth to pay for our murders!" cried out Benjamin.

The men responded with another angry outcry.

"Listen! Listen to me! We have almost a year," reminded Mordecai with strength and calmness he did not understand.

"We have eleven months to seek the face of Elohim. We will pray, we will not go as sheep to slaughter. We will make our presence known to all, without fear. They will send spies to find and identify us, but we will not hide. We will publicly cry out to our God; we will let it be known that He is our defender. So continue your businesses and your relationships with the people around us, but do not yield to turning against one another. Hashem will give us directions, and we must listen to Him. Above all, we must not panic or see everyone around us as the enemy. We will seek no other help besides Hashem. When our nation has been mistreated due to our own rebellion, idolatry, and immorality, yes, Hashem allowed, and even moved our enemies against us! But when we are the prey to evil men because of our worship of Hashem, El-Sabaoth (the God of Armies) will defend us! Examine yourselves! Instruct your wives and children to look to El-Nissi (God our Banner) for deliverance. And we will continue our lives as we have in the past. In the meantime, we will pray; we will wear sackcloth and ashes and make our appeal to our Deliverer. We will do it in public to all the eyes of the gentiles."

Frightened eyes sought other eyes for assurance, but none was found. They watched as Mordecai raised his hands and face upward and began to pray aloud a familiar prayer and song that David prayed when Saul sought his life. Slowly and quietly some of the men in the garden with trembling hands raised, and with tears streaming down their faces, joined in as some of the younger ones watched in stunned silence and then stormed off.

> *"Deliver me from my enemies, O My Hashem;*
> *Defend me from those who rise up against me.*
> *Deliver me from the workers of iniquity,*
> *And save me from bloodthirsty men.*
> *For look, they lie in wait for my life;*
> *The mighty gather against me,*
> *Not for my transgression nor for my sin, O Hashem.*
> *They run and prepare themselves through no fault of mine.*
> *Awake to help me, and behold!*
> *You therefore, O El-Elohe-Israel (the God of Israel),*
> *Awake to punish all the nations;*
> *Do not be merciful to any wicked transgressors. Selah* (Psa 59.1B-5)

✡

Chapter Twenty-Six

Sackcloth and Ashes

When Mordecai perceived all that was done, Mordecai rent his clothes, and put on sackcloth with ashes, and went out into the midst of the city, and cried with a loud and a bitter cry; (Est 4.1 KJV)

The next day after Mordecai had read from his scroll, he did not go to meet with his brethren for prayer and the *Torah*, nor did he plan to attend his booth. Instead, even before the sun had risen, he went into his garden shed where he selected a large, empty feed-bag, went to the ash heap and filled a second bag with ashes. With these in hand, he walked with purpose and determined courage to the village square.

Even before the men, women, and children were stirring and preparing to go about their business, a few devout *Yehudi* men moved like shadows from their homes to gather in the streets and meet with Mordecai. With solemn and bold faith in Elohim Roi (the God who sees) they stood in the center of the village, took hold of the neckline of their garments and ripped them from top to bottom as they released a loud guttural cry and began to publicly cry out to El-Gibor (the Mighty God).

It did not take long for lanterns to be lit inside homes, and with alarm, men opened doors to stare in stunned silence at their neighbors in sackcloth pouring ashes over their heads and smearing blackening over their faces and arms, all the while wailing and weeping.

Then with a desperate heart, and a soul full of sorrow, Mordecai led them through the village where at times they fell on their knees, placed their heads on the ground and with great anguish and bitterness of soul publicly cried out with loud wails and groans to Hashem Elohim for the deliverance of their people.

———————הפסָקה———————

Woe to those who devise iniquity,
And work out evil on their beds!
At morning light they practice it,
Because it is in the power of their hand.
(Micah 2:1 NKJV)

SACKCLOTH AND ASHES

From within the chambers of his home, Haman opened his eyes, furrowed his thick brows, and strained his hearing to determine what had awakened him. The dimness of the morning made him think he had awakened from a dream, or perhaps one of the children in the house had awakened with a night terror. As he lay there, it slowly became clear that from somewhere in the street there was the sound of a man's voice.

Slipping from beside Zeresh, he crept to the balcony and stepped out into the open. Standing with his head high, tilted to the side, and with his eyes closed to focus his mind and ears, he listened closely. He realized it was perhaps the sound of someone getting bad news. Then a warm feeling filled him like the warmth that comes with a drink of his best wine. No . . . it was more than a man. It was the sound of many men, and the sound, although distant, was definitely the sounds of men wailing and crying.

With a bit of surprise and with much pleasure, a smile spread across his face and widened until his teeth gleamed in the moonlight.

Ah, of course, the news has spread. Now Mordecai, see what you have done? Do you still hold honor among the men of your cursed and captured race? How will you respond to these fearful Yehudim now that they know their lives are taken from them?

From inside the room behind him Zeresh awoke. Realizing he was standing on the balcony, she called to him.

"Haman, my *azazim* (dear), what are you doing? What is happening?"

He turned toward her still grinning, and practically floated across the room and fell on the bed beside her.

"My dear, the *Yehudim* have received the decree—and not quietly. Some of the men are in the streets wailing and crying."

"What if it reaches the palace? Will King Ahasuerus remove the decree?"

"He cannot. He is bound by his own word to fulfill it. Do not worry. These people live by their lusts and emotions. The noise of it will quieten before the palace awakens. Do not stress yourself, *Azazim*. I fully expect them to try to go into hiding. None will be so foolish as to draw attention to themselves. Most of our province do not know which men are *Yehudi* except for a few of the most radical, but my men and their hired spies are organized to identify every one of them."

Zeresh fell back onto her pillows and yawned.

"Good. They have embarrassed and humiliated you enough. It seems the plan will succeed. May the months pass quickly."

"It will succeed, my *azazim*. The gods are with me; the stars have aligned to the perfect date. My committee is committed to spreading whatever word is necessary to see that on the appointed day, our men will take up weapons and with vengeance and determination wipe out these cursed worshippers of Mordecai and his blind, uncaring god."

In the streets as the sun rose, the men were fully visible in the stark light of morning. They continued their mission intent on carrying it to the palace gates. More and more *Yehudi* men, also in sackcloth and ashes, joined in the procession of the public display of their despair and desperation.

The Shushan residents responded. Some were peeping through cracks and shaded windows with wide-eyed terror. Such terror strikes at the heart of humanity when the actions and cries of men in anguish raise an alarm. Some watched in disgust that men would degrade themselves, and others watched mocking their neighbors who were so foolish as to reveal their association with those now under a decree of death.

On horseback Haman reached the palace gates just as the men were also arriving. It took him a moment to evaluate the scene. It was not the reaction he expected.

They are more ignorant than I thought!

Looking down on them, he sought out the subject of his hatred and finally spied Mordecai. The sensation of pleasure he felt seeing his enemy in ragged feed bags, smeared with ashes, his hair unbound, and his feet bare was exhilarating.

You stupid fool! You didn't hide! What are you thinking? Now everyone knows what you are! And you have convinced others to swallow the sword! Good! You make my task easier.

He reined his horse through the center of the men. When he reached Mordecai's side, he sneered as he jerked his horse's reins. The sudden movement caused the beast to shove Mordecai to the ground. Although tempted to rear the horse and crush him, instead, a better image filled his head. Haman proceeded through the gates.

My time will come when the whole of Shushan will see you crushed.

Guards barred the *Yehudi* men from following Haman through the gates by yelling at them to disperse and leave. They forcefully reminded the men no one was allowed entrance to the royal grounds while wearing sackcloth. The guards found the scene of grown men dressed in such a manner with blackened faces, shaved heads or unbound hair ridiculous. No self-respecting Persian would ever publicly degrade himself by publicly weeping and wailing. An irrational hatred and disgust arose against the men in the hearts of the Persian guards.

SACKCLOTH AND ASHES

Before Haman reached his office and quarters in the palace, he saw Keyvan and Anwir sitting outside his door. When they saw him, they both quickly arose and stood impatiently waiting for him.

"What are you two waiting for?" Haman asked. "I can tell by your expressions that something is off."

"Have you seen the mob of *Yehudim* in the street wearing sackcloth and with ashes on their heads?" asked Anwir. "They are in an uproar!"

"I have. So what of it?"

Haman opened his office door, entered and threw open the large doors that swung out onto his balcony garden. Sunlight flooded the room. Turning, he saw the two standing with confusion written all over them.

"What's wrong with you two? Have you never seen someone in sackcloth and ashes?"

"Of course, I have," croaked Anwir with irritation, "but never in the streets wailing and crying! That kind of lamenting is usually done in private or in a temple entrance! Not in the streets here in Shushan! It is obvious that the *Yehudim* are not going into hiding because of the decree! They have taken to the streets! In my section the men have met and laid a plan to appeal to Hashem for deliverance! They intend to proceed with these public displays of distress as their prayers to Him."

"I have instructed the eunuchs and servants not to spread the word of it," added Keyvan, "but the sound of it grows as the number of men grows! I can't keep this from the king much longer. Soon the entire palace will be aware of it."

"You worry about nothing. So what if the king knows? Let him know. We have done nothing but follow his instructions."

Haman sat and leaned back in his chair. His entire demeanor was one of unconcern.

"But will he suspect you? Will he not be angry that you have deceived him?" Keyvan's voice was low, almost a whisper.

"Suspect me? I haven't deceived him! I've done nothing but report to him what Masoud, Behzad, and Javad reported to me. The action of these *Yehudim* are just more of their rebellious and extreme emotional reactions to any type of news they regard as threatening. It will pass. Calm yourselves."

Keyvan was stunned. He was puzzled by this man who had laid out a plan to wipe out an entire race of people. He and the others had not considered that instead of trying to hide, or to conceal their identity, they would make a spectacle of themselves! Nor was it conceived that they would pour into the streets of the city and bring their complaint to the palace gates! That was not in their minds as possible. A sudden sound at the door to the room made Anwir and Keyvan startle. Turning, they saw Masoud, Behzad, and Javad waiting for permission to enter. Keyvan could tell they obviously had heard Haman's last words.

Haman waved them to enter and signaled for them to shut the door behind them.

The three men wore dark expressions and had the look about them that spelled their concern.

"You will not lay this on us," spat Masoud quickly to Haman. "Don't even think of making this something that we have devised."

Behzad and Javad moved slightly away from him. Their hands twitched.

Anwir noted a slight tremble in their knees.

"Watch your tone and remember to whom you are speaking." Haman's voice was low, but the threat was loud and clear.

"No one would ever give credit to you three fools. You don't have the ability to pull off a plan that would cause this kind of uproar. But you will be blamed if it isn't stopped." Haman turned toward Keyvan.

"Keyvan, summon Farzad and the royal guards that are not in attendance to the king. Move, man. Now!"

As Keyvan scurried out the door, Haman eyed the four men in the room with him.

"What a pathetic lot you are. What did you think would come from reporting the name of a rebel to me? Did you think I would just let it go? Did you think I would ignore the information and just allow it to continue? No! You wanted to gain my trust and you wanted a reward. And you got it! Your positions are elevated; your salaries are doubled. You didn't care what happened to Mordecai in regard to your report. You only thought of yourselves. You were digging weeds and hauling dirt when you came to me. Now look at you! Dressed in the finest and appointed as special counsel to the second highest seat in Shushan. And now you come crawling to me in fear? Making threats to me? What if I do lay the blame on you? What will you do? Who will you convince that you are not to blame?"

The three stood faint and paled before him. There was no response to be given, and if there had been their tongues were glued to the roofs of their mouths inside their locked jaws. Guilt and lack of understanding in regard to their actions overwhelmed them until they could no longer look at Haman.

"Look at me!" Haman ordered. "Do you understand?"

"Yes, Sire," they mumbled in unison.

Haman burst out laughing. The sound rose from deep within him and rose in volume until the very floor seemed to tremble. Anwir, and the three mute men raised their heads, looked from one to another not quite certain about the source of the laughter had rose to an almost hysterical high pitch. It stopped as suddenly as it began.

"Look at you," Haman sneered. "Cowards, all of you. Well, straighten your backs and change your faces because this is just the beginning of accomplishing our goal—and it is *our* goal. Did you think this plan would be an easy ride? Did you think it wouldn't change Shushan? Did you think your participation wouldn't be recognized? You will be heroes! Think about it. In eleven months we will pick up swords and clubs and weapons of every kind and pierce through the heart of every man in the street down there bawling his eyes out and yelling to a god that has no power; a god who won't answer them, and a god that doesn't see them. And if he did, he wouldn't care. You know why? Because he put them here in the first place. And don't forget that. He's a cruel, angry god—if he even exists! I happen to think they are weaklings, driven by pride, religion, and rules. They deserve to be wiped off the face of the earth. And we are the men that will do this empire the service of doing just that. So stand up, straighten your shoulders, stop whining and get a backbone!"

Farzad's entrance broke the spell over the room. He entered with an air of military authority and posture, then bowed to Haman.

"You sent for me?"

"I did. There is a disturbance at the city gates and I need you and your men to clear it out. Get those rebels back to their own streets and away from the palace. They are vermin. If they oppose you, strike them down."

Farzad, made no expression. He simply bowed again, spun on his heels and left the room. Haman stood and left his position from behind his desk and approached the four men standing abashed before him. Keyvan who had quietly slipped in behind Farzad took his place at a distance.

"Feel better? The mob will be dispersed. The sounds will be quieted; the grounds will be quiet and back to normal. So return to your duties.

"Anwir, since the *Yehudim* do not intend to hide or run, I suppose your services are no longer needed. You may return to your *Yehudi* wife and your mistress. Let the traitors you have hired know that their services are no longer needed until the day to take up arms."

Slightly deflated and suddenly feeling unnecessary, Anwir bowed and backed from the room while desperately trying to concoct some reason to give to Haman that would continue his profitable employment as a spy. But for the moment, he was completely blank.

"You three are dismissed," he said to Masoud, Behzad, and Javad.

He turned his back from them and went outside into the garden where he could see Farzad and his squad of men on horseback headed for the palace gates. However, as he stood there, the sounds from the gates increased with the sounds of loud orders and commands mixed in with the cries of the *Yehudim*. Sure that if they did not move from the gates their day of death would come suddenly, most of them melted into the crowds gathered to witness the scene, and returned to their homes where they took up their laments in smaller groups or alone.

When Haman was satisfied that the worst was over, he turned back to his now empty office. Suddenly, he felt his knees give way, and a cold sweat broke out on his forehead.

How will I explain this to the king?

He grabbed an urn of wine, poured himself a cupful, and threw it down his throat. He went into his private chamber of worship to report to Āz and to make an offering for a new plan. He now had to devise a lie to hide the fact that he had connived to get the king's permission to decree a massacre.

———————— הַפְסָקָה ————————

Just outside the palace gate, one lone man in sackcloth, took his position near his booth, covered his head with more ashes from his sack, then rocking back and forth and in low moans and cries, he began his private petition to his melek, Elohim Avinu.

> *And in every province, whithersoever the king's commandment and his decree came, there was great mourning among the Yehudim, and fasting, and weeping, and wailing; and many lay in sackcloth and ashes.* (Est 4.3 KJV)

✡

Chapter Twenty-Seven

The Tailor

So Esther's maids and her chamberlains came and told it her. Then was the queen exceedingly grieved; and she sent raiment to clothe Mordecai, and to take away his sackcloth from him: but he received it not. (Est 4.4 KJV)

Darius grabbed a lock of Esther's hair and tried to put it in his mouth. His expression matched her delighted face so close to his own.

"O my little prince, must everything go into that mouth?"

Esther laughed as she gently pulled each chubby finger apart to loosen the tight fist of hair. With his hand empty, he grabbed at her necklace and immediately began to pull on it intent on learning its taste.

"I think he is becoming quite the grabber," laughed Saroya. "Perhaps I will go to the nursery and find him a suitable toy to chew."

"Don't bother. I love his grabbing and holding on to me. May he always hold on."

Esther looked into his large, dark sparkling eyes.

"Do you understand, Darius? I am your mother, forever."

Darius answered his mother with hiccups which brought giggles from the handmaidens gathered around them.

Still enthralled by the bundle in her arms, Esther ignored a rapid, soft rapping on the door to her quarters. The handmaidens' attentions were immediately captured. Saroya moved quickly to the door, opened it just enough to see who it was, then stepped out of the room.

"His knees show signs of crawling," cooed Esther. "They are pinker than his legs. He will soon be walking!"

"Yes, My Queen. He is very fast when allowed on the floor. He is curious about everything. We must keep our eyes on him at all times," said Renayar. "He is fascinated by birds, bugs, and worms. When we take him into the garden, he wants to taste everything."

Esther laughed and tugged at Darius' chubby toes. "You mustn't eat the worms! You are chubby enough!"

"Does he eat well for you, Renayar? Solid food, I mean?"

Esther smoothed his dark hair and kissed his cheek. She longed to nurse Darius herself, but the king had strictly forbidden it. Renayar had nursed Darius since he was three months old and had faithfully attended to him.

"Oh yes! He is especially fond of fruit. Of course, I still have to make it soft and remove any chunks that might choke him."

"He gets that from me," said Esther. "I think I could live my life only eating fruit."

"It's the sugar in it that he loves," chimed in Meradin, the stoutest of Esther's handmaidens and Renayar's young apprentice with a love for all things sweet.

"Of course, it is!" laughed Renayar. "I must be careful that he doesn't get too many sweets or he will not be strong and muscular like his father!"

Esther smiled with her head bowed toward Darius and thought of the softness around Ahasuerus' middle that he tries so desperately to hide. When his favorite belt would not fit anymore, he had thrown it across the room and cursed it, then demanded that his tanner be whipped for making it too small.

Esther's attention was finally drawn toward the door as she handed Darius to Renayar after he began to fuss and hold his arms out to her. Renayar and Meradin left the room for the nursery, and Esther started toward the door. Saroya had been outside too long.

Esther wondered if there might be a problem.

When she opened the door, she was surprised to find Hathach, Saroya, and two other attendants standing with grim faces obviously in deep conversation. Hathach immediately grew silent, and the three females watched her with silent dark eyes and tight lips.

"Is something wrong, Hathach? Saroya? Darai? Tezaria? What is wrong? Why are you standing here in a huddle?"

Esther's heart rate increased and she felt her mouth go dry. The four of them obviously dreaded to tell her the nature of their discussion.

"I demand that you tell me!"

The skin on the back of her neck grew hot and something moved deep in her midsection. She put her hand on the wall to steady herself. Her sharp mind immediately began playing scenes of possible scenarios. Her first thought brought up old scenes from her people's history—of men, women, and children being slaughtered or taken into captivity, their cities ravaged and burned. Esther understood that the destruction and captivity came upon her people because of their refusal to repent from idolatry, adultery, and following after the ways of other foreign cultures and worship. The *Yehudim* had refused to heed warnings from the prophets of Adonai until finally He had allowed them to lose their land and they were taken into captivity to Babylon.

During the first year of the reign of Cyrus, after seventy years of captivity, Cyrus allowed the *Yehud* Zerubbabel to lead the first group of *Yehudim* numbering 42,360 to return from the Babylonian captivity to Jerusalem and Judea. He also decreed that the temple could be rebuilt on its original foundation and that the expenses for it were to be paid from the king's treasury. Furthermore, the gold and silver articles of the temple were restored to the *Yehudim*.

During Darius' reign, letters started coming from Tattenai, the governor of the region. He was attempting to stop the rebuilding of the temple. However, Darius searched out the records from Cyrus and instructed the governor and his men to let the workers alone. He also decreed that the expense of the work be paid from taxes collected. The work would be paid at the king's expense. Further, Darius decreed that funds should be given to the elders over the work immediately. Darius went on to instruct the governor that anything needed for burnt offerings and sacrifices were to be provided to the priests, as they requested.

Hashem had moved king's hearts, and Esther and those of her people who remained in Babylon and Persia recognized it as the work of Elohim. In the letters Darius had sent to Jerusalem and Judea, he made it clear his motivation was in recognition that the *Yehudim* God was to be honored. He even decreed that anyone, even if it be a king or ruler who tried to alter his decrees, should be hanged and his house made into a heap. Darius wanted the blessings of Elohim, so he requested that sacrifices and offerings be made for his life and his sons. *Would Ahasuerus continue the work?*

Recent messages from Mordecai revealed there was new trouble brewing in Jerusalem from letters Ahasuerus had lately received from the Babylonian, Persian, and other leaders sent to oversee the provinces beyond the Euphrates. The letters were concerning Samaria and Jerusalem, in particular.

Rehum, the commanding officer, and Shimshai, the secretary were over Jerusalem. They had sent the most recent letter to the king specifically to complain against what they referred to as a "rebellious and wicked city," meaning Jerusalem. They informed Ahasuerus that the captives he had given permission to return to Jerusalem were trying to rebuild the walls. This was of great distress to the Persian and other officials. They claimed that if the walls were rebuilt, the *Yehudim* would no longer pay taxes, tribute, or duty to the empire and the result would be a dishonor to Ahasuerus. To keep that from happening, they strongly suggested that a search in the royal archives be done to see what the previous kings had recorded about their dealings with Jerusalem. In Rehum's opinion the records would prove that the city walls of Jerusalem should not be allowed to be rebuilt.

Ahasuerus ordered Haman to oversee a search, and records confirmed that the city did indeed have a long history of revolt against kings. Jerusalem was recorded as "a place of rebellion and sedition." In fact, the city had proven to be very powerful against other kings in surrounding areas and had demanded taxes, tribute and duty to be paid from them. In light of Haman's report, Ahasuerus had ordered that the rebuilding of the city be stopped immediately. Esther feared the news she was about to hear was somehow related to her people and the order against them by her husband.

But they do not know I am a Yehud. Do they? Maybe the empire is under attack . . . the Greeks? Another rebellion or insurrection?

Fear seized her.

"Let us tell her, Hathach," said Saroya, "but stay with us."

She turned to Esther and said, "It is about your friend, Queen. The man called Mordecai."

Saroya moved her hand toward Esther's door, palm up to indicate her desire. Let us return to your quarters. There are ears that do not need to hear the message."

At the mention of Mordecai's name, Esther immediately felt a shockwave of fear that brought with it nausea. By the looks of the servants' faces, she knew it was grave news closer to her than she had imagined. She turned to enter her room, but instead of sitting, she proceeded with determination toward the outer garden.

If harm or death has come to Dod, I know I shall faint.

The air outside was cooler in the afternoon than in the room, and there was also a breeze from the sea. She braced herself by placing her hands on the low garden wall and took a deep breath. She turned toward Saroya and the other two women with Hathach and softly spoke.

"Hathach, tell me."

Since he had been the one that rapped on the door, he was the obvious one to ask.

"I know the eunuch, Keyvan, who has become very closely dedicated to Haman, the king's Vice-Regent. Keyvan reported to me, the eunuchs, handmaidens, and staff that a rebellion has arisen in Shushan against the king, and it will possibly spread into the other provinces. The rebels are wearing sackcloth and ashes; they are publicly weeping, and wailing to disrupt businesses. They have caused quite a stir. I don't think the king is aware of the full extent of the rebellion because according to Keyvan, Haman is dedicated to stopping it. He has ordered Farzad and the royal guards to forbid the mourners from coming near the palace gates. He threatens to hang them or send them to prison.

"But what about Mordecai, my . . . friend? What has he to do with these rebels? And what is the reason for this rebellion?"

"My Queen, I am not informed about his reason for it, but Mordecai has joined them. He has also refused to leave the area outside the gate. He is in sackcloth and covered in ashes, rocking and weeping while muttering and moaning. Since the rebellion began, he has not left the gate. This puts him in great harm from the guards following Haman's orders."

Esther stood so still that even the wind dared not ruffle her hair. Hathach watched her and although she showed no emotion, all color had drained from her face. He could almost hear her mind's distress.

When she finally spoke, her voice was not the voice of the tender mother of Darius, nor the entertaining story-teller of miracles and heroes and righteous kings whom the women of the palace gathered to hear. It was the voice of the most powerful woman in the empire.

"Saroya, call Davzadi the tailor . . ."

"But My Queen . . ."

"Saroya, now!"

Startled, Saroya spun on her heels and in haste left to find Davzadi, the most recognized and gifted tailor in all of Shushan.

"Thank you, Hathach for informing me. Do not let anyone know that I am a friend to the man Mordecai. Gather as much information as you can about the rebellion and report to me only as soon as you know more. You may take your leave now."

After the handmaidens and everyone else was gone, Esther fell across her bed and wept until every tear in her had been released. A knock at her door interrupted her intention to pray—something that she suddenly realized had been forsaken for all too long.

When she opened the door, Saroya was accompanied by the tailor. Esther quickly ushered them both in, then immediately sent Saroya to get some wine and refreshments.

As soon as Saroya was gone and the door was shut, Esther took Davzadi into the outer garden and whispered.

"Davzadi, I have been told that an old friend of my father is sitting at the palace gates in sackcloth and ashes in support of some kind of rebellion. I want you to take him some clothes and plead with him to forsake this effort and to go home. I greatly fear he will be hurt or killed."

Davzadi suddenly seemed taken aback by her request. She noticed a sudden change in his countenance—a faint wave of sadness—or fear?

"I understand your hesitation, Davzadi. Why would the queen send clothes to an old man involved in such as this, and perhaps get you accused of being involved? I'll see that you are paid and more if you will do this for me. I don't want to draw attention to myself as a supporter of a rebellion, or I would send one of my known attendants. So please do this for me. His name is Mordecai. Do you know of him? Have you seen him?"

She watched as Davzadi seemed to be struggling by her request.

Maybe he is afraid that he will be accused of supporting the rebellion, or worse, disobeying someone over him.

"I'll sent Hathach with you. Or better, I'll request one of the palace royal guards. He will protect you."

"That isn't necessary, Queen," Davzadi said quickly, and she realized that what she had seen on his face was fear. *But why? What is he afraid of?*

"I will collect appropriate clothing and find the man Mordecai. I will let him know that you are sending him a change of raiment, and you wish for him to go home and stop the involvement in . . . what is happening."

As Saroya returned, Davzadi was leaving. She noticed that the queen seemed quite animated and anxious following her conversation with the tailor. After she set the small table with wine, fruit, and bread, she asked.

"Are you quite all right, Queen?"

"Oh, yes! I am much better now. I think he will stop his support of it. Thank you for the refreshments, Saroya. You may retire now. Ask Yasmin to come. I am going to enjoy this food you brought and then prepare for bed. It's been a full day. I will see you in the morning. Sleep well."

"You as well, My Queen."

———————— הַפְסָקָה ————————

It was not hard to find Mordecai. He was sitting on the ground with his back against a booth near the gates. Except for the two guards at the entrance to the palace, he was the only person still on the deserted street.

Davzadi stood in shadows watching Mordecai and wondering how he could approach him without the guards seeing him. Trying to explain his mission to them, if he were stopped, would be hard and possibly threatening to his position. He took the route through the gates, then proceeded in the opposite direction from Mordecai. Weaving his way through the darkened side streets, he approached him from behind the booth where Mordecai was seated.

The man was a wretched sight—a crumpled old man on the ground covered in ashes, unwashed, his knees raw from kneeling in prayer. Davzadi's heart twisted with pity. He did not know Mordecai, but he did know many *Yehud*, and he was confused as to why the king had suddenly decided to do away with them. He wondered how he and other Persians would take up weapons to slay their neighbors. Some of his *Yehudi* neighbors were skilled craftsmen, honorable, hard working, and peaceable men. He also acknowledged that many of the Persians resented the captives that took land, jobs, crafts, and positions from them. Perhaps taking arms against them might not be as impossible as he might think. The thought made him shiver.

As he watched the guards for the opportunity to approach Mordecai, Davzadi recalled his conversation with the queen. He was positive Queen Esther did not know about the decree, but he also knew it was not his place to tell her. He had a request to fill, and he would do it because she was Queen, and also because she was beloved of all who knew her. He was grieved for her sake that her friend would soon be murdered like a common criminal.

Mordecai was exhausted, hungry, and hoarse from prayer filled with crying and calling out to Adonai. Unaware that he was being watched from a close position, Mordecai had no idea there was someone close enough to hear his prayers.

"Have I brought this upon Your people because of my own refusal to obey the king's decree? Let it be to me only, My Adonai. I cannot bear the weight of the result. I am overwhelmed with grief and sorrow. Must I see my brethren slaughtered in this captive land? Is captivity not enough? Must we also come under the sword?

"Will You save us? Will Elohim deliver us from this decree that cannot be retracted—the one that I have brought upon us all? If I have behaved righteously before You, You hear; if I have not failed to worship and obey You, You will hear my cries and deliver. Show me Your path, O Elohim Rohi (my Shepherd)."

When a deep moan rose from Mordecai's chest, Davzadi felt hot with shame that he had intruded upon a conversation he was not entitled to hear. A conversation he realized was prayer he did not quite understand, but the grief of the man was so strong Davzadi felt it, too.

"Mordecai?" he whispered.

Mordecai turned toward the shadows and looked up to see a man in a long cloak bearing the crest of the palace. He recognized the man as the palace tailor.

"Yes?"

"I am Davzadi, a servant to the king and queen. I am here at the request of Queen Esther."

At the sound of her name, Mordecai's heart skipped a beat. *She has not been discovered.* A wave of relief went through him.

"I have clean clothes for you and some food. She wants you to go home."

Mordecai placed a hand on the ground and pushed himself to his feet as if she were before him.

"The Queen?"

"Yes. She is most concerned that you not participate in this rebellion. She greatly fears for you."

Davzadi watched his face for some response but saw nothing but weariness and sadness.

"I am appreciative that you would seek me out and relay the message from her, but I cannot accept the clothes. I do not want the food. It seems she does not understand the situation that brought me here."

"Sir, I fear you are correct. There are many more that do not understand. Is there anything I can do for you?"

Mordecai stood there with his head dropped. Davzadi heard him take a deep breath. He raised his head to look Davzadi full in the face. The tailor saw strength and determination in Mordecai's expression that caused him to admire this *Yehud*, even in his present state.

"Just tell the queen what I said. I cannot accept the clothing, as fine as I'm sure they are, and I will not accept the food. Thank her for me. *Shalom*, Davzadi."

And he sank to his previous position.

Davzadi feeling at a loss and dreading to relay the message, he knew this man was not going to suddenly change his mind. So he turned back to the hidden route he had taken from the palace and made his way to the queen's chamberlain, Hathach, to let him know the answer to give the queen.

But in the first year of Cyrus the king of Babylon the same king Cyrus made a decree to build this house of God. (Ezr 5:13)

Now in the second year of their coming unto the house of God at Jerusalem, in the second month, began Zerubbabel the son of Shealtiel, and Jeshua the son of Jozadak, and the remnant of their brethren the priests and the Levites, and all they that were come out of the captivity unto Jerusalem; and appointed the Levites, from twenty years old and upward, to set forward the work of the house of the LORD. (Ezr 3.8)

The hands of Zerubbabel have laid the foundation of this house; his hands shall also finish it; and thou shalt know that the LORD of hosts hath sent me unto you. (Zec 4.9 KJV)

And in the reign of Ahasuerus, in the beginning of his reign, wrote they unto him an accusation against the inhabitants of Judah and Jerusalem. (Ezr 4.6 KJV)

Then ceased the work of the house of God which is at Jerusalem. So it ceased unto the second year of the reign of Darius king of Persia. (Ezr 4:24 KJV)

✡

Chapter Twenty-Eight

The Mission

Then called Esther for Hatach, one of the king's chamberlains, whom he had appointed to attend upon her, and gave him a commandment to Mordecai, to know what it was, and why it was. (Est 4.5 KJV)

The night was restless, the room too hot, the bed uncomfortable. Esther's thoughts were going in every direction, and yet, going no where. When sleep would approach, a heavy darkness would try to smother her, and she would startle fully awake. Multiple times she miserably sat up waiting for the day to come. Finally, exhausted by it all, she fell asleep.

Esther could hear Mordecai moving around putting the bread into the oven, singing psalms in his scratchy, deep, rich voice. Still lying with her eyes closed and without having to look into the room, she knew he was getting his scroll to read aloud with her. Now, he would be settling into his most comfortable chair. Her dreams were filled with him. She was a maiden again living in the small bedroom with the open window and the singing birds. She stretched in delicious peace and happiness.

Suddenly awakening she was not in her little room in Mordecai's home they had shared. She was in a room as big as his house, a room with elaborate furnishings and the soft, muffled sounds of the attendants preparing for her to arise.

She bolted upright and loudly called out for Saroya.

Saroya burst through the door alarmed.

"My Queen! Are you quite all right? What is the matter?"

"I am well. But I must speak to Hathach first thing. Summon him, Saroya, and call for Yasmin to attend to me."

"Yes, My Queen. Right away."

Preparing for the day with Yasmin's assistance, Esther was impatient and worried. She was anxious to know how successful the tailor had been.

When Hathach was finally ready to meet with her, she could not believe his report from Davzadi.

"He refuses? He would not leave the gates? He would not go home?"

What is the matter with him? Has he lost all reason? Can he not take advice? Does he want to be killed? Or am I missing something?"

Esther did not know what to think, but she knew Mordecai—or at least she believed she did. This did not sound like Mordecai.

"I must speak to him. I must hear his reasons. Hathach, is there any way I can speak to him? Can he come secretly to the palace, or to the gardens, so I can approach him?"

"My Queen, he cannot approach the palace. He is in sackcloth. The guards will kill him before they let him in."

"I will go to him."

Even as the words left her lips, she knew it was impossible.

"Queen," Hathach whispered. "You cannot."

Hathach looked at her with deep compassion and sorrow.

What kind of family friend was a man that would cause the Queen of Persia to risk her life to speak to him?

"Tell me what you want to say to him, and I will relay the message."

——————— הפָסְקָה ———————

So Hatach went forth to Mordecai unto the street of the city, which was before the king's gate. (Est 4.6 KJV)

Hathach wove his way through the crowds going about their business in the early morning. The smells of freshly baked breads and sweets filled his nose and reminded his stomach that he had not taken time to eat. A low rumble came from his gut to agree with the nose.

Mixed in with the merchants and their customers were men in sackcloth walking randomly among them while groaning and beating their chests. Men shoved up against them in disgust, while women ducked and twisted from their course to avoid them, dragging their curious children along.

Hathach looked into one ash-darkened face and then another while asking, "Mordecai?"

Most ignored him, some hurried away. It was not until he reached the city square that he finally recognized the man she had described to him, and one he had often seen working the booth near the gates. To be sure he had found him, he asked to be sure.

"Mordecai? Mordecai?"

The weary man would not answer, so finally Hathach leaned in and whispered, "Are you the friend of Queen Esther?"

"What do you want? What do you have to do with me?"

"I must speak to you in private, Sir. I am sent by Queen Esther who is filled with fear for you."

Mordecai turned and led Hathach toward the city gates and then into his booth where he left the curtains drawn and the candles unlit.

"Say what you were sent to say."

"It is not so much what I have to say to you, Sir, as it is what you will answer. The queen is convinced that the truth of why you and others are participating in a rebellion against the king is hidden. She wants to know from you why you are publicly in sackcloth and ashes."

"First, tell me . . . how is it that the queen and you who are in the palace do not know about the decree issued against the *Yehudim*?"

"A decree? I am sorry, sir, but I have no knowledge of a decree."

"Here, I will show you." Mordecai pulled from his counter a written notice with the seal of the king on the bottom. He handed it to Hathach without a word.

After Hathach read it, he looked at Mordecai in astonishment.

"So this is a rebellion against the decree?"

"It is not a rebellion. It is a public call, a cry for help from Hashem Elohim, whom we worship. When enemies come against the *Yehudim*, we are told by Hashem to call for fasting and prayer. Sackcloth and ashes are our humbling before him to pray for deliverance in the face of evil."

"This is an act of prayer?"

"Yes. As you can see we are sentenced to death within ten months."

"But why, sir? Why would the king decree such an order? Do you know?"

"You are the one that lives in the palace."

"I do, sir, but there are many in the palace who do things of which I am not aware. At one time I was the king's attendant, but due to his trust in me and my faithfulness to him, he appointed me as attendant to Queen Esther. I am not privy to the goings on with the king as I was once. None of us that serve the queen were informed of this decree or the intent."

"So you are also not aware that Vice-Regent Haman has promised to pay into the royal treasury 375 tons of silver to the officials over the treasury once the *Yehudim* are destroyed?"

"I did not know!" Hathach seemed not only shocked, but surprised that he was unaware.

"Men in power have risen up against us because we serve the unseen god. We have lived in peace among the nationalities here in the city without problem. But now, because of our refusal to bow to another god, we are under an order of destruction by the influence of one man. If you can stay a bit longer, I will give you a full account to give to the queen. She needs to know it all.

"Here, take the decree to the queen and explain to her all that I will tell you. Command her, in my name, to approach the king and beg for his favor . . . to plead with him personally for her people.

✡

Chapter Twenty-Nine

My People

And Mordecai told him of all that had happened unto him, and of the sum of the money that Haman had promised to pay to the king's treasuries for the Yehudim, to destroy them. Also he gave him the copy of the writing of the decree that was given at Shushan to destroy them, to shew it unto Esther, and to declare it unto her, and to charge her that she should go in unto the king, to make supplication unto him, and to make request before him for her people. And Hatach came and told Esther the words of Mordecai. (Est 4.7-9 KJV)

By mid-morning Esther had done everything she knew to do to make the time pass. Her time with Darius had provided a bit of distraction, but now he was back in his nursery enjoying his nap, and Esther was pacing the floor. *Where is Hatach?*

In the garden her handmaidens were enjoying their mid-morning refreshments, and she could hear their voices sprinkled often with laughter.

"Queen, if it pleases you, we would love to hear another story. It has been some time since we have heard one and the day is so beautiful," begged Hadarah.

Esther stopped pacing and looked toward the seven young women all looking at her with expectant eyes and relaxed smiles. For a moment she considered declining their request, but she realized that it would be another way to fill the time until Hathach returned from speaking with Mordecai.

"Very well, but I must warn you that I am expecting Hathach to return from an errand, and I may be interrupted."

She took her seat with them and forced her mind to cooperate by putting Hathach and his message out of front and center.

"We are still discussing the story of the man that the huge fish swallowed!" exclaimed Ariana.

"His name was Jonah, Ariana," reminded Daria. "When you tell us stories, Queen Esther, it is as though we can see it happening! I think I could smell fish!"

"Ah. Well, let me see what I can tell you today that will fill your mind with images! I will tell you of a man and his wife that had an angelic visit.

They lived long ago during the time when there was no man as king in the land. The people lived with the Creator God as their unseen king, and by messengers He would appoint men as judges to keep peace and safety in the land."

"Oh, how dreadful! I cannot imagine a world without a king in a palace! Were these judges like our regents, or the satraps over the provinces, or were they like gods?" asked Nima.

"Perhaps that is a way to understand it, Nima, because the regents and satraps have no power except that which is given under the authority of the king. In the land of the judges, they were empowered by the Mighty King, and they would seek out prophets at times for directions—if the king did not send an angelic messenger."

"Oh, can you imagine seeing a being from the stars to speak some urgent message to you?" Ariana's eyes sparkled at the thought. "I would love that!"

"I would find it terrifying," responded Farah. "I prefer to get my instructions from humans."

"While you imagine what it would be like, I will tell you of the couple that experienced it," said Esther.

The girls settled themselves and were ready for the story.

> The people of the land had made Mighty King angry because they refused to do what He told them to do. So He brought an enemy against them that overpowered the people and made them slaves. For 40 years they were under the power of this cruel and violent king and his people. Of course, the people who remembered what life was like under the rule of Mighty King, would offer sacrifices and prayer to Him to deliver them and to allow them to live in their land as He had instructed them.
>
> A man named Manoah was married to a wife named Susai that was barren. One day an angel sent from the King appeared to her and said, "Listen to me! You are barren and have not been able to have a child, but you will conceive and have a son. But I warn you, do not drink any wine or strong drink, and do not eat anything that Mighty King has said is unclean. For, you will conceive. When your son is born, do not cut his hair or put a razor on his head, for the child will be special to Mighty King from the time he is in your womb, and he will begin to deliver your land from the enemy that is over you."
>
> So Susai ran to her husband and told him about the man that had told her she would have a son who would deliver their people.

"What did the messenger look like?" Manoah asked.

"Oh, he was amazing! He looked like an angel!" Susai said. "He was glorious and terrifying. I asked him where he came from, but he would not tell me, and he would not tell me his name!"

She repeated the angel's instruction to her husband.

"He told me that our child would be special to Mighty King from the day he was conceived until the day of his death!"

Well, of course, this was hard for Manoah to believe. He wasn't sure if his wife had heard or remembered the message correctly.

So he prayed to the King and said, "O My King, send the man again which you sent to my wife, and let him teach us what to do for the son whom he said would be born."

So Mighty King being the good king that He is heard Manoah's request and sent the angel to Susai again while she was sitting alone in the field.

As soon as she saw him, she jumped up and ran to find her husband and said, "Lo and behold! The man has appeared to me again! The same man that came the other day!"

"So what is it about a man that he cannot believe the report of a woman? I mean are we just such liars until everything we say has to be verified?"

"Why are you interrupting, Daria?" asked Farah. "The Queen already said this story may be cut short. Let her tell the story!"

"As to your question, Daria, I have no answer. We would need to interview Manoah to get that answer. It is a good one, however. I will continue."

So Manoah and his wife ran back to the field, and there he was! Still, Manoah had to be sure, so he asked, "Are you the man that gave my wife a message?"

"Seems to me that Manoah can't trust anyone!"

"Daria, let it go!" said Saroya giggling.

And the angel said, "I am."

Then Manoah excitedly said, "Oh, let it be true! How are we to raise him, and what shall we do with him?"

The angel said to Manoah, "Do as I instructed Susai! She must beware not to eat anything that comes from the vine, nor drink wine or strong drink, nor shall she eat any unclean thing. Everything that I have commanded, she must do."

"Can you imagine how excited they were? Can you imagine how special they felt?" Esther asked.

"I don't know about that," said Saroya. "Isn't wine necessary for life?"

The girls burst out laughing!

"Only for a drunkard!" squealed Zahra.

"Ladies, you must let me tell the story, or I will never finish!"

"I hate it when we have to hurry, Queen." Leeza sighed.

"I'm sorry, Leeza. I can wait until tomorrow, it you girls prefer."

"Now, look what you have done!" Farah cried. "I don't want to wait."

"If you want me to continue, raise your hands. All right, then."

> Manoah said to the man, "Please stay until we can prepare a meal for you." Manoah said this because he believed the angel was a man and not an angel.
>
> But the angel said, "You may ask me to stay, but I will not eat your bread. If you decide to offer the meal as a burnt offering, offer it to Mighty King."

Daria started to speak but Farah glared her eyes at her and she stopped.

> So Manoah was still thinking he was a man and asked, "What is your name? When the child is born, we want to honor you! We will give him your name!"
>
> That may have sounded like a wonderful idea if the angel were a man, but since he was not a man, instead he said to Manoah, "Why do you ask my name? Don't you understand? It is a secret."
>
> So Manoah decided to kill a kid goat, place it on a rock, and make a burnt offering in thanks to Mighty King. Then the angel did a wondrous thing!

By now the maidens' eyes were wide, and they were leaning forward in their seats to hear the next words.

"What? What did he do?" exclaimed Roya.

The others chimed in, "Tell us! Quickly!"

"Oh . . . I don't think you really want to know," Esther teased. "Maybe I will tell you another day."

"Oh, My Queen! Do not torment us so. We cannot rest until we know what he did!" exclaimed Saroya who usually restrained herself in these times in order to maintain her superiority among them. Apparently, the suspense was too much, even for her.

Esther laughed and continued.

> When the flame of the offering rose toward the heavens from the altar, the angel ascended in the flame. Manoah and Susai fell on their faces to the ground when they saw it.

Gasps and expressions of shock and surprise were what Hathach heard as he neared the garden where the queen and her audience were in a close and deep conversation. He knew she was telling them another story. He waited a moment before he interrupted especially since his knocking on the outer door had been ignored or unheard. He had entered without permission. Esther was speaking to the handmaidens so enraptured they did not see him.

> Finally, Manoah knew the truth. It was indeed an angel and suddenly he was terrified. He grabbed his wife and cried out, "Surely we are going to die because we have seen Mighty King!"
>
> But the wife calmed him by saying,"Husband, if Melek had wanted to kill us, he would not have received the burnt offering from us. Also, he would not have shown us all these marvelous things, nor told us this wonderful news!"
>
> And later, just as the angel had said, Susai gave birth to a baby boy, and she named him *Like-the-Sun*.

Suddenly Saroya jumped to her feet. "My Queen! Hathach is here!"

Esther turned toward her room, and saw him standing sheepishly near the opening to the garden.

"Hathach! I did not hear your entrance."

The handmaidens were scrambling.

"Please forgive me, Your Majesty, I did knock, and I have urgent news; but I finally supposed you could not hear me. I could hear your voice from the doorway, so I entered."

Esther turned to the maidens standing in a close knot.

"Please, all of you except Saroya leave me."

Once they were gone she turned toward Saroya.

"Saroya, I requested that Hathach should send a message to a man in the city, and what we discuss now will not be revealed until I say so. Do you understand?"

"Yes, My Queen."

Esther turned to him, "Hathach, what is the word? Did anyone see you?"

"I don't think anyone noticed me, and I fear you will not like the message I have to deliver."

"It doesn't matter if I don't like it; I must hear it."

"Very well. I found Mordecai and he did explain to me why he is involved in actions as those of the others who are also wearing sackcloth and ashes and making public their distress. But, My Queen, they are not rebels."

"Not rebels? Then what?"

"They are *Yehudim*, My Queen. They are praying."

Esther felt behind her for the arm of her chair. Saroya moved closer to her as she eased herself into it.

"I don't understand, Hathach."

Her voice had a slight quiver to it. "What are they praying for?"

Hathach reached inside the cloak he was still wearing and pulled out the decree and handed it to her.

"My Queen, I think this may help me explain."

Hathach stood silently tense as she took the paper and began to read.

TO ALL PROVINCES OF PERSIA BY THE ORDER OF KING AHASUERUS AND ACCORDING TO THE SEAL OF HIS SIGNET:

CITIZENS OF EVERY PROVINCE ARE TO TO DESTROY, TO KILL, AND TO CAUSE TO PERISH, ALL YEHUDIM, BOTH YOUNG AND OLD, LITTLE CHILDREN AND WOMEN, IN ONE DAY, ON THE THIRTEENTH DAY OF THE TWELFTH MONTH, WHICH IS THE MONTH ADAR. CITIZENS ARE ALSO COMMANDED TO TAKE THE SPOIL OF THEM FOR A PREY.

He noted that she did not read it once, but twice before she laid it in her lap and looked up at him.

"Did you know about this, Hathach?"

Her eyes were dark, her brows drawn together, and her face had lost its color.

"No, My Queen. I only heard it today from Mordecai when he handed the same note that you now hold in your hand."

She looked down at it again. Rising from the seat with the paper in hand, she began to walk aimlessly in the room. Finally, she turned to him and spoke.

"What did Mordecai say to you? I mean what did he tell you to say to me? I can tell from your face there is more."

"There is more." He stated it flatly. "I will repeat the words he said and I beg you to remember they are his words and not my own."

Esther smiled at him weakly.

"I know him, Hathach. He is a man of bluntness, but he is also a man of integrity and truth. Whatever he said, I will hear. Speak."

"He told me when Haman was given the position as Vice-Regent, the king ordered that when in the presence of Haman, every servant of the palace and those who do business in the city booths near the palace gates should bow in honor to Haman. I can assure you that the order is true. I knew about it. However, it soon became known to the citizens near the gate that Mordecai would not bow. They questioned him and warned him. His own neighbors met and accused him of disobeying the king and putting their lives in danger because he refused to bow. Even when he explained to them why he could not obey the king's order, and asked them to trust in their god to keep them safe, they still feared they may be endangered.

"One of the eunuchs that Mordecai knows well and trusts, told him that Haman had been told his name and that he refuses to bow to honor him. Soon after that, Haman formed a committee of his closest friends, and they came up with a plan to destroy all the *Yehudim*.

"When Haman offered the king 375 thousand pounds of silver to the treasury of the king for the complete destruction of the *Yehudim* ethnic group, he also convinced the king that they were a group that refused to obey the king's commands and were a threat. The king gave Haman permission to write a decree to have them destroyed. Haman picked the day by casting lots and using astrological signs in the heavenly bodies for the date and month that did not favor the *Yehudim*."

"How does Mordecai know all this? It is as if he lived in the palace!"

"He was approached by a man named Anwir that had been hired by Haman to spy out the *Yehudim* by identifying them and finding where they work and live. Haman and his committee assumed the *Yehudim* would hide or try to leave Shushan. But when they started wearing sackcloth and ashes, wailing and crying and appealing to their god in the public, Haman told Anwir he no longer needed him. So Anwir thought perhaps Mordecai would pay him for information.

"Anwir also believed the report from those closest to him, that the king is not aware that the decree is determined to wipe out so many people. The king believes it is a small number of rebels only in Shushan. I really doubt that the king knows the decree was issued to every province.

"Mordecai knows Haman is the instigator of the decree. Mordecai says the reason he will not bow to Haman is because Haman bears the image of a false god on his raiment, and he will not bow to anyone but the god of the *Yehudim*. The basis of the decree, according to Mordecai, is that from long ago the people of Haman's tribe attacked Mordecai's people in a most vile and evil manner, destroying the weakest of the people and stealing their supplies. Because of that, the god of the *Yehudim* cursed Haman's heritage with a promise that they would be destroyed. Since that time there has been animosity between the two tribes. Haman is somehow the source of the decree even though the king's seal is on it, as you can see."

"Is there more?"

"You read me too well, Queen Esther."

"You are a good man, Hathach, but I do know you. I know when you still hold back some of the full message. I must hear it all."

"Mordecai said, and I quote, 'Command her, in my name, to approach the king and beg for his favor . . . to plead with him personally for her people.'"

Esther froze in her place. . . . *her people*. Mordecai had told Hathach the *Yehudim* were *her people*. She watched his face, but it was a mask that she could not read. Her mind was spinning. Her palms dampened. She raised her chin a bit and tried her best to appear as someone calmly and unemotionally facing a huge challenge.

"Yes. He is right. A huge portion of our city and of the empire is being threatened, and yes, I am their Queen. It is reasonable that as their Queen I should do all I can to intervene for my people. As far as I know, these people being sentenced are not a threat, nor a people that should be killed because of their god."

She watched his face to see if Hathach distinguished between Mordecai's words and hers. There was no tell at all. She could not say more. When it came to the royal decree in her hand, she must not reveal her identity. She hoped Mordecai had not already done it.

"However, Hathach, you know as well as I do that I cannot do what he asks of me. Return to him and give him my reply. Tell him all the king's officials and the people of the royal provinces know there is a law that for any man or woman who approaches the king in the inner court without being summoned, they shall be put to death. There is only one exception—unless the king extends the golden scepter to them and spares their lives. Thirty days have passed since I was called to go to the king. Tell him that, Hathach."

She watched his face, but she only saw the face of a man who obediently takes orders.

Oh, Adonai, may this man be trustworthy! May he not repeat Mordecai's message to any other!

"Hathach, I want Saroya to go with you. She will act on my behalf as a witness to the conversation."

Of all the servants of the palace, she trusted Saroya most. She had been with her for a long time. Esther knew if Hathach should tell the messages between Mordecai and herself to anyone along the way, Saroya would inform her. Also, if he were tempted, having Saroya with him would make it impossible, or at least more difficult to do.

"Right away, Queen Esther. I will return to Mordecai with your message . . . and with the maid Saroya. Do not fret, My Queen. You can trust me." Hathach turned away from her and his heart was heavy with grief. Although she had made a good attempt at hiding the truth, Hathach knew what Mordecai had made clear about the *Yehudim* was also a death sentence to the queen. Hathach vowed in himself that he would do all within his power and position to protect his beloved queen, no matter what.

Esther turned to Saroya, "You go with Hathach, but do not speak to anyone coming or going. What you hear I will discuss with you later, but for now you are simply to act as a witness to what Hathach and this man say in the event there is an investigation. Do you understand?"

"Yes, My Queen," Saroya smiled.

"Hathach, take care that you remain as invisible as possible. I do not want it said that you or I are attempting to support what is being called a rebellion against the king."

"Of course. I will conduct myself as you wish."

After the two of them were gone, Esther paced the floor again. Her mind was in a turmoil.

I know Mordecai will not be pleased with my message to him. Oh, if only I could meet with him and explain! He doesn't understand my position. I have no power here! I do my duties when called, but I live under the threat of being exiled or even killed it if I approach him at a time when he is angry or occupied by someone else's attention. What Mordecai asks is too dangerous! He has no idea what my relationship with my husband is like. If he does away with me, he has a harem full of beautiful women to replace me! Then what would happen to Darius? He would become as the other ignored and abandoned children living in The House of the Women.

In her distress, she mentally searched for some words from Mordecai's scrolls that would give her some relief from the frantic feelings of helplessness that overwhelmed her. Her mind was too full of fearful and confusing thoughts to remember any of them. Through tears she looked around the room that she called hers and realized as never before that none of it was hers. She was simply another possession of the king, someone to be used at his beck and call and easily replaced when her beauty and usefulness were gone.

> *All the king's servants, and the people of the king's provinces, do know, that whosoever, whether man or woman, shall come unto the king into the inner court, who is not called, there is one law of his to put him to death, except such to whom the king shall hold out the golden sceptre, that he may live: but I have not been called to come in unto the king these thirty days.* (Est 4.11 KJV)

✡

Chapter Thirty

In the Garden

> *And they told to Mordecai Esther's words. Then Mordecai commanded to answer Esther, Think not with thyself that thou shalt escape in the king's house, more than all the Jews.* (Est 3.12-13)

The two of them made their approach toward Mordecai in the market square. He recognized the eunuch Hathach but this time he had a woman with him. When he saw them coming, he immediately began moving in the direction of the city gates and his booth. Since Hadassah had sent two this time, he knew his work of convincing her was not finished. He suddenly felt weak and old. As he made his way to meet with them, he silently prayed to El Shaddai (God who providers) for wisdom, guidance, and strength.

Once in the booth for privacy, Mordecai turned to face the two of them and the realization that all of this—his people in the streets in sackcloth, the revealing of Hadassah's full identity—was because of his refusal to bow down and honor a man that he knew was an enemy who lived under the curse of Hashem. The guilt and remorse fell on him like a heavy weight. He felt the tension in the eunuch but he also felt something else he could not fully identify that surrounded them like the darkness in the heavens before a destructive storm.

"You have returned."

"Yes. I come with a reply to your request of the queen."

"Who is the woman with you?"

"She is the handmaiden of Queen Esther. She is here to bear witness to the conversation should I be arrested for meeting with you."

———————הַפְסָקָה———————

Once the eunuch and the handmaiden had left him, Mordecai left the booth, passed through the city square, and made his way home. He needed to be alone; he needed the garden and the quiet; he needed to hear from *Avinu*.

From the well, he drew water and stripping away the sackcloth, he washed himself. The black of the ashes had by now seeped deeply into the pores of his skin. He looked down at his naked body and saw the skin sagging on his frame from the loss of weight from days of fasting.

From his grief and guilt, he fell to his knees and cried out.

"Hashem Elohim, do not rebuke me in Your anger
   or discipline me in Your wrath.
Have mercy on me, Adonai, for I am faint;
   heal me, Adonai, for my bones are in agony.
My soul is in deep anguish.
   How long, Adonai, how long?
Turn, Adonai, and deliver me;
   save me because of Your unfailing love.
Among the dead no one proclaims your name.
   Who praises you from the grave?
I am worn out from my groaning.
All night long I flood my bed with weeping
   and drench my couch with tears.
My eyes grow weak with sorrow;
   they fail because of all my foes." (Psalm 6.1-5)

"What are you doing, Mordecai?"

He did not look. He knew he would not see anyone, but he recognized the voice he heard in his spirit.

He fell on his face, arms stretched outward. He had no explanation and even if he had any, he could not speak. It was as if he suddenly was sinking deep into the earth he was lying upon. He was overcome by weakness and wondered if he were dying.

"Do not be afraid or dismayed by the threat against My people. I am their sword and their shield; I am present in the time of trouble. Those who call upon My name shall be delivered; They shall prosper; they shall see the enemy destroyed. Now take peace, Faithful Servant, and know I will send all that is needed to win this battle."

Hope flowed through him as well as strength.

"I fear for Hadassah, *Avinu*," he whispered.

"Fear not, Mordecai. Your words to the eunuch are true. For many years now you have grieved because she was taken from you, and you prayed for her safety. But her appointment was ordained by Me, and I am with her, even now.

"Remember the words I spoke to Moses when he asked Me to show him grace by going with him and my people. I give you the same grace, Mordecai. I am with you, and I will do the same thing for you. I made a covenant to my people, and that covenant stands today. Remember that covenant."

> I will perform wonders in the presence of all your people that have never been done in the whole earth or in any nation. All the people you live among will see Hashem Elohim work, for it is an awesome thing I will do with you. (Deu 34.10)

A warm breeze blew over Mordecai and peace that started in his mind flowed through him. Still lying naked on the ground, he felt hope, and strength overwhelmed him. Rising from the ground, he turned his face upward and with a voice strong and confident, declared his faith.

"Away from me, all you who do evil,
    for Hashem Elohim has heard my weeping.
Hashem has heard my cry for mercy;
Hashem accepts my prayer.
All my enemies will be overwhelmed with shame and anguish;
    they will turn back and suddenly be put to shame." (Psalm 6.6-10)

✡

Chapter Thirty-One

The Reply

For if thou altogether holdest thy peace at this time, then shall there enlargement and deliverance arise to the Jews from another place; but thou and thy father's house shall be destroyed: and who knoweth whether thou art come to the kingdom for such a time as this? (Est 4.14 KJV)

"Hathach, what does it all mean?"

"I am not allowed to speak of it, Saroya. You heard the queen. We are to keep the words of the man Mordecai only for the queen."

"But I don't understand. What did he mean? Is the queen in danger?"

He would not look at her lest his face reveal his own thoughts. But he knew the fear he heard in her voice was real. It was as real as the fear that was now gripping his own heart for the queen.

"These questions are not for me. You must ask the queen. If she wants you to have the answers, they are hers to give."

"It seems this man is commanding the queen to do something that will have her killed! Who is he that he has the right to command the Queen of Persia! Why does he include her with those decreed to be killed? Is she *Yehudi*? Should we not report him to the king? Should we not do something to stop him? I found him very cold and dangerous!"

"Hush, woman! Or I will take you to the guards and tell them that you speak treason against the queen! Did she not command you to be silent! Stop your questions! If you are to know anything, it will be at the pleasure of Queen Esther, not me!"

Saroya stopped her mouth, but her mind was a torrent of questions—flooding not only her mind, but also her spirit. She frowned in confusion and fear that Queen Esther who she loved and honored was in danger. As she tried to understand it all, she hated herself for her lowly position and inability to even speak against the idea that her queen was in danger. *Am I to simply stand quiet and do nothing to save her if all of this that I heard is true?*

As they reached the door to Esther's quarters, he turned to her.

"We are not to interpret Mordecai's words; we will not add to them, nor take away any of them. We were sent to deliver a message, and now our responsibility is to give her the reply. Do not show any emotion or reaction to any of what will happen once we enter this room. Do you hear me, Saroya?"

Her face said it all.

Why do women have to show in their faces every thought they have? Hathach thought with aggravation.

She did not respond and it did not matter. They were at the queen's door.

Daria opened the door and held her forefinger to her lips.

"Darius has finally fallen asleep. He has been very cranky today. Please wait here until Renayar and Meradin leave with him," she whispered.

Saroya leaned around Daria to try and catch a glimpse of Queen Esther. She knew the queen must be frantic with worry if Darius was showing any signs of distress or sickness.

"Is he sick?" she whispered.

"Oh, not to worry. He is cutting teeth and that always causes babies to drool, gnaw their fingers, and whine more than usual."

Saroya listened to the maiden describing Darius' symptoms and giving diagnosis as though she were an expert in child rearing. She chuckled at the maiden's pretense of knowledge which Saroya was sure were the very words she was repeating from what the nurses had said to Queen Esther's same questions. She and Hathach moved to one side so Renayar and Meradin could pass with the red-faced, exhausted baby.

Hathach did not know if they should give the report to the queen now or if they should wait. After what was most likely a stressful visit with her baby, the queen may not want the message now. However, the decision was not his to make. Esther saw them and immediately motioned for them to enter.

The two of them bowed and faced her with stoic faces. Hathach noted that she seemed calm and ready to hear whatever they had to say. Saroya noted that she seemed quite at ease in spite of the visit with her cranky baby.

"Please, report your visit, Hathach."

"When we gave your reply to Mordecai, he replied with this answer, 'Do not think that because you are in the king's house you alone of all the *Yehudim* will escape. For if you remain silent at this time and hold your peace, relief and deliverance for the *Yehudim* will arise from another place, but you and your father's family will perish. And who knows but that you have come to your royal position for such a time as this?'"

Hathach and Saroya saw her face change, but they did not know what it meant. What they also did not know was that since the day she had been brought to the palace, she had worn a veil of secrecy about her heritage.

Silently, she stood looking from one to the other. Her next expression was one of relief or perhaps pleasure—they were not sure, but it was not what either of them had expected.

"Very well."

She continued to stand with that same look of calm resignation. It was the kind of expression that often comes when someone accepts that a private, protected secret is openly revealed, and no amount of effort will hide it again.

She looked around the room at the faces of her handmaidens. From their expressions, she realized she had kept her secret well. None of them as yet had been informed of the decree. But they were confused by the mysterious messages and the unknown relevance of their meanings. However, the words *escape*, *deliverance*, and *perish* hung in the air with the significance of a drawn sword.

Hathach broke the silence.

"My Queen? Do you wish to reply?"

Surely she will deny his accusations and decline this ridiculous suggestion that she is part of this, and that somehow she is going to save the Yehudim! he thought.

Hathach hoped she would openly declare the man a lunatic and command the order for him to be dragged to the palace prison and executed. Family friend or not, he was making claims that would get the queen slaughtered with the rest of the rebels in the streets. *That is not going to happen!* But Hathach suddenly realized his position could not save himself when it was all revealed, much less save the queen.

When Saroya saw the calm expression and the hint of a smile, she felt much relief and conviction that the man in the city square covered in sackcloth and ashes was mad. *Send me to report him, Queen. I'll see that he's properly stopped from his insane rantings.*

With a calm and authoritative voice, Esther instructed her handmaidens to go into the garden.

"We need to finish the story we started yesterday."

She smiled at them and watched as they turned and with wide-eyed looks at one another, filed out into the garden. Then she turned to Hathach.

"You've had a busy morning and most of the day. Please, go refresh yourself. I will continue my story to the maidens, and later I will speak to you again." She smiled at him and nodded.

He felt concerned that she was not immediately taking action.

Is she really going to dismiss the entire events and tell her maidens a story?

With nothing to say, he bowed and quietly said, "As you wish, My Queen."

Once outside the door, he stood with his back against the wall. He laid his head against it and stared at the ceiling then closed his eyes.

What is going on? Who is this man Mordecai and who is this queen? Is any of what has happened in the past two days real, or was it all just the result of one man's delusions and madness?

Convinced he had no idea of what was real or insanity and he did not want to believe the implications of what he had seen and heard. He suddenly decided he was hungry and emotionally drained. *I can't calm my spirit or solve these mysteries, but I can calm the gnawing animal in my gut.* He headed down the hall to do what he could do.

In the peace of the garden, Esther faced the seven maidens and wondered how to proceed.

"Are you going to tell us about the baby?" asked Zahra. "The one born to Manoah and his wife?"

"Wait," said Saroya. "Just wait a minute. My Queen, is it true?"

"The story? It was true for Manoah and Susai."

"Not the story!"

She spoke in a manner so boldly and so rudely the others were startled.

"The message of the old man Mordecai in the city dressed in sackcloth and ashes? Is it true what he said?"

The others looked at Saroya with eyebrows raised, then at the queen to see what she would do or say concerning the report just given.

"My dear, all questions will be answered and time will be given for understanding, but I have called you here to finish the story we started yesterday. Please give me the respect and time to do it as I desire."

Saroya blushed in shame and hung her head.

"Forgive me, My Queen. I don't know what came over me."

"You are weary from the trip into the city, and you have not had time to refresh yourself. We have all had a full morning. I will call for a meal to be brought. We will eat in privacy while I finish the story.

"Farah, please send one of the eunuchs to bring us our mid-day meal. We will eat it here in the garden."

While they waited for Farah to return, Esther excused herself into her closet to wash her face and take a moment to still her heart and her thoughts. She sat on her vanity stool and crossed her arms to cushion her head on the table.

I must remember the words of Hashem. I must remind myself of His promises.

At first her mind seemed empty.

"O Hashem, help me," she whispered. "Do not forsake me or leave me to my own devices. I am but a woman in a foreign land, but I am one of Your chosen people, and I need You. Please . . ."

Suddenly the words came like light into darkness. Her heart leaped with joy when she heard the words in the beautiful rhythm of Mordecai's voice:

> *Hashem Elohim is your refuge, and underneath are the everlasting arms.* (Deut 33.27)
>
> *When the righteous cry for help, Hashem hears, and rescues them from all their troubles.* (Psa 34.17)
>
> *In repentance and rest is your salvation, in quietness and trust is your strength.* (Isa 30.15)

Without knowing how it happened, she suddenly knew what she must do to help save her people. The answer was as clear as her face in her mirror. Filled with assurance, and now with a solid plan, she raised her hands in praise. She then wrapped her arms around herself and whispered.

"My soul magnifies My Savior."

When she returned to the garden, she knew by the sudden embarrassed quietness among the maids that there had been some discussion while she was gone. However, as soon as the eunuch entered with the meal, a relaxed and peaceful atmosphere replaced the tension as they eagerly gathered around the table to enjoy the meal and the sunshine.

Esther dismissed the eunuch and took a drink from her cup of wine.

"Now, let us finish the tale of the promised son who would deliver his people."

✡

Chapter Thirty-Two

An Appointed Life

> Then the LORD put forth his hand, and touched my mouth. And the LORD said unto me, Behold, I have put my words in thy mouth. See, I have this day set thee over the nations and over the kingdoms, to root out, and to pull down, and to destroy, and to throw down, to build, and to plant. (Jer 1.9-10 KJV)

The meal had given the girls a satisfied and contented feeling. Any concern for the queen seemed to have disappeared. Afterall, she was relaxed, smiling and at ease.

"Are you ready? Shall we have the tables cleared?" Esther asked.

"I will get the servants, Queen."

Leeza rushed to the door and called the waiting servants. They entered, and cleared the tables while the maidens went to wash their hands and refresh themselves.

As soon as they returned, Esther started where she had left off.

> When the son was born to Manoah and Susai, she named him Samson which at that time and place meant *like the sun*. From his early youth he grew up under the instructions given to his parents by the angel.
>
> When he was a young man, he saw one of the women of the enemy's tribe and thought she was most pleasing.
>
> He told his father and mother, "I saw a young woman in a nearby village, and she is very pleasing to me; I want to marry her. Get her for me."
>
> His parents were horrified!
>
> "Isn't there even one maiden in our tribe that you can marry? Why must you marry this maid from the tribe of our enemy?"
>
> But he was very insistent and said, "Get her for me! She pleases me!"
>
> As you can probably tell, this young man had come to believe he was more important than everyone, even his parents!
>
> The poor father and mother of this strong-willed young man did not understand that Mighty King was working in the heart of

Samson to bring about the defeat to the enemy.

Soon the parents and Samson headed to the village where the maid lived. On the way there, when he was out of his parents' sight, a lion suddenly attacked Samson.

Now, at that very moment, a spirit of strength and power from Mighty King came over him. It made him fearless and so strong that he ripped the lion's jaws apart with his bare hands!

Esther noted the girls wide eyes and surprised expressions.

However, he did not tell his parents about the sudden power given by Mighty King to rip apart a lion.

"Queen, why do you think he didn't tell his parents? If I did something like that I'd tell everyone."

The girls all burst out laughing.

"It's true! She's right! Ariana can't keep a secret! Anytime we need to know something, we just ask Ariana!" said Roya.

Ariana shrugged her shoulders and gave a sheepish smile.

"Ariana, it is probable that this was the first time this power had been felt by Samson, and he was most likely very surprised by it, or maybe it scared him a bit. Anyone have an idea why he didn't tell?"

Faces showed they were thinking.

Suddenly, Zahra's face lit up. "Oh! Maybe he didn't want them to tell anyone. Maybe he was waiting until he knew if it was a one-time thing!"

"That's reasonable, Zahra. If he found the ability never happened again, he would have been embarrassed."

"Yes . . .," Roxana said nodding slowly. "Boys can keep secrets. They really don't like to brag and then everyone find out it isn't true."

"Did it happen again, Queen?" Farah asked. "Or was the lion old or sick?" she giggled. "Maybe Nima could kill a sick lion."

"Well, I wouldn't be afraid to try!" agreed Nma.

Everyone laughed again.

"Warrior Nima! Killer of lions!"

"I'll continue and we'll see if it happened again. Maybe that was a sick, toothless lion."

Esther grinned, and the girls responded with nodding heads and smiles of their own.

When they reached the maid's home, an agreement was made with her parents for them to be wedded.

Later, when Samson and his parents were on their way to the village for the wedding, he left his parents on the path and found the carcass of the lion. He was amused to see that in the carcass was a swarm of bees and the honey they had made. So he scooped out some honey with his hands and ate some of it, gave some to his parents, and they ate it on the way to his wedding. Again, he did not tell his parents about the lion or the honey.

Before the wedding, Samson, and thirty young men who were selected by the bride's parents as companions for him, were having a party. So Samson said, "Let me tell you a riddle. If you can solve it during the seven days of the bridal celebration, I will give each of you fine linen robes and festive clothing. But, if you can't solve it, then you must give me thirty linen robes and thirty sets of festive clothing."

"All right," they agreed, "let's hear your riddle."

So he said, "Out of the one who eats came something to eat; out of the strong came something sweet."

Three days later they were still trying to solve the riddle. On the fourth day they said to Samson's wife, "Convince your husband to explain the riddle for us, or we will burn down your father's house with you in it! Did you invite us to this party just to make us poor?"

Now you may be able to understand how distressing this was to the poor young wife. So she went to Samson in tears and said, "You don't love me! You hate me! You have given my friends a riddle, but you didn't tell me the answer!"

Samson was surprised by her and said, "I haven't even told my parents the answer! Why should I tell you?"

Obviously, that was not the right answer for Sampson to give his new wife because she cried every time she was with him. Her crying continued for the rest of the celebration.

Finally, on the seventh day, he could not take it anymore, so he told her the answer to stop her from tormenting him with the crying and the nagging.

"Guess what she did?"

"She pulled an Ariana!" said Nima.

Hysterical laughter burst from the girls again. Even Ariana nodded and joined in with the fun.

"You're right!" said Esther.

She went straight to her friends and explained the riddle.

Before the sunset on the seventh day, the young men came to Samson and said, "We have the answer. What is sweeter than honey? What is stronger than a lion?"

"Oh. She's in trouble!" said Leeza. Her green eyes gleamed.

All the girls agreed by nodding and giving each other knowing looks.

"Can you imagine how betrayed Samson felt?" Esther asked. "Can you understand his anger?"

He said to them, "If you had not plowed with my heifer, you wouldn't have solved my riddle!"

Now the laughter was at a such pitch that Esther herself joined in.

"Heifer! He called his wife a heifer!" Zahra did not know whether to be shocked or tickled.

Suddenly the same power and strength that came over Samson to kill the lion, came mightily upon him again. He went down to another town of the enemy, killed 30 men, took their clothes and belongings and gave the clothing to the men who had solved the riddle. But Samson was so furious about what his wife had done, that he went back home to live with his father and mother.

"It happened again! It wasn't a one-time thing!"

"You're right, Roxanna," agreed Esther. It was not."

Later, when he had calmed down, Samson took a young goat as a present to his wife.

"Now there's a man that knows the key to a woman's heart."

Esther got so tickled, she had to stop to wipe the tears from her eyes after Ariana's comment.

"Girls, if you don't stop laughing, I will never finish this story."

They stifled their giggling.

When he arrived, he told her father, "I am going into my wife's room to sleep with her."

But her father stopped him and said, "I truly thought you must hate her, so I gave her in marriage to your best man. But look! Her younger sister is even more beautiful that she is. Marry her instead."

Rage filled Samson, and he said, "This time I cannot be blamed for everything I am going to do to the enemies of my people!"

He went out and caught 300 foxes. He tied their tails together in pairs, and fastened a torch to each pair of tails, lit the torches, and let the foxes run through the grain fields of his enemies. He burned all their grain to the ground including the sheaves and the uncut grain. He also destroyed their vineyards and the olive groves.

When the men knew what had happened, they said, "Who did this?"

Someone said, "It was Samson! His father-in-law gave Samson's wife to another man. This was his revenge upon us all."

So the men went to the home of the wife and burned down the house with her and her parents inside and burned them to death.

Now Samson was angry with the men that killed his wife and her father, so he sent them a message. "Because you did this, I won't rest until I take my revenge on you!"

So he attacked the men and killed many.

Then he went to live in a cave.

"Shall I stop now?" Esther asked.

"No! We will have many questions when you finish!" they said.

Well, as you can imagine, the people of the enemy were very angry. So they went into the populated section that belonged to Samson's tribes and set up camp.

The men of Sampson's tribe said, "Why are you attacking us?"

And the men of the enemy camp said, "We have come to capture Samson. We have come to retaliate for what he did to us!"

Now Samson's own people were frightened and angry that Samson had brought great trouble to them. So 3000 of them went to the cave and found Samson.

They asked, "Don't you know that these men are our enemies and they rule over us? What are you doing to us?"

Samson said, "I only did to them what they did to me."

"We have come to tie you up and deliver you to the enemies."

"All right," Samson said, "but promise you won't kill me."

"We won't kill you," they promised.

So they tied him with two new ropes and brought him to his enemies.

When the enemy camp saw the men bringing Samson, they jumped up and starting shouting in triumph. But suddenly, the power of Mighty King came upon Samson mightily, and he snapped the ropes off his arms like burnt flax, picked up the jawbone of a donkey's carcass and killed 1000 of the enemy.

You might think that he was exhausted. But no, he was filled with pride! No one could defeat him, even a thousand men!

So while standing in the midst of the broken and dead bodies, he raised the jawbone and cried out.

"With the jawbone of a donkey, I've piled them in heaps! With the jawbone of a donkey, I've killed a thousand men!'

Then he threw the jawbone away and named the place *Jawbone Hill*.

After all that killing, he was very thirsty, so he cried out to Mighty King.

"You have accomplished this great victory against the enemy by the strength of your servant. Must I now die of thirst and fall into the hands of these pagans?"

So Mighty King caused water to gush out of a hole in the ground and Samson drank. Then he named that place, *The Spring of the One Who Cried Out.*

Samson judged his people for 20 years during the time when the enemies of Mighty King ruled the land."

Esther picked up her cup and took another drink. The maids looked at her in expectation.

"Is that all? Is that the end of the story?" asked Nima.

"Not quite. But before I tell the end, I must explain the events of today or rather the past days to you."

"Farah, ask the eunuch to clear the tables while we refresh ourselves to listen. It may take a while."

The maids left the table and the garden to tend to necessary matters. Esther, now alone in the garden, closed her eyes. She quoted a scripture.

> *"For the glory of your name, O Adonai, preserve my life. Because of your faithfulness, bring me out of this distress."* (Psalms 143.11)

In faith, trust and confidence in the words she remembered, she stood still hoping to feel the same power that had overshadowed Samson.

O, Hashem, was my life appointed as You appointed Samson's?

The idea seemed ridiculous, and the concern that what she had to say would come back to take her life tried to creep into her spirit and destroy her trust. *To lose my life would not be the greatest heartache, but to leave my son without an eema would be disastrous.*

She remembered a morning conversation she had with Mordecai after he had read from Jeremiah's writings. He read it to her and said, "Remember these words, Hadassah. In your future you will need to draw strength from them."

> "Before I formed you in the womb I knew you, and before you were born I set you apart and appointed you . . ." (Jer 1.5 KJV)

"But *Dod*, those words were spoken to Jeremiah!" she had replied.

"Hadassah, they are the words of Adonai and do you think that He did not form you? Do you think He did not know you before you were born? Do you think your life is an accident? Elohim gives life and purpose. You were born as part of His plan, and He has laid a plan for your life, if you will receive it; He has appointed you for His service . . ."

Her thoughts were interrupted by the chatter and some laughter as her handmaidens were returning and were probably discussing the events in Samson's life. Once they entered the garden, they quietly took their seats and waited to hear her.

✡

Chapter Thirty-Three

Rending the Veil

Now the serpent was the most cunning of all the wild animals that the LORD God had made. He said to the woman, "Did God really say, 'You can't eat from any tree in the garden'? In fact, God knows that when you eat it your eyes will be opened and you will be like God, knowing good and evil. (Gen 3.1,5 NKJV)

"I have much to tell you. First, I will tell you that the captives from the cities of Jerusalem and Samaria and the regions around them are the religious and ethnic group known as the *Yehudim*. They are scattered from Babylon to Egypt in the 127 provinces of this empire. They have been portrayed to the king by Vice-Regent Haman as rebels who must be destroyed. Vice-Regent Haman has offered to pay into the king's treasury 375 thousand pounds of silver to those who help with their total annihilation. A decree has been issued into all of the king's provinces."

She pulled the decree from her pocket.

"I am reading to you from the decree.

"'On the thirteenth day of the month Adar, the people of Persia are to destroy, to kill, and to cause to perish, all *Yehudim*, both young and old, little children and women in one day and to take the spoil of them for a prey.'"

The maids were stunned. She saw several starting to ask questions, but she held up her hand to stop them.

"I will answer questions when I have finished. That was the first thing I wanted to tell you. Here is the next. I am *Yehudi*. We serve one God, and we have many names for Him. In every way that He interacts with us, we have a different name, but He is the One True God. He is our King.

"My parents are both dead, and I was adopted by my cousin, Mordecai. When the virgins were taken after Vashti was removed, I was brought into the palace, as you were. My cousin warned me to keep my heritage identity secret because there are enemies to the *Yehudim* people throughout the empire. Mordecai knew Haman to be one of them.

"Now I know there is at least one in the palace that has enough influence with the king to convince him to destroy my entire religious heritage and race of people. We identify as the children of Father Avraham. We consider him the father of our nation. We worship, Elohe-Yisarel, the God of Israel. We are called to live by the commandments and laws given to us by Elohim through Moses who was called to deliver our people from slavery in Egypt. He gave us our own land and many promises of blessings.

"The foundations of our faith and nation were given to Avraham, Yitzchak, and Ya'acov our forefathers. God made great and awesome promises to them and their future generations if they would obey and worship Him. God wanted them to be different from the other nations who worship many gods.

"But my people forsook the faith. They turned away from Elohim. They began to worship the gods of the nations around them. They intermarried other people groups who were not *Yehudim*. That was contrary to the commandment of Elohim. Hashem Elohim forbids us to worship or bow down to an idol or image of another god. Our God is a jealous God.

"Prophets, messengers, teachers, and even shepherds and farmers were called by Elohim to tell our people to repent and forsake all other gods or He would turn His favor away from us. My people refused to obey. They shrugged their shoulders and stopped their ears and refused to hear. They made their hearts as hard as stone. They refused to obey the law given to us by God that would show other nations that we are His and who He is.

"Finally, Elohim sent His wrath upon my people. He sent strong kings against us to destroy our cities, burn our temple, ravage our land, and carry my people into captivity. Still my people did not repent. My God is an awesome God of power, love, blessings and peace to those who will love Him and obey Him. He desires to bless us. But we must be obedient.

"Here is another thing you must know. The stories that I have shared with you these many years are not stories of fantasy or dreams. They are stories of real men and women who are *Yehudi*. They were anointed by Elohim, the Creator God and Father, to do mighty works, preach righteousness, declare judgment, and announce punishment and destruction to the wicked and the enemies of Melek, the King of Kings.

"You may wonder what the purpose was for Eloheenu, the Lord our God, to choose a people as His own. To explain that to you, I must tell you another story."

Esther paused to observe their expressions. She wondered what they were thinking, what they were feeling. Do they feel deceived by me? Noting that they were fully attentive, she decided to continue.

I may as well tell them.

In the beginning Elohim, the Eternal Creator, created the world and all that is in it in seven days.

On the sixth day of creation, He made a man from dust and named him Adam. He placed Adam in a garden called Eden. Adam was given authority over everything that Elohim had made. Then Elohim told him about one of the trees.

"Adam, you are free to eat from any tree in the garden, but you must not eat from the Tree of the Knowledge of Good and Evil. If you do, on the day that you eat from it, you will certainly die."

After that warning Elohim said, "It is not good for Adam to be alone. I will make him a helper."

He caused a deep sleep to come over Adam. Then He took one of Adam's ribs and made him a wife. Adam named her Eve.

Elohim said, "It is very good."

In Heaven a beautiful, created angel named Lucifer had become so proud, he wanted to be God. He wanted to be worshipped. Of course, there is only one God, so Elohim cast him out of Heaven. Lucifer convinced one-third of the other angels to go with him.

Now that Lucifer was not in heaven, he saw Adam and Eve who Elohim had created and given authority over everything in a perfect world. So, Lucifer decided he wanted what Elohim had created. He decided if he couldn't be the god of Heaven, he would be the god of the earth. So he made a plan to take the earth away from Adam and Eve and to destroy them. He used the most beautiful and cunning creature Elohim had made.

A beautiful creature said to Eve, "Did Elohim really say, 'You can't eat from every tree in the garden?'"

Eve said, "We may eat the fruit from the trees in the garden; but the fruit on the tree in the middle of the garden, Elohim said, 'You must not eat it, or touch it, or you will die.'"

The beautiful serpent said, "You will not surely die! Elohim knows that if you eat that fruit your eyes will be open to see things differently; you will be like Elohim! You will know good, and you will know evil."

Eve looked at the tree. The fruit looked delicious. It was beautiful fruit. She believed the serpent and believed the fruit would make her more than Elohim had made her to be, wiser than He made her to be. She believed the serpent and was deceived to believe that Elohim was keeping her from being all she wanted to be. So she took the fruit and ate it. She gave it to Adam and he ate.

Suddenly their eyes were opened, and they saw things differently! They suddenly knew they were naked. They looked at each other, and for the first time since they were created, they felt shame. They picked fig leaves and sewed them together to make themselves coverings.

Then they heard Elohim walking in the garden, and for the first time, they felt fear. Feeling ashamed, afraid, and guilty, they hid themselves in the trees.

Elohim called to them, "Adam, where are you?"

Adam replied, "I heard Your voice in the garden, and I was afraid because I am naked! I hid myself."

Elohim said, "Who told you that you were naked? Have you eaten from the tree I warned you not to eat?"

Adam said, "The woman You gave to be with me, she gave me the fruit and I ate it."

Elohim said to Eve, "What have you done?"

Eve replied, "The serpent deceived me, and I ate."

Elohim said to the serpent, "Because you have done this, you are cursed above every animal. You shall go on your belly and eat dust all the days of your life!"

Because Adam and Eve disobeyed Elohim, they were made to leave their beautiful garden. No longer would they live forever. They would grow old and die and return to dust.

The earth and all mankind is cursed because of their disobedience. Weeds and thorns make farming hard. Women giving birth must go through terrible pain, and no longer was woman as Elohim made her. She was made to be under the rule of man.

Evil came into the world. Lucifer had taken Adam's authority and position, and he became the prince of the world.

But Elohim made a wonderful promise. A woman would give birth to a child who would crush the head of the serpent. He would destroy the evil of Lucifer and those who obey him to do evil and to tempt all creation to worship him instead of Elohim.

Since that promise, many other prophesies have been given about that child. He will be born to a virgin from the tribe of a *Yehudi* man named David. Every *Yehudi* girl lives with the hope and dream that she will be the one chosen by Elohim to bear the Son of Elohim who will save the world from sin and evil and make Judah, or as we say *Yehudah*, His eternal kingdom of peace.

The maids were speechless. They had never heard such a tale. Some of them had furrows in their foreheads, and Esther wondered what they must be thinking and feeling. She knew she had to continue.

"I had that hope. I wanted to be the virgin that brought forth the promised Son of God. But instead I was taken from my cousin Mordecai, just as you were taken from your families. I was brought to the palace to become the property of the king.

"From what my cousin Mordecai said today through the message you heard, he thinks that Hashem Elohim has placed me in the position as Queen and as the wife of the king to save the *Yehudim* people from this decree of death. To be honest with you, I don't know that I can do anything. But I am not just Queen Esther, I am Hadassah; *I am a Yehud*. I am one of the chosen people by Hashem Elohim and my life is to serve Him. If He chooses for me to die for Him, I am ready to die. It means that as His servant, He can use me as He pleases to accomplish whatever He desires.

"I must be willing, and so I call on you to support me to see the salvation of my people, the people of Yehudah."

The silence was long. She had given them much information. She had bared her soul and given them opportunity, if they wanted it, to see her hanged or beheaded.

Suddenly a flood of questions came from all of them.

"You mean there was a real Samson?"

"There was a real Jonah?"

"A real David?"

"A real giant killed by a stone?"

"Was Moses really raised in the palace of the Egyptian king? His army drowned in the Red Sea? That's real?"

Esther laughed.

"Yes. The stories are real; the people are real; Hashem Elohim is real. So now, from a real *Yehudi*, who is a real queen, speaking to her real handmaidens, will you help me in my efforts to save my people?"

Roxanna, the youngest in the group, looked at her with eyes the color of the sky.

"How can we help the queen? We are just handmaidens. We have no power or influence."

"Roxanna, remember the power that comes from Hashem. Remember the stories I have told you about what He has done and realize what He can do. Put your life under that power. We must put our trust and hope in His power as He works through us.

"I intend to take three days to fast and pray for the deliverance of my people. That may be very strange to you, but it is a sure way to be made strong enough to do what I have planned. What I will do after the three days of fasting and prayer will only succeed by Hashem Elohim's favor.

"I will also request that the *Yehudim* of Shushan fast and pray the same three days. We will pray for the God of Heaven, Hashem Elohim to stop the enemy and his evil plan. I do not know how it can be done, but I know, and now you know, that He is powerful and can do the impossible.

Will you fast and pray with me? Do you want to see His power? Do you want to be used by Him?"

✡

Chapter Thirty-Four

A Battle Plan

Then Esther bade them return Mordecai this answer, Go, gather together all the Jews that are present in Shushan, and fast ye for me, and neither eat nor drink three days, night or day: I also and my maidens will fast likewise; and so will I go in unto the king, which is not according to the law: and if I perish, I perish. So Mordecai went his way, and did according to all that Esther had commanded him. (Est 4.15-17 KJV)

The palace was quiet. Esther was wide awake, her mind a turmoil of thoughts. By her request to her handmaidens, she had put all of them in danger. It was one thing for her, a *Yehud*, to be in danger, but to call for these young women under her influence to fast and pray for three days also put them in danger. For them to intercede for her and her people was a risk that Esther knew they probably could not comprehend.

She smiled slightly as she remembered their wide eyes, their faces, their love for her, their eagerness to participate in something completely foreign to them. Every one of them had been through so much; it was easy for them to understand captivity, loss of family, loss of freedom to choose. They had a strong and binding connection to her. She had given them a choice, and they had chosen to follow her example.

Most of them had been taken from pagan homes that followed idolatry; a couple of them were from homes of men and women so poor and so mistreated that they had no belief in any kind of god, especially an all-powerful, all-seeing deity. Esther's stories had been pure fantasy to them.

After Esther revealed her heritage to the girls and they went to their quarters, Saroya had lingered behind the others.

"May I have a moment with you, My Queen?"

"You may, Saroya."

Saroya sat down and Esther noticed that she was struggling to hold back tears.

"What is wrong, Saroya. Have I upset you?"

She dropped her head. Raising her eyes to Esther she began.

"You did not upset me. I must make a confession to you."

Esther felt her heart quicken. Saroya was her closest confidence concerning the message to Mordecai.

"Please. Tell me, Saroya. Whatever you need to say, I will listen."

When she raised her head, tears were slipping down her cheeks.

"My Queen, I am the daughter of a Yehud. My mother was given in marriage to a Persian man in payment for a debt. I am sure my mother is knowledgeable about the *Yehudim* beliefs and heritage, but in order to live in peace with my father, she must have forsaken it. She never told me about my heritage. Actually, my father is not really much of a worshipper of any god either.

"From your stories for the first time in my life, I have learned about my people and my history."

Her eyes glistened with tears, and her face shone with love and gratitude.

"Oh, Queen Esther, thank you! For the first time in my life, I know that I truly belong to a people; I have a history; I have a future."

She threw her arms around Esther, and they both wept.

As she remembered those moments with Saroya, she longed for Mordecai with an ache that she could not relieve. He had faithfully taught her. She knew he loved her with a love that she did not deserve. For months she had gone without thinking of him. Then he would send her a letter and tell her about the births, marriages, and deaths among the *Yehudi*m in her village.

In earlier days the news was from reports Mordecai received from Jerusalem and Judea. The city was in ruins and decay. Many of the *Yehudi*m had moved from the city and returned to farming and animal herding.

Then after the first captives were allowed to return to Jerusalem, the news was about the amazing restoration and rebuilding of the temple. The work had been supported by letters from kings Cyrus and Darius. Those two kings had financed the work and provided for the workers and the priest over the temple. Darius even asked for the people to pray for him and his son, Ahasuerus. Now the work was halted.

Mordecai often grieved over Jerusalem and especially those of his people who still did not obey Hashem after all that had happened, after all the prophecies, visions, and calls to repentance.

Mordecai wrote to her about the men moved on by the Spirit of Hashem to give the people warnings, encouragement, and predictions of a time when Jerusalem would be completely restored and under the kingship of David. When she received these letters, she always felt guilty because she had forgotten the struggles of her people. She had become entangled in the life of the palace far from all things *Yehudi*. Her lack of prayer for them and the total lack of concern for them was the source of her guilt.

She suddenly felt trapped and remembered the words of the psalmist.

> *"Oh that I had wings like a dove for then would I fly away and be at rest."* (Psalm 55:6 KJV)

Pushing those thoughts aside, she knew she still had to take Hathach into her confidence. Gnawing on her lip, she wondered if he would betray her and her handmaidens. When they did not call for food for three days, he would wonder; he would notice.

What might he do? What is he hearing in the quarters of the eunuchs and servants? Is he tempted to inform them of what he knows? Would he feel it his duty to tell the king?

These and other thoughts crashed around in her head like the waves of an angry sea. Putting her hands on the sides of her head, she repeated words from the psalmist.

> *Vindicate me, Adonai, and champion my cause against an unfaithful nation; rescue me from the deceitful and unjust person.*
> *For you are the God of my refuge.*
> *Why have you rejected me?*
> *Why must I go about in sorrow because of the enemy's oppression?*
> *Send your light and your truth; let them lead me.*
> *Let them bring me to your holy mountain, to your dwelling place.*
> *Then I will come to the altar of Adonai, to Adonai, my greatest joy.*
> *I will praise you with the lyre, Adonai, my Hashem Elohim.*
> *Why, my soul, are you so dejected?*
> *Why are you in such turmoil?*
> *Put your hope in Hashem Elohim, for I will still praise him, my Savior and my God.* (Psalm 43)

She repeated the final part of the psalm.

"Put your hope in Hashem Elohim. . . my Savior and my God. I will do that," she whispered. "I am resolved to hope in Him. Why do I fret? I cannot change a man's heart or mind. I know what the scripture says about a king's heart."

> *The king's heart is in the hand of Adonai, as the rivers of water: He turns it whithersoever he will.'* (Psalm 21:1)

"Surely the heart of every man is in His hands. Hashem will take care of Hathach. I put him into Adonai's hands."

> *I will bless Hashem who counsels me —even at night when my thoughts trouble me.*
> *I always let Hashem guide me. Because He is at my right hand, I will not be shaken.*
> *Therefore my heart is glad and my whole being rejoices; my body also rests securely.*
> *For you will not abandon me . . . ;*
> *You will not allow your faithful one to see decay.*
> *You reveal the path of life to me;*
> *in your presence is abundant joy;*
> *at your right hand are eternal pleasures.* (Psa 16.7-11)

———————— הפסקה ————————

When Saroya opened the queen's room the next morning, she was surprised to see that she was still in bed. She opened the drapes over the doorway to the garden and the light flooded into the room. Moving over to the bed, she gently pulled back the filmy curtains surrounding the bed to see if the queen was stirring. For a brief moment, Saroya's heart skipped a beat.

"My Queen?" she whispered. "My Queen?"

As lightly as she could, she touched her hand. Relief flooded her when warmth was present.

Since she knew the queen was to meet with Hathach after breakfast, she wondered if she should awaken her. More thoughts flooded her mind.

Is she sick? She doesn't look sick. What should I do? Do I wake her? If I don't wake her she will miss her meeting with Hathach and may also lose her time with the little prince.

The problem was solved when she heard the queen taking a deep breath, and stretching. She opened her eyes and seeing Saroya, she mumbled.

"Saroya? What time is it?"

Putting her arm over her face she said, "Oh, my, the sun is very bright!"

Sitting on the side of her bed, she pulled her robe around her and started for her private spa where the handmaidens were waiting. On the way, she issued her instructions.

A BATTLE PLAN

"Saroya, please see that the chamberlains bring a light breakfast up to me. I fear I have lost precious time this morning from staying up too late. Ask the nurses to bring Darius in the early afternoon before his nap, instead of this morning. I do not want my meeting with Hathach to interfere with my time with him. I will send two of the girls from the spa to help you see that everything is ready for my meeting with him. I also want you to be present when we meet. I will take care of my bath and preparations as quickly as possible."

Esther stopped a moment in her rush. She looked at Soroya and smiled, then crossing the room to her, she gave her a quick hug.

"Good morning, *achot*."

Saroya responded with a soft smile. When Esther was gone, she informed the chamberlains who had been waiting outside the door that the room was now ready for them to enter and make it ready.

"The queen overslept and intends to hurry though her bath and dressing, so now you will need to work quickly!"

When Hathach and three other eunuchs arrived with breakfast trays, Saroya ushered them into the queen's private dining area which the chamberlains had prepared. The food was placed, and Saroya approved everything just as Queen Esther and her handmaidens emerged from the entrance to the spa.

The handmaidens left the queen's quarters to have breakfast with the other servants of the king and queen in the servant's hall. However, since Esther had requested that Saroya be present for her meeting with Hathach, she waited in the bed chamber to oversee the cleaning while the queen had her breakfast.

Hathach and the eunuchs watched her take her seat at the table that could have easily seated twenty. She gave a brilliant smile to each of them and a nod of her approval. The eunuchs noted that this queen was so unlike Vashti who never looked at any of them in the eye. They took their places along the dining room wall to serve as needed.

Waving her hand to them in dismissal, she said, "Oh, you may leave me. I will get one of the handmaidens to send for you to return and remove the service when I am finished. It will not be long. Then flashing a smile at them, she turned her attention to Hathach.

"Please wait a moment, Hathach, I have an urgent message I need you to deliver."

To Paresh, the last eunuch leaving the room she said, "Paresh, please ask Saroya to come in."

Once she and Hathach were alone in the room, she waited until Saroya was present and the adjoining rooms were vacant.

"I have a reply to send to Mordecai. Before I give it to you, Hathach, I want to say that I am aware of the danger I have put you under by sending you to communicate with him. I think it is only right that I explain to you my reasons for doing so. Actually, you may already have an idea for my actions.

"Mordecai is my cousin. When my parents died, he adopted me and made me like his own daughter. He and I are *Yehudi*. When the captives from Jerusalem and Judea were allowed to return, Mordecai decided not to leave Persia. We have lived here all of my life, and we have many friends here. We have been content to live, worship, and do business here. Also, Mordecai receives news from Jerusalem very often, so we know that there is much trouble there from the overseers appointed to the region.

"The reason Mordecai did not leave when the last group returned to Jerusalem is because I was brought into the palace. When I was taken from him, he warned me not to let anyone know my heritage. Mordecai has had dealing with the man Haman from years ago when he was an employee of Mordecai and when he was a barber. Haman has a long standing hatred for *Yehudim*. His ancestors once attacked the *Yehudim* when they were in a very vulnerable position. Since that time, the *Yehudim* and the Agagites have been enemies. When Haman was promoted, Mordecai refused to bow to him as commanded by the king, so the decree is Haman's way to get revenge and to destroy all of us.

"Telling you this is putting my life into your hands. I cannot command you to keep what I am telling you a secret. Actually, I'm quite tired of secrets. It's a heavy burden. I am *Yehudi*. I believe in the *Yehudim* God, and I put my confidence and trust in Him to protect me as He has my forefathers before me. But now I am in a position of danger because my husband, I believe innocently, gave Haman his seal to sign our death warrant.

"Adonai has placed within me a plan to save my people, but it depends on the faithfulness and support of my closest associates. I intend to expose Haman's plan, and if my God is with me, Haman will be the one destroyed. That is what Mordecai meant when he told you to tell me that perhaps I am here for such a time as this. He and I know the history of Hashem's dealings with the *Yehudim*, and He is a delivering, saving Melek, a King to us.

"Saroya was informed of my status last night, as well and all of my handmaidens. I trust you, Hathach, and as I said, my life is in your hands. My life is in the hands of my handmaidens, but more than that, my life is in the hands of Hashem, my God, and because of your assistance to me, so is yours.

"Return to the city and find Mordecai and tell him to gather together all the *Yehudim* that are present in Shushan to instruct them to fast for me for three days, night and day. Let him know I and also my maidens will fast likewise. Tell him I will go before the king, which is not according to the law since he has not summoned me; and if I die, I die."

Saroya stood pale and drawn hearing the message while tears rolled down her face and dripped off her chin.

Hathach stood unmoving and silent. He had never been told that any service he offered was of such importance. When she said, "My life is in the hands of my God and because of your assistance to me, so is yours," he felt a strange sense of fearlessness come over him and a reason for living that he had never experienced. Basically his life had been one with no reward and many losses. Looking into her face, he suddenly realized he had a purpose, and he also determined to learn more about a god that would use such as he to help save the lives of other captives.

He bowed, not from the waist, but to his knees and placed his forehead to the floor. Then still on his knees he spoke.

"My Queen, my life for yours."

She suddenly felt more assurance by that one act than she had ever felt from anyone in the palace. Her eyes met his in a bond of understanding, bravery and trust.

"*Adonai, Elohaynu, melekh ha-olam,*" she replied. Then explained to him, "That is to say: Blessed are you, Lord our God, King of the universe."

✡

Chapter Thirty-Five

The Third Day

Now it came to pass on the third day, that Esther put on her royal apparel, and stood in the inner court of the king's house, over against the king's house: and the king sat upon his royal throne in the royal house, over against the gate of the house. (Est 5.1 KJV)

For two days quiet and rest settled over the streets of Shushan. The men in sackcloth and ashes had gone home. The moaning, crying, and wailing had ended. Businesses hung fresh banners in their windows advertising special deals to shoppers. The people rejoiced that the confusion and disturbing sights were over.

On the first day that the men in mourning did not appear, Haman was delirious. On his ride to and from the palace, he rejoiced over the city that he had empowered with his decree. He longed for the thirteenth day in Adar when he and others could slash the throats and push spears through the hearts of the arrogant believers of a god that would put a curse over the heads of his ancestors and him. He dismounted his horse and strutted into his home.

"Zeresh! My *azazim*! The protest against the kingdom has stopped! The *Yehudim* have given up and gone home with their tails tucked under like the whipped dogs that they are!"

He grabbed his wife and swung her around laughing in joy for the success of his plans and the weakness of the *Yehudim*.

On the second day of quiet, he and Zeresh prepared a huge meal and invited his neighbors, his committee, the spies, his sons and their wives to his home to enjoy a time of delicious food, music and dancing. He was so high on his success that he even gave bottles of wine to all of his guests.

———————הפְסָקָה———————

Ahasuerus awoke with a headache and a thirst that had stuck his tongue to the roof of his mouth. The woman beside him was making gurgling noises that made his head hurt more, so he took his foot and shoved her off the edge of the bed, and she hit the floor.

"Get out," he ordered.

She scrambled to grab a robe and while wrapping it around herself she shuffled toward the door. Opening it, two burly guards startled to attention, then seeing it was the woman with very little covering and her hair disheveled, they both grinned and leered at her. Red-faced and humiliated, she tossed her head, sneered at them, then straightened herself. With as much dignity as she could muster, she proudly walked down the corridor, her bare feet slapping on the tiles while the two men twisted their heads to watch her departure.

"Hargazah! Bring me wine! And be quick about it!"

Sprawled on a couch nearby and sleeping, the king's eunuch was accustomed to these nighttime demands, so jumping up quickly, he made a dash to the niche where had the stash of wine hidden just for these occasions. Grabbing the urn, he rushed into the chamber of the king, and poured his goblet full. He noticed that the bed was a wadded mess of linens and covers.

"Shall I remake the bed, sire?"

"What? What for? I like it this way!"

Ahasuerus gulped the wine then asked for a cold towel to wrap his head.

"You tell Shaashgaz not to ever send that woman back to me! She snores like a donkey braying!"

"Yes, sire." Hargazah bit his lip so he wouldn't laugh.

"Can I get you another one, perhaps?"

"Another what?"

"Another woman, Sire."

"No. What I need is sleep and a potion for my head. Can you manage that?"

"I will go immediately."

Hargazah left to awaken Savara, the apothcarey. The two of them were old friends by now after multiple times of being awaken in the middle of the nights when the king had enjoyed himself too much. They had accepted the fact that these nighttime demands were no reason to be angry with each other. In happier times of fellowship, they enjoyed a game of imaging ways to kill the king with potions mixed into wine.

After he left, Ahasuerus fell back onto his pillows after beating them into different shapes. He was too hot; the room was too hot; and the wine was too hot. In a foul temper he threw off the covers, stripped off his remaining clothing and threw open a window hoping a gale force wind would hit him.

It did not.

"Where is Hargazah? Where is my powder?"

The guards outside his door, looked at each other with eyes blared open hoping he wouldn't call one of them in. Unfortunately, he did.

"Tolgar! Where is Hargazah?

Marcazi grinned at him and whispered, "You're up!"

Tolgar bolted into the room, snapped to attention and replied in his most military voice.

"He has gone to get you a powder, Sire. Shall I fetch him?"

"By the gods! Do you have to yell? Get out, you worthless dog! If you go after him, I will be waiting on two to find their way back here!"

Tolgar retreated gladly to rejoin Marcazi who was biting his fist to hold back the laughter.

"Better you than me, brother!"

"He is fit to be tied," said Tolgar shaking his head.

At the end of the corridor, they could see Hargazah running toward them, his robe fanning out behind him like wings.

"The bird of paradise returns," snickered Marcazi.

Hargazah ignored the brutes and rushed past them with the vial of powder in his hand.

"Shall I mix it with the wine, Sire?"

"Use your brain, dog."

Hargazah stirred the powder into the goblet, poured more wine to fully dilute it, and wished Savara had given him poison.

Ahasuerus gulped it down, then still completely naked, fell back onto the bed, and almost immediately fell asleep.

When morning awakened Ahasuerus, his headache was gone. He enjoyed an ice cold dip in his pool followed by a long hot bath in his spa. After that, several beautiful and very fit women with arms that would shame most men, massaged him down with heated oil. He finished off his morning with a huge breakfast and topped it off with enough wine to make him quite the jolly fellow. In fact, he was feeling so good, that when Sergazi handed him his daily roster, he tried to make a joke about how popular he was, and Sergazi rewarded him with a hardy, although hypocritical laugh.

When he took to his throne, he was still in quite the jovial mood, but as the business of the day droned on, his upbeat mood began to fade and his mind wandered.

———————— הַפְסָקָה ————————

THE THIRD DAY

On the third day of the fast, Queen Esther arose early. With her handmaidens present, she led them in prayers she had taught them, and others that they had never prayed to a god they did not know, but to whom they had entrusted their lives.

Esther put on her most beautiful royal apparel. Her maidens combed her hair and allowed it to fall like ringlets around her beautiful face and shoulders. They placed the jeweled crown on her head that declared her as Queen of Persia, and then she asked them to anoint her with perfumed oil and pray with her.

"A holy prophet named Isaiah wrote a beautiful passage in his writings, a thanksgiving prayer to Hashem Elohim. As I pray this prayer, repeat the words with me, and may Hashem, the God of the *Yehudim* bless me and protect me as I make my approach to the king."

Standing in the middle of the room in her royal attire, the hidden star of Yehudah prepared to reveal herself to the king, and to seek his favor to her request. She led the prayer written years before with her handmaidens repeating it back to her.

> "*In that day you will say:*
> '*I will praise you, Hashem.*
>   *Although You were angry with me,*
> *Your anger has turned away*
>   *and You have comforted me.*
> *Surely El-Gibor is my salvation;*
>   *I will trust and not be afraid.*'
> *Hashem, Hashem himself, is my strength and my defense;*
>   *He has become my salvation.*"
> *With joy You will draw water from the wells of salvation.*
> *In that day You will say:*
> '*Give praise to Hashem Elohim, proclaim His name;*
>   *make known among the nations what He has done,*
>   *and proclaim that His name is exalted.*'
> *Sing to Hashem, for He has done glorious things;*
>   *let this be known to all the world.*
> *Shout aloud and sing for joy, people of Zion,*
>   *for great is the Holy One of Israel among you.*"(Isa 12)

When the prayer was ended, she kissed each maiden and blessed them. "Hashem bless you and keep you; Hashem make His face shine upon you, and be gracious to you; Hashem lift up His countenance upon you, and give you peace." (Num 6.24-26)

With Hathach as her escort to the king's house, Esther left him outside the doorway then made her way to the inner court of the king's house where she stood.

✡

Chapter Thirty-Six

The Scepter and the Gallows

And it was so, when the king saw Esther the queen standing in the court, that she obtained favour in his sight: and the king held out to Esther the golden sceptre that was in his hand. So Esther drew near, and touched the top of the sceptre. (Est 5.2 KJV)

The satrap could tell he was losing the king's attention. He tried to change the volume of his voice, then the tone, and even wondered if singing his petition would help. Finally he gave up, bowed and hoped that Sergazi had made good records of his report and maybe one day the king would take the time to review it.

Esther could see the king sitting upon his throne. As he watched him, she waited knowing that at any moment he may order the guards and his attending eunuchs to forcibly remove her for approaching him without a summons. Her heart was pounding, but her spirit was fierce to stand her ground.

From her vantage, Esther counted possibly a dozen or more men in the king's throne room waiting to speak with him. The last one presenting his case, seemed to have tried multiple ways to keep the king's attention, but she noticed that the king seemed distracted and somewhat bored by the proceedings.

Then just before the mid-morning break, Ahasuerus caught his breath when he saw her. After the previous night, the wonderful bath and massage, and the boring hours since then, she was to him a wondrous sight.

Did I call for her? I don't remember calling for her, but why in the name of Aka Manah have I not called her? Look at her! Never has any woman held such beauty and grace!

Completely captivated by her and somewhat intrigued that she would appear in his inner court without a summons, he locked his eyes on hers. He waved his hand to Sergazi, the guards, and attendants to dismiss the men in the court.

As the men began to leave, Ahasuerus raised his hand holding the golden scepter and held it out toward her.

He watched grace and beauty in motion as she approached him still with her eyes locked on his. When she was close enough, she bowed before him, and when he laid his scepter on her shoulder, she stood and laid her hand on the orb of the scepter. She saw a smile playing on his lips.

"Queen Esther, welcome to my throne room."

Leaning forward, so he could smell her fragrance, he admired the glow on her face, the softness of her skin, and the curve of her lips.

"What do you wish? Make your request, and whatever you want, it shall be given to you up to half the kingdom!"

Knowing that the king had just made a statement without meaning except to express favor, Esther smiled and answered.

"If it will please the king, let the king and Vice-Regent Haman come today to the banquet of wine that I have prepared for you, and tomorrow I will tell you."

He held his head to one side and looked at her wondering why she would take such a risk just to invite him to enjoy sweets and wine with her.

She must really miss me! But why invite Haman to join us? Ah, perhaps it is it to restrain her desire for me.

Pulling himself back to his seated position, he answered.

"It pleases the king. I will see that Haman is informed and we will attend your banquet."

To her surprise, he arose and took her hand. He laid it on his arm and walked her to the inner court and out the door toward her palace. Standing at the entrance, he kissed her hand, stroked her cheek and whispered with a wink.

"To the banquet."

He turned and with guards in tow, returned to his throne room where Sergazi and Hargazah were waiting. Once there, he commanded Hargazah.

"Bring Haman quickly."

The eunuch bowed in response and left the room as though there were a fire and he had the only water bucket. On his way to fetch Haman, he wondered what had just happened.

No woman has ever approached the king's throne room. But this Queen had done it, and lived! Ha! Lived? She practically wrapped the king around her little finger!

Thinking about the sight of her, he could understand why even the King of Persia could not resist that woman.

He reached Haman's office doors out of breath. Keyvan was perched on a bench outside the door, and when he saw the king's eunuch, red-faced and panting, he immediately jumped up.

"What's wrong?"

"I have to speak to Vice-Regent Haman."

"Why? What's happened?"

Ever protective of his own position, Keyvan knew it would remain strong if he delivered an important messages.

"I have a message for Haman. Is he here?"

"Of course, he's here. I will give him the message!" Keyvan insisted.

"Not this time, Keyvan. Not this message! This message I'm going to give!"

He tried to push his way to the door, but Keyvan stepped in front of him and barred his attempt.

"What are you doing? I have a message from the king for Haman! Move out of my way!"

Suddenly the door threw open and Haman looked at them with his brows melted together into one bushy, black mass.

"What is going on out here? Keyvan, what's the problem? I can hear you through the door!"

Before Keyvan could speak, Hargazah blurted out.

"I have a message from the king, sir. It is urgent."

Haman glared at Keyvan, grabbed the eunuch Hargazah by the collar of his robe, yanked him through his door, and slammed it in Keyvan's face.

"What's the message?"

"Sir, you're choking me!"

Haman let him go, and demanded again.

"What's the message?"

"The queen came to the king's throne room this morning, and . . ."

"What? She did what? Was she summoned? What did the king do? I mean, he has a law about that."

"I'm trying to tell you. No, he didn't summon her . . ."

"Ha! Another Queen exiled! Or maybe he'll kill this one. I don't especially like her."

"You're jumping to the wrong conclusions, Sir. He dismissed every one in the court and invited her in."

Haman straightened into what can only be described as someone who suddenly fears he's being followed and freezes into his position to listen for footsteps. His eyes even shifted back and forth.

"Wait. Is that the message? What is that to me?"

He relaxed into his usual posture and started making his way toward his desk and chair.

"What it is to you, Sir," said Hargazah with an icy tone, "the queen has prepared a banquet of wine for the king."

He paused just to aggravate Haman who had stopped in his tracks and turned around to face him.

". . . and you."

Haman felt something inside him start jumping up and down. His mind commanded his face not to show it. The corners of his mouth twitched and tried to pull back into a toothy grin. The muscles in his cheeks fought not to bunch in to tight balls that would then wrinkle his eyes.

"Well," he said, hoping he sounded controlled and calm, "that seems like a very nice thing to do."

"The king wants you to come immediately to the throne room. I'll leave you now."

Hargazah was not fooled at all by the battle going on in Haman to stay calm and unemotional.

Once he closed the door, he and Keyvan heard an awful racket behind the door. Keyvan jumped up alarmed and started to enter.

"Don't!" warned Hargazah. "Let the man have his moment."

"Is he all right? Did you hurt him?"

Keyvan's fist were in balls and his entire demeanor was like an animal about to attack.

"Oh, he's more than all right! What you hear is a man rejoicing. He'll be out right away—or as soon as he can compose himself."

Hargazah turned to leave with a grin on his face.

"I hope he deserves this."

———————— הַפְסָקָה ————————

> That day Haman left full of joy and in good spirits. But when Haman saw Mordecai at the King's Gate, and Mordecai didn't rise or tremble in fear at his presence, Haman was filled with rage toward Mordecai. (Est 5:9 CSB)

The house was filled with music, wine, laughter and congratulations as Haman and Zeresh celebrated with relatives, friends, business acquaintances, his selected council of eleven, and his three spies. Masoud, Behzad, and Javad were invited by Haman with the hope that the celebration would be reported to the other guards and servants of the palace. Several times the crowd called for Haman to make speeches related to his great success, riches, promotions and how he had advanced himself above all the other officials and servants of the king. He lined up all ten of his sons and his grandchildren who were dressed in their finest attire to be displayed as his greatest blessing from Āz. Some of the children sang, some danced, some quoted lines, and all were declared as the most beautiful, or handsome of the kingdom. Everyone agreed, Haman was a man to be honored and envied.

"But today, my friends," Haman announced proudly, "today I was honored to attend a banquet of wine prepared by Queen Esther for no one except myself . . . and the king, of course."

The crowd applauded until he waved them quiet.

"A splendid array of sweets, pastries, delicately designed towers of delicious desserts and the finest wines in the empire. She spared nothing from us for honor and delight. And not only that, my friends, but tomorrow the king and I are invited to a full banquet of the highest honor also prepared by the queen. It seems she has a special request to make . . . so . . . I may have an even greater announcement to make to you tomorrow evening!"

And the crowd went wild with cheers and congratulations as the music swelled and the noise of celebration rose to a fevered pitch.

Haman stepped down from the elevated dais his sons had made for him for just this kind of announcement. He joined his council of eleven along with Masoud, Behzad, Javad and Keyvan. They surrounded him with grins and slaps on the back.

Shapur lifted his wine glass and made an announcement.

"Great speech, Haman! Everyone is envious of you tonight. You are the word on everyone's lips!"

Suddenly confused by Haman's expression he asked, "What's with the dark look on your face? You should be proud and moving through the crowd to be congratulated."

"Don't you understand, Shapur? Darab, Bijan, my friends, don't you men understand?"

He glared at the men and they responded with confused expressions.

"None of this means anything as long as I see that filthy Mordecai sitting at the gate when I pass! He still refuses to bow to me! There is no tremble, no fear of me! I hate him! The whole village wonders at him. He makes a public show of disgrace!"

Zeresh overheard his comments to his council and quickly moved closer to them before anyone noticed his angry face or heard him.

"Haman," she hissed, "do as your sons and I have suggested! Tell your friends here and see if they do not agree!"

The council members and his three spies looked from her to Haman.

"What? What is the suggestion, Haman?" asked Darab.

"Tell us Zeresh, if he will not."

"He needs to kill Mordecai. He can order his attending guards to thrust him through the heart! Be done with the man!"

She spoke through her teeth and impatiently glared at Haman.

"Hire other men to do it, if you do not want his life taken by your own command!"

"No . . ." interjected Javad. "Haman has the king's ear—his favor. He can ask the king's permission for Mordecai to be hanged. Then the death of the man will be done by royal permission.

"Haman, command a gallows to be built! Then go to the king and tell him that Mordecai has refused his command to bow to you! That's all you have to do!"

"And make the gallows tall enough to be seen in all of Shushan," Zeresh added, her eyes glowing. "Let the whole of Shushan see the death of one who dared to dishonor you and disobey the king!"

"She's right!" Bijan said in full agreement. "Seventy-five feet tall should do it! Then everyone can see it. Have it built tomorrow! Then after he's displayed before the palace and all of Shushan, you can go happily to the banquet with the king!"

Haman stood looking into the faces of his wife, spies, and friends and slowly a broad smile broke through above his sharp, pointed chin and under the hanging moustache. His black eyes became slits in his face.

"You're right! I *can* persuade the king. I do have his ear! That is exactly what I shall do. I shall build a gallows! Well, not me, personally but . . ."

And he turned to face the three former yard sweeps who also at times had built gallows

"You three can certainly do it . . . tonight!"

Javad's face fell. Behzad choked on his wine and Masoud's mouth dropped open.

"But, sire . . ." Masoud finally spoke, "we are not gallows builders anymore. We are . . ."

"Whatever I say you are. Right?"

Haman interrupted joyfully.

"And tonight you are gallows builders!"

He held his wine goblet up as he continued.

"I want it to be at least seventy-five feet tall, and built here, in my own yard. That way everyone in Shushan will know I was dishonored, and they will be able to see what happens to a man that dishonors someone like me!"

Zeresh beamed with pride. It was so rare that she got to see her husband be so forceful.

"O Haman, my *azazim*!" she cooed and fluttered her eyelashes.

The council members and the three spies stood speechless.

"Now? You mean tonight? Here?" asked Behzad.

"I do! Let's toast to the plan! Why wait? I want this done right away!"

Everyone but the three spies clinked their mugs together, but they stood slack-jawed and solemn. Then Javad spoke up hopefully.

"But don't we have to have an order from the king to build a gallows?"

The other two straightened up and started nodding.

Still glowing from the idea, Haman grinned.

"No! Not at all! That's why I want it built here! In my courtyard! Then we can all see the hanging. So go! I have what you will need in my storehouse. Gather the supplies and build it!"

He pointed across the crowd to Keyvan and another eunuch assigned to him. "

Look! I have two eunuchs here. They can help you, as well as any of my friends! I'm sure they will want to help!"

So while Haman's joyous celebration continued well into the night, three of his guests, two eunuchs, and a few council members were in his courtyard building a gallows under the direction of the recently promoted yard sweeps.

✡

Chapter Thirty-Seven

A Matter of Record

> And it was found written, that Mordecai had told of Bigthana and Teresh, two of the king's chamberlains, the keepers of the door, who sought to lay hand on the king Ahasuerus. (Est 6.2 KJV)

The king awoke suddenly. The dream was still in his head and he was sweating. His heart was pounding in rhythm with a far away drumming sound connected to his bad dream.

"Abagtha, Mehuman! One of you get in here! Now!"

The door flew open and Abagtha burst through.

"Yes, Sire?"

"Open the balcony door! This room is too hot! And get this woman out of here."

Ahasuerus sat up on the side of his bed while the young woman, who was now no longer a maiden, scrambled for her clothes. She was embarrassed and shocked by the presence of Abagtha, and hurried out the door.

Abagtha opened the door to the balcony, and Ahasuerus glared toward the doors and growled.

"What's that awful banging?"

"Sire, I don't know. It sounds as if someone is perhaps building something?"

Abagtha waited for the next instructions.

"Well, shut the doors. By the gods! What kind of fool is building this time of night?"

"Sire, I don't know, Sire."

"Well, aren't you just a spring of information! Get Mehuman in here!"

Glad to be replaced, Abagtha darted for the door.

"And get some fans! I'm dying here."

Mehuman entered and stood waiting for orders while he observed the king's state. The king was nude, sweating, and in a dark and foul mood.

Abagtha returned with two large fans and nodded toward Mehuman to take one of them.

"No. Mehuman, I don't want you to take a fan. I want you to arouse Sergazi and tell him to bring me a record of daily events."

"All of them, Sire?"

"Of course not, fool! Tell Sergazi to bring the ones for the past six months. And be quick about it."

Mehuman bowed slightly, then backed from the room. Once out the door and out of earshot of the king, he mumbled.

"Oh, Sergazi is going to be happy about this, but I wager no one in the palace is getting any sleep with that fool pounding outside!"

Back in the king's quarters, Abagtha was using the large fan to cool the king still sitting on the side of the bed with his head hanging down. His wine urn was empty, but his mind was filled with images from the few minutes he had managed to sleep. Rising from his position, he mumbled to Abagtha.

"I'm going to the pool to cool off. When Sergazi arrives, if I'm not back tell him to join me there."

Abagtha, happy this time that the king was relatively calm under the circumstances, left the room to take his position on the couch outside the king's doorway to wait for Sergazi and Mehuman to return.

Ahasuerus, alone in the cool misty spa, stepped into the pool and laid his head back onto a pillow. He closed his eyes under the frown that furrowed his brow.

Slipping uncalled from his mind, the events of the day and the visit with Esther gave his lips a slight smile, but then . . . the images of the dream came back and pushed her out.

The frown returned.

His mind was a jumble of flashing images. Battle scenes in Ionia and Athens, storms blowing away flimsy cords and boards, horses floundering in mud-filled trenches, men bleeding, and swords clashing. He tried to push the defeat out of his mind, but then images of himself with young girls barely thirteen crying and shamed filled him with guilt. He had been commanded by an unknown force to be cruel. He remembered others coming into his room perfumed and with faces painted under veils. They had made great effort to seduce him. Instead they were just more of so many more.

Then . . . Esther.

Tall, well-formed, perfection. He had seen those qualities by the hundreds. But she . . . she overwhelmed him by . . . *what? Her spirit? . . . Her complex simplicity?* He shook his head. None of that made sense! But He couldn't contain her. He did not . . . could not capture her. There was something in her he had longed for, tried to reach all his life but had not because he didn't know what it was.

When she spoke it was with intelligence and interest, sound judgment, and a strange openness that he had not experienced from a woman. There was no guile in her, and no hidden agenda. He realized it made no difference to her at all the outcome of the night. She was there as if it were a divine appointment somehow. Whatever he decided about her would not change her. She conversed with him as an equal, and he knew she had come to face him without fear, expectation, or timidness. In an effort to somehow surpass her, he had quizzed her to see if she had the ability to answer him on his level of intelligence. She answered his questions and discussed with him historical records and events. She had obviously studied famous men, and battles won and lost. He realized she was beyond him—more than he. She described cities in detail that he knew she had never seen but had researched from his own library. He didn't know how he had ever been blessed by the gods to have her.

———————— הַפְסָקָה ————————

Through the marble-tiled corridor, the sound of footsteps interrupted his musings. Sergazi appeared, bleary-eyed, puffy faced, and with him two of his young apprentices holding several large volumes of records.

"Sire."

Ahasuerus arose from the pool, grabbed a sheet-sized wrap and proceeded to bind it around himself.

"It's too damp in here. Let's go back into my quarters."

From Mehuman's report about the king's mood, Sergazi was somewhat taken back to find him calm—almost melancholy.

Thank you, Mithra, for protecting me! he silently prayed.

The king went straight for his bed, propped himself up on several pillows and commanded.

"Read from the records. I can't sleep, so I may as well get caught up on some of the records I missed, use the time wisely, so to speak."

Sergazi wondered if he had thought about the fact that he was also using up his time which was the few hours of the clock that he had to sleep and be away from recording all the mundane events. Instead, he opened one of the volumes.

"Do you have a particular time period you want me to review with you?"

"No. Just open and read. I have no way of knowing what I've reviewed previously or what I haven't."

With great effort to avoid using a tone that would indicated his intense irritation, Sergazi opened the book and began to read. An hour later, one of the apprentices took over the reading. When another hour had passed, Sergazi took over again.

Is this man ever going to sleep? Sergazi yawned.

From the bed, Ahasuerus with closed his eyes, listened to the droll of Sergazi's voice as he read dates, names, events, questions, and commands that he had made.

Sergazi, completely bored and reading in a monotone continued.

"... and on the twentieth of the month, a message was received during the meeting by King Ahasuerus from the hand of Regent Haman. The message was sealed and once opened the king read it, then handed it off to Sergazi the scribe to record. The message said, 'My King, I have overheard this day two chamberlains, Bigthana and Teresh, plotting to take your life. Your humble servant, Mordecai.' Then the king . . ."

"Wait!" Ahasuerus shouted.

The two apprentices jumped to their feet, and Sergazi completely startled, almost dropped the book. He grabbed it and looked at the king who had sat completely straight up. He was holding out his hand, palm facing Sergazi.

"Read that again," he ordered.

"From what point, Sire?"

"The message. Read the message again."

"'My King, I have overheard this day two chamberlains, Bigthana and Teresh, plotting to take your life. Your humble servant, Mordecai.'"

"Mordecai? I don't remember that. All this time I've credited Haman with saving my life," he said slowly. "And he let me!" he said angrily jumping up from his bed.

"Who is this Mordecai, Sergazi?"

"I think he is a scribe, Sire. I believe he has a booth just outside the palace gates. I have asked him to copy work for . . ."

"Read on! What did we do for him? What honor, reward, or special recognition has been given to Mordecai?"

"Well, nothing, Sire. Nothing has been done for him. The reward was given to Regent Haman."

"Yes. It was, wasn't it?" Ahasuerus suddenly felt very irritated. "Is anyone in the court?"

"At this hour, Sire, I wouldn't think so."

"Well, send Mehuman or Abagtha to see!"

Sergazi noted the sudden change in the king's mood, so he moved quickly to open the door. The two young men scrambled behind him. Both eunuchs jumped to their feet at Sergazi's appearance.

"What?" asked Mehuman startled.

"Relax." Sergazi grinned at the two of them. "I need one of you to go to the court and see if there's anyone there."

"This early? No one will be there!"

Abagtha looked at Sergazi like he was personally asking for the errand that in all their minds was foolish.

"Abagtha, thank you for volunteering. Now go!"

Sergazi watched as he started down the corridor, then yelled after him. "And hurry!"

Then grinning, he watched little chubby Abagtha jog down the hall.

✡

Chapter Thirty-Eight

Haman's Big Idea

So Haman came in. And the king said unto him, What shall be done unto the man whom the king delighteth to honour? Now Haman thought in his heart, To whom would the king delight to do honour more than to myself? (Est 6.6 KJV)

Haman did not sleep. He was too excited. He and his committee had watched the construction and drunk wine throughout the night. When the gallows was finished, and the last guest had finally left his house, Haman bathed, carefully combed his hair and moustache, changed into his official clothing and hung the seal of the Vice-Regent around his neck. He admired his image in the mirror.

"Ah, now that is what my neck needed today." He kissed the seal.

Kissing Zeresh lightly on her cheek so he didn't awaken her, he slipped out of the house, mounted the steed, and galloped in the morning's cool refreshing mist toward the palace.

When the palace came into sight against the dark blue of the pre-dawn morning, Haman looked back toward the direction of his house. Grinning from ear to ear, he was pleased that a full-moon in just the right position, outlined the new gallows standing tall and finished above the city skyline.

Haman reared up his horse, and sat still and tall in the saddle still grinning at the sight.

"O Āz, if only I were an artist!"

He sighed. Then spurring into the horse's haunches, he sped toward the palace. He wanted to be in the court early, so he could be done with the hanging to enjoy the rest of the day. He would happily go to the queen's banquet with the business accomplished.

He hurried across the palace yards just as the sun was rising. He stopped briefly and turned to see if the gallows was visible from the palace. Satisfied, he lifted his face toward the sunlight, closed his eyes to feel the warmth, and lifted his hands in joy.

When Haman entered the court, he startled Abagtha who was just turning to leave.

"Abagtha?"

Abagtha wheeled around in shock to see him.

"Haman! Just the man I need to see! Come with me!"

Knowing Abagtha and Mehuman had replaced Bigthana and Teresh as the kings's doormen, Haman, was surprised and excited beyond measure. He picked up his pace to catch up with the eunuch.

His mind was in a spin of possibilities. Grinning behind his moustache, his heart was racing, and his curiosity was mounting. Haman felt sure he was headed for something big.

When they arrived at the king's chamber, Haman was surprised to see Sergazi leaning against the wall. Two young men holding books were sitting on a couch. Mehuman was pacing back and forth.

"Haman?" Sergazi asked, pushing himself upright, "Why are you here so early? I'm surprised to see you."

"I have business to discuss with the king."

"Well, first, he wants to see you. We're out here while his attendants assist him to get dressed."

"Why are we meeting here and not in the court? Is he ill?"

Haman hoped the king was well and able, especially today.

"He's well enough. He didn't sleep last night. Noises outside, some fool building something. And of course, it was hot, and so . . ." Sergazi's voice trailed off.

"Oh," Haman replied and hoped with all his heart the king wasn't asking to see him because he knew Haman had ordered construction during the night and the noise kept him awake. He suddenly felt his arm pits get wet.

The door opened and the two eunuchs Biztha and Harbona exited.

"He's ready for you now," they said to Sergazi.

Sergazi motioned for Haman to enter first, then he and his two assistants followed. Ahasuerus was seated at his desk and as soon as he saw Haman he wasted no time.

"Haman! Good. What should be done for a man the king wants to honor?" Ahasuerus demanded quickly.

Haman wished to his god that he had a beard so the king would not see the blush that suddenly came not only to his face, but to his entire body. Springs of joy filled him, and immediately he thought, *Oh! Who is the man the king would want to honor more than me?*

He took a minute to calm himself so he would not speak too quickly. He could not say anything that would let the king know he had often dreamed this day would come.

He cleared his throat, tilted his head to one side and lifted his sharp chin.

"For the man the king desires to honor...," he started pronouncing each word distinctly, "have your attendants to bring a royal garment which the king himself has worn..." he paused as if thinking, "... and a horse the king himself has ridden, which has a royal crest on its head, so everyone will know it is yours."

He paused to smile at everyone.

"Then put the garment and the horse under the charge of one of the king's most noble officials. Have him clothe the man the king wants to honor, parade him on the horse through the city square, and proclaim before him, This is what is done for the man the king wants to honor!'"

Haman opened his arms in a flourish, bowed slightly then clasped his hands and stretched himself to his full height.

Ahasuerus contemplated a moment then slapped his hand down on his desk.

"Haman! Hurry! Do just as you proposed!"

Turning to one of the young men he said, "Ask Mehuman to come in and I will select one of my robes for Mordecai. Haman, I will order Abagtha to go with you to the stables. Select my horse. Be sure to tell the boy to put the royal crest on his head. Mehuman will bring you the robe and go with you and Abagtha to prepare Mordecai who is at the palace gates."

The king was suddenly in a very pleased disposition, pleased that Haman had proposed such a reward so quickly. The king motioned to Haman to leave, but Haman seemed completely immobilized for a brief moment.

"Now Haman, you may go," said Ahasuerus. "Do as you suggested. Brilliant ideas. Just brilliant!"

With a sudden jerk, Haman bowed, looked around at the others in embarrassment, and quickly left the room.

Once he was out of sight of the king's chamber, he stopped, grabbed the regent seal with one hand and his chest with the other. He closed his eyes and waited for his mind to catch up with what had just happened.

Shaking his head he muttered, "No, no, no, no."

Behind him Abagtha asked, "Are you all right, Sir?"

✡

Chapter Thirty-Nine

The Temptation

Then the king said to Haman, Make haste, and take the apparel and the horse, as thou hast said, and do even so to Mordecai the Jew, that sitteth at the king's gate: let nothing fail of all that thou hast spoken. Then took Haman the apparel and the horse, and arrayed Mordecai, and brought him on horseback through the street of the city, and proclaimed before him, Thus shall it be done unto the man whom the king delighteth to honour. (Est 6.10-11 KJV)

Mordecai put his hands on his head and his elbows on his knees. His spirit was downcast. It was the third day of the fast, and he felt more hopeless than he could remember. He felt a weight in his spirit dragging him into a sadness like he had never experienced. Thoughts tormented him. They came in strong memories of events from his youth into the present time. The torments focused on failed decisions, losses, mistakes, and the times he had stood up against "evil" for the "right" reasons, at least he thought they were right reasons. Instead, they brought disaster on himself, Hadassah, his closest friends, and lately the whole of Shushan. He felt ashamed, tired, and like Elijah, he prayed to die. *What is there to live for, anyway?*

Regrets filled him. He should have gone to Jerusalem and taken Hadassah with him when the last captives were given permission and means to go there. If only he had left, Hadassah would not have been taken. She would have been spared from going through what he could not bear to imagine. Her whole future as a happy, blessed *Yehud* was shattered.

He should not have reported the conversation he heard behind the booth. Perhaps Haman would not have been promoted, and two men would not have been killed.

He should have just gone along with the order of Ahasuerus and bowed when Haman passed by. The *Yehudim* community would not be suffering now, fasting and praying because of the decree that Haman had devised and somehow got the king to endorse.

In his mind faces flashed. Faces filled with anger, fear, and confusion that he had brought by his actions.

THE TEMPTATION

What makes me think I am acting righteously? I'm not righteous! I'm a disgrace. I have pleaded with Hashem. But did He save Hadassah? Did Hashem save her from a life separated from her heritage, her family, her friends? Why did Hashem take her? Was it because of my sins? Did I fail Hashem and this is my punishment? My joy, my hope, my reason to live is destroyed.

Scriptures pressed into his mind, but he refused them.

Where is the deliverance? Where is the Mighty Melek? Where is the Hashem of Armies? Maybe I just pray scriptures, live by them, proclaim them and it's all just something that was made up long ago. How do I really know I am the one that is right? Where is Hashem?

The thoughts and feelings were dark, tormenting, foreign and evil. He shook his head trying to make them stop. ran his hands through his hair and pulled with his fingers. He groaned and looked upward, He hoped that like Avram he would see three strangers coming to give him a promise and a chance to make a bargain with Elohim to rescue the righteous from Shushan and the palace while fire and brimstone fell from heaven and consumed them. But all he saw were people up and down the street bowed to the ground. Coming straight at him was Haman, leading a horse and two eunuchs. Mordecai hoped they were coming to take him to the dungeon where he could stay and die.

That's what I deserve, he thought, *for all this chaos is my fault.*

He stood up as Haman stopped and stood in front of him.

"I'm ready," he said softly. "I've been expecting this."

"Really? That's strange. How did you know I was coming?" Haman's tone was flat, painful, sarcastic.

"Well, Haman, because I deserve it. The decree, the fear among my people, the sackcloth and ashes, the prayers—all of it is because I would not shame Hashem by bowing to you. This is the work of Hashem."

Haman felt shame and weakness wash through him at the thought that a god he had scorned, disregarded and spoken against might be real, that could actually be behind all of this.

"What about Bigthana and Teresh? What about the message you sent to the king, the one I hand-delivered? Is that why you deserve it?

"Yes," Mordecai said softly and his head dropped. "Let's just do what has to be done. You have me where I am supposed to be, so do what you have been commanded to do. I will not resist you."

Without another word, one of the eunuchs moved to Mordecai and said, "Raise your arms."

Mordecai obeyed and felt himself engulfed in a robe. Looking down at it, he was completely confused. "What is this?"

"It is one of the king's robes," Haman said, "Now, get on the horse."

Without a word, with the help of the two eunuchs, Mordecai was lifted up to mount the huge beast. Mordecai noted that the crest of the king was on the horse's head. He became overwhelmed by the realization that he was about to be paraded before the town while his acts against the king and his people were being proclaimed. He closed his eyes as Haman led the horse to the main street. With no one else to call for help, he silently cried out to Hashem, the one he had just doubted and accused because he knew that if Hashem were not real, nothing was.

───────── הַפְסָקָה ─────────

And Mordecai came again to the king's gate. But Haman hasted to his house mourning, and having his head covered. (Est 6.12 KJV)

When Haman had finished with the last announcement, he took Mordecai back to the palace gates where he had been. He helped him dismount, handed the reins of the steed to Abagtha and Mehuman, and made his way quickly home through alleys and side streets with his head covered by his mantle. He hoped no one would know who he was. Occasionally, with no strength to stop it, a groan of mourning would pour out of him. He was totally abashed.

Reaching his home, he entered quietly since he arrived on foot. He heard voices coming from the center of the house, and shrank against the wall. Trying to peek around the corner to see exactly who was there, he saw his sons, their wives, his closest neighbors, his eleven advisors, and the three men who built the gallows. His wife was being consoled in the center. Suddenly, one of his son's daughters saw him, and excitedly pointed him out and squealed.

"It is *pedar bozorg*! It is grandfather!"

Zeresh ran into his arms, her face streaked with tears, and her hair in disarray.

"Oh, my *azazim*! Tell us what has happened!"

With absolutely no desire to tell anyone about the humiliating day, but too exhausted to resist, he started from the time Abagtha met him in the court and related the events up to taking Mordecai back to the gate. Of course, he did not relate that he thought he was the one the king wanted to honor.

"But *Azazim*," whined Zeresh, "why did you make the honor so extravagant? So public? Could you not have made it less?"

As Haman looked around at those in the room all waiting for his reply, he did what he knew best. He lied.

"I thought he was speaking about Admatha, one of the other regents. I learned when I was promoted, that the king had originally planned to promote him, so I wanted to be fair about it."

Sad faces showed sympathy to their friend.

"Oh, *Azazim*, from what you've said about Mordecai, if he is indeed of the seed of the *Yehudim*, it is certain that since this has befallen you today, the plan to hang him has failed, and he has risen to such honor, you will not be able to prevail against him."

Haman looked at her as though she had spat in his face.

Kazem, one of his chosen advisors, spoke up.

"I have done a bit of investigation into the *Yehudim* since our meetings to see them destroyed, Haman. It seems they are either a very lucky people, or they have woven some very fantastic lies about themselves, or they do indeed serve a very powerful god. He is quoted as having said, 'I will bless those that bless you; I will curse those that curse you.'"

All in the room became quiet at the words of Kazem.

Haman suddenly remembered Mordecai's words. 'This is the work of Hashem.' A sick feeling washed over him. Weary in mind, spirit and body, Haman just wanted them all to leave. He wanted the day to restart.

While others in the room started asking Kazem more information about what he had learned, there was a loud rapping on the door. One of the servant girls came running into the room and made an announcement.

"Sir Haman, two men from the palace are here to escort you to the palace for the queen's banquet. They requested that you hurry."

Haman turned to see Harbona and Abagtha standing at the door talking to one of his servants. He left the room to change his clothes and to escape from the crowd in his house.

Haman met Harbona and Abagtha at the door and wondered what else this long day had in store for him.

✡

Chapter Forty

The Queen's Request

So the king and Haman came to banquet with Esther the queen. And the king said again unto Esther on the second day at the banquet of wine, What is thy petition, queen Esther? and it shall be granted thee: and what is thy request? and it shall be performed, even to the half of the kingdom. (Est 7. 1-2 KJV)

Once inside the banquet hall, Harbona and Abagtha left Haman alone to wait for the king and queen. The serving staff were finishing up the table settings while several eunuchs were waiting at the entrance of the kitchen ready to serve.

With sideways looks and quick glances which the eunuchs had perfected, they watched Haman's arrival and noted his face, drawn and pale. Already the gossip concerning the morning conversation with the king had been repeated several times. Haman seemed nervous and did not know what to do with himself. While he started walking around the table to see what was being served, Harbona and Abagtha were telling the other eunuchs about the visit to Haman's house and what they had seen there and what they had learned.

The table was spread with baskets, trays, and bowls of foods; but what drew Haman's attention were the candles and flowers which filled the room with a soft haze and a pleasant odor. Unlike the banquets hosted by the king, this banquet had a definite flourish of feminine touches. Beautiful silks and yards of purple, blue and gold cords twisted into ropes separated the dishes and trays of food.

The realization that the queen had asked the king and him to this banquet suddenly gave Haman a hopeful lift in his spirit.

I wonder . . . I hope the queen's request will somehow have something to do with me, . . . my future, my position . . . so this day will end differently than it started.

His thoughts were interrupted. The king entered the hall with Queen Esther on his arm. As always when he saw her, Haman acknowledged that the king had indeed found the most beautiful woman in all of Persia. He noted with a warm feeling that in her modesty and plan to speak on his behalf, she refused to look at him.

Typical to his impatient nature, once seated at the banquet table the king leaned toward Esther.

"You have kept me waiting for two days. Tell me now, before we dine. What request has brought you to my court and what is the reason for us to be invited to this second banquet? What is your petition, Queen Esther? Whatever it is, I will grant it! What is your request, and I will see that it is done, even if you are requesting half of my kingdom!"

Haman's eyes widened as he realized the queen already owned half of the kingdom. *Will the entire kingdom be hers?* he thought. He watched her closely to see if at last she would reveal her request to him.

Esther looked down for a moment then raised her head and smiled at the king. The king and Haman leaned slightly forward, waiting for her to speak.

Esther's heart was beating so hard she felt a bit lightheaded. She had given much thought about how to present her request. She knew Ahasuerus was not a man to make wait, and he was also a man of intense curiosity. She had put him off as long as she could. At the banquet of the wine, he had pressed on her throughout the evening to tell him what she wanted. She knew she could not delay any longer.

My King, I do not want more of the kingdom. I want this man Haman, my enemy, removed from power, she thought. With confidence El-Roi (the God who sees) was watching over her, she knew the time had come to speak. She made her well-thought out request.

"If I have found favor in your eyes, Your Majesty, and if it will please the king, let my life be given to me . . ."

King Ahasuerus leaned further toward her at her first words. Immediatley, he was completely confused. Haman, on the other hand suddenly felt disappointed that he wasn't the basis of the petition. Suddenly he wished he had not been invited.

". . . and the lives of my people at my request." Esther saw the confusion on the king's face. Glancing at Haman, she confirmed that he had no idea that she was *Yehudi*.

"We have been sold, my people and I, to be destroyed, to be killed, and to be annihilated."

She saw the king's expression and confirmed her belief he was not aware of the decree.

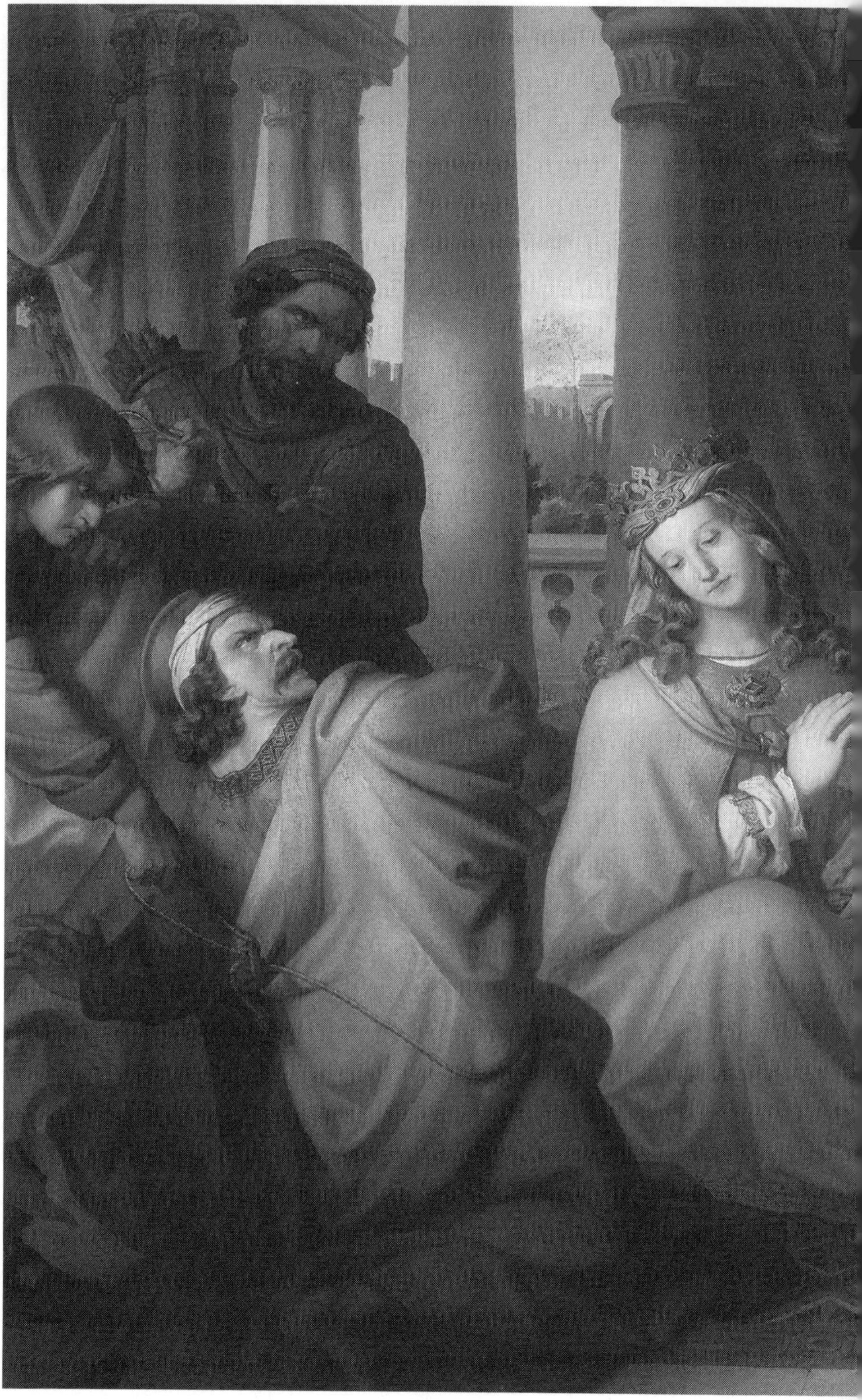

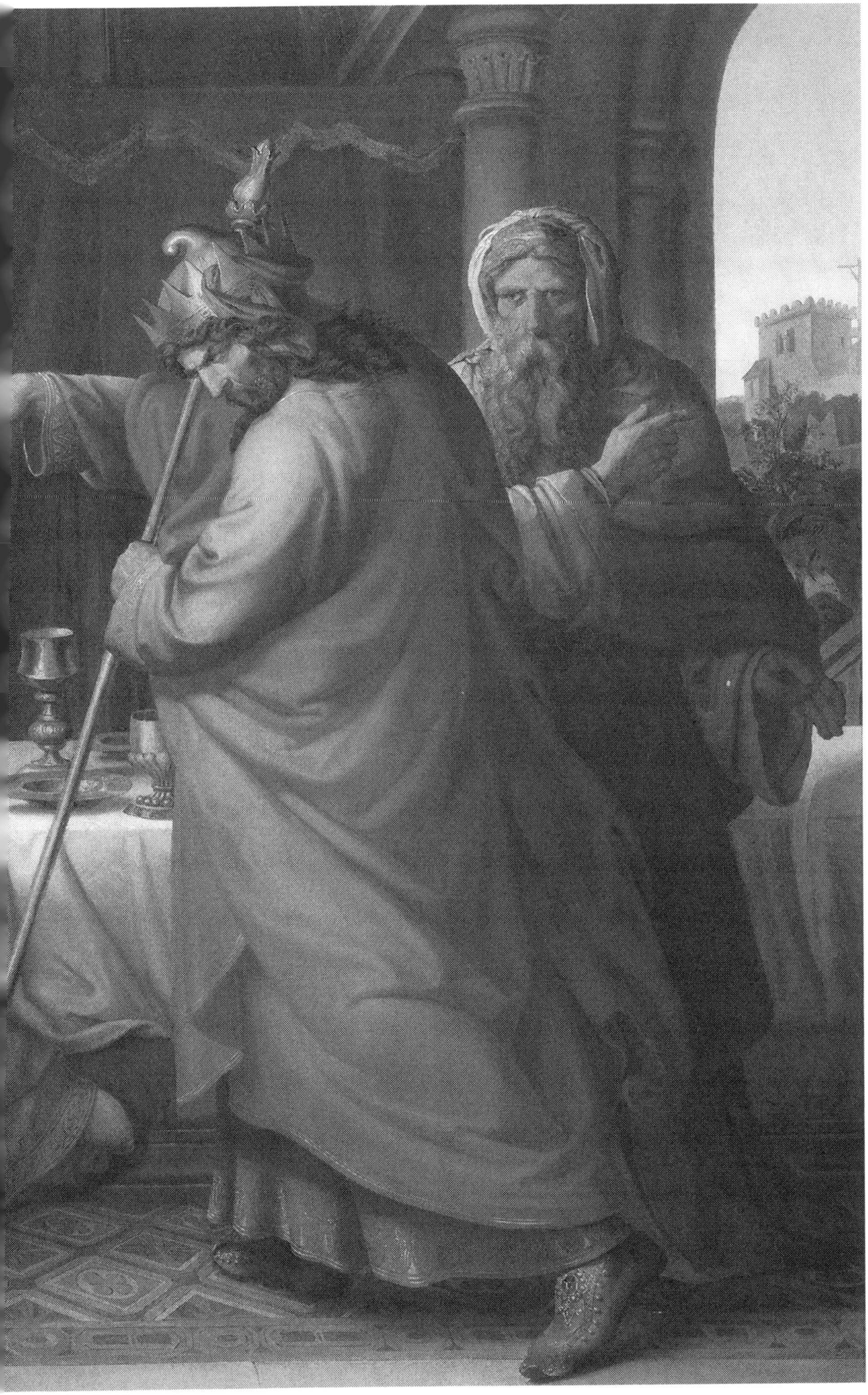

"If we had been sold into slavery as male and female slaves, I would have kept silent, although the enemy could never compensate for the your loss."

Completely lost by her words, Ahasuerus leaned back, looked at her and suddenly wondered how it was possible that an enemy had crept into his kingdom to harm his wife, and the mother of his son without his knowledge. He was stunned that Esther seemed to be speaking of some planned attack to kill him and the people of the kingdom. Apparently, a price had been paid by an unknown enemy to annihilate his people. His face flushed with anger, but also rage was building like a volcano that his princes, advisors, and regents had not informed him of a planned attack. *What if they knew, and the plan was to kill me?* He glanced at Haman who was wearing a blank expression, and Ahasuerus wondered why, as the vice-regent, he wasn't also angry by this news. *Is he in on it?*

"Haman! Are you informed of some attack against the kingdom?"

Startled by the sudden question, Haman sat up straighter. With a wry smile, Haman sighed then responded in a dismissive tone.

"No, My King. I have no knowledge of an attack against our Queen's life, or in fact, of any one of the Persian population."

What Haman wanted to say was how utterly disappointed he was by the queen's build up for a request that was obviously founded on some false imagination in a foolish woman's mind.

Feeling somewhat relieved that Haman had not heard of such a plan, Ahasuerus turned back to Esther.

"Who is this enemy? Where is he who would dare have the audacity in his heart to do such a thing?"

Esther looked the king in the eyes and with calmness and without hesitation answered.

"The adversary and enemy is this wicked Haman!"

Haman strangled on his wine and dropped his cup. Suddenly the queen had his full attention. Fear like a vice gripped him as realization filled him with such clarity of revelation that the room seemed to spin. He and the king both immediately stood up. Haman's eyes met the king's and what he saw filled him with a terror so strong his knees weakened. He fell back onto his couch. He had never seen the king as he saw him now, so he shut his eyes.

Glaring at Haman, what Ahasuerus saw confirmed Esther's words. Overcome with the desire to kill Haman, and filled with wrath, he stalked out of the banquet room and into the garden.

Esther felt peace come over her. The king didn't know! The king had somehow been deceived and manipulated to allow his signet to sign the decree that had terrorized her people by the evil man coming toward her. Looking calmly up at him standing in front of her horrified and trembling, she was assured that she had overcome her enemy.

"My Queen, please . . . forgive me. I did not know you are *Yehudi* or I would not have planned . . ." he couldn't bring himself to say it. "Forgive me! Intercede for my life! He will have me killed."

Weeping, frantic, and overcome, Haman stumbled and fell across her couch and upon the queen.

Sobbing, and wallowing he continued to plead.

"I beg you, My Queen. Please! Help me!"

At that moment, Ahasuerus returned with three guards, members of the Ten Thousand Immortals, his eunuch Harbonah, and Sergazi the scribe. Seeing Haman lying across the couch and on top of Esther, he roared.

"Will he also assault the queen while I am in the house?"

As the words left the king's mouth, the three men pulled Haman still begging from Esther, then covered his face with the hood of execution.

Harbonah, who had seen for himself the tall gallows in Haman's courtyard and knew the reason for it, quickly spoke up with a strong declaration.

"In Haman's courtyard there is a gallows, fifty cubits high, which Haman had built last night to hang Mordecai, the *Yehudi* who spoke on the behalf of the king to reveal the murderous plan to kill him."

Ahasuerus didn't miss a beat. Turning to the men he said, "Take him there and hang him on it! But before you go, I have something I need to get from him."

And the king himself grabbed Haman's hand and took possession of the ring that he had given to Haman to sign the death decree against the *Yehudim*.

The guards wrestled Haman through the doors of the banquet hall while he begged, pleaded and cried hysterically.

Esther and the king watched in silence.

✡

Chapter Forty-One

Shattering Secrets

And Esther spake yet again before the king, and fell down at his feet, and besought him with tears to put away the mischief of Haman the Agagite, and his device that he had devised against the Jews. (Est 8.3 KJV)

Once Haman was out of sight and could no longer be heard, the king took Esther's hand and looked at her gravely.

"I did not realize what he was doing, Esther, but you with great wisdom have revealed much to me. He came to me with a report of rebels which he intended for me to think were a few unruly characters. He picked the time to come after a long night of drinking when I wasn't thinking clearly. I blame myself for trusting him, and I don't understand how one of the regents or advisors didn't tell me."

"I think it is because he had the promotion and your ring, My King. I feel sure your men had no idea of how it all came about either. He is a man of evil devices and a wicked heart. I also am aware that Haman has spread rumors in the palace that he revealed the plot to have you killed. He was crafty and sly."

Ahasuerus suddenly straighten himself as he thought back on the morning.

"It is very funny to me now to think how Haman must have felt leading the *Yehudi* man, Mordecai, to the city square proclaiming his honor."

He paused. "You are *Yehudi*," he stated it, but he was actually making a confirmation. "Did you know of this man Mordecai?"

"He is my cousin, My King," she said quietly. "When my parents died, he took me in as a child and has been like a father to me."

Esther felt something in her burst open. The secrets were fading as truth brought light and a release into her. Just the freedom to say Mordecai's name, declare his relationship to her, and make known who she was felt comparable to the feeling birds must experience when a cage is opened and they are allowed to fly.

The king was staring at her almost in shock.

"Your cousin? I must see him personally. It is not enough that Haman took him out publicly. Now that I know him, I'm quite sure it was less than what I intended to be done to honor him. Yes, I must honor him myself."

Ahasuerus motioned for Harbona to approach.

"Go to the city gate and find Mordecai, the scribe. Bring him to me right away."

Harbona bowed with a slight smile on his face. Turning toward Esther, he bowed again. As he walked away, he counted the rumors Haman had spread, the hatred he had plotted, the devious ways he had used his position to try to destroy the *Yehudim* and the queen. He couldn't wait to hear the conversation between the king and Mordecai.

Mordecai was still in his position against the palace wall near the gate. The events of the previous day were real enough, but the reasons for them was a complete mystery which neither Haman nor the eunuchs had bothered to reveal. Mordecai did however know that a very tall gallows had been built during the night in Haman's courtyard. Mordecai knew evil intent well enough to know that somehow Haman intended it for him.

The merchants on the street looked at Mordecai differently after the announcement by Haman, but they did not know what Mordecai had done to deserve the honor that had been given. Haman did not announce the service for which Mordecai was being honored. So he was an even greater mystery to them all.

When the guards exited the building with a man wearing a hood, everyone had grown quiet enough to hear the man begging, crying, and pleading for his life. They knew all to well that he was going to be executed, and according to the direction they were going with him, they supposed that Haman had something to do with who was going to the gallows.

Mordecai recognized him immediately by the idol embroidered on his cloak, and even if he had not see that, he knew the voice of the man that hated him enough to kill off an entire race of people.

By the time he saw Harbona making his way toward him, Mordecai did not know whether to stand and greet him or try to hide. Whatever was going on in the palace was not being announced on the street yet, and Mordecai already knew surprises had a way of coming out of there regularly.

When the eunuch started grinning, Mordecai was completely taken off guard. He decided to stand and meet the man, whatever his message.

"Mordecai, King Ahasuerus has requested your presence."

"But I am not dressed to face the king, Sir. I need to clean myself and change my clothes," Mordecai was still wearing the clothes he had put on the night before after the embarrassing and confusing ride through the town with Haman and this same eunuch.

"Sir, you are under order to come immediately. The king and queen are waiting for you."

The eunuch did not have to say more. The words ". . . and the queen" suddenly changed everything.

Hadassah! My Hadassah! I can see her. I can perhaps speak to her, he thought and almost choked on the tears that sprang to his eyes.

Weak from fasting and prayers, Mordecai was suddenly given strength to follow the eunuch who was walking much too slowly to suit Mordecai.

Entering the banquet hall, Mordecai saw the king sitting on the couch across from Esther, their heads were together in quiet conversation. Hearing them enter, she turned and looked at Mordecai with eyes suddenly wide and filling with tears. She asked the king a question to which he nodded and motioned his hand indicating permission. She sprang from the couch and ran to him weeping. She fell into his arms.

The servants and the eunuch in the doorways and along the walls watched in amazement. They wondered who this man was that had caused the queen to run to him with such emotion. Harbona slipped in to join them.

"Apparently the queen likes the man," Harbona said out of the corner of his mouth.

Quiet chuckles and snickers behind hands broke the tension of the past moments. They watched as Esther took Mordecai by the hand and led him before the king. Mordecai bowed and waited. The observers stood motionless and mute with ears honed to catch every word. There would be much to discuss that evening in the servants hall among the others.

"Sergazi," said the king, "record the following."

"Mordecai, are you the cousin of Queen Esther?"

"Yes, Your Majesty," Mordecai replied.

"And are you the man who sent the note to reveal the plot against my life?"

"I am, Your Majesty."

"And were you taken to the village square by Haman to receive honor for saving my life?"

Mordecai looked up at the king in surprise.

"I am the man," said Mordecai stunned by this bit of information.

"And did you know why Haman took you through the village?"

Ahasuerus didn't miss the surprise in Mordecai's face and voice.

"I cannot say that I knew, Sir. It was unexpected and . . . done dutifully by Haman," said Mordecai with as much grace as he could muster.

Pulling his ring from his finger, Ahasuerus looked at Mordecai intently.

"Give me your hand, Mordecai. This is my ring that I gave to Haman. It is the same ring that he used to seal the decree to sell your people to be murdered and annihilated. It would please me if you would become my new Vice-Regent."

Before Mordecai could say anything, Esther knowing that more must be done before this meeting with the king was over, fell on her knees before him weeping. Ahasuerus was somewhat stunned by this, but held out his scepter to give her permission to make a request.

"O King, put away the plot that Haman the Agagite has devised against my people."

Taking her hand, he pulled her to her feet so that she stood before him.

"A written decree sealed with the king's ring cannot be reversed."

"But . . . if it is pleasing to the king, and if I have favor in your sight, and if what I suggest seems right to the king, let it be written in such a way to reverse the letters that Haman wrote to bring about the destruction of the *Yehudim*. A new decree can give permission to the *Yehudim* to arm and protect themselves. Let that decree be dispersed throughout the empire in all of the king's provinces. For how shall I endure to see this great evil that will come upon my people? Or how can I endure to see the destruction of my family?"

Without replying to her, he turned to Mordecai.

"The guards have taken Haman to be hanged on the gallows that he built with the intention to kill you, Mordecai. He dared to lay his hand on the entire race of *Yehudim* in my kingdom, so, I have ordered his death on that very same gallows. Also, I have given the house and lands and all that he possessed to Queen Esther. She has said that she wants you to live in that house and be master over it."

He nodded toward Esther and continued.

"Mordecai, write a letter to say whatever you desire for the protection of the *Yehudim*. Seal it in the name of the king with my ring, so it cannot be reversed by any man.

"Now," said the king, "we have before us this table filled with food and drink. Let us eat and drink to celebrate uncovered evil intent, justice upon the head of the deceiver, and days ahead of joy and gladness!"

And for the first time in much too long a time, Mordecai and his Hadassah enjoyed a meal together with gladness and thanksgiving, and not for the last time in the palace of Shushan.

✡

Chapter Forty-Two

The Postscript

Write ye also for the Jews, as it liketh you, in the king's name, and seal it with the king's ring: for the writing which is written in the king's name, and sealed with the king's ring, may no man reverse. (Est 8.8 KJV)

In the month of Sivan which was the third month of the year, on the twenty-third day of the month, the king's scribes were called together to make copies of the decree written by Mordecai. It was to be dispersed to all the *Yehudim*, the lieutenants, the deputies, the rulers, satraps, and governors of the 127 provinces of Persia from India to Ethiopia. The decree was written in the language of every people of the provinces and to the *Yehudim* in their language and according to their writing. Mordecai wrote the decree in the name of King Ahasuerus, and sealed it with the king's ring.

The letters were sent by couriers on horseback, mules, camels, and young one-humped camels bred for fast travel to every province in the empire.

TO ALL PROVINCES OF THE PERSIA EMPIRE BY KING AHASUERUS:

ON A SINGLE DAY IN THE MONTH ADAR, ON THE THIRTEENTH DAY OF MONTH, YEHUDIM IN EACH AND EVERY CITY ARE GIVEN THE RIGHT TO ASSEMBLE AND DEFEND THEMSELVES: TO DESTROY, KILL, AND ANNIHILATE EVERY ETHNIC AND PROVINCIAL ARMY OR PERSON HOSTILE TO THEM, INCLUDING WOMEN AND CHILDREN, AND TO TAKE THEIR POSSESSIONS AS SPOILS OF WAR.

A COPY OF THIS TEXT, IS ISSUED AS LAW THROUGHOUT EVERY PROVINCE AND DISTRIBUTED TO ALL THE PEOPLE SO THE YEHUDIM CAN BE READY TO AVENGE THEMSELVES AGAINST THEIR ENEMIES ON THAT DAY.

So the decree went out with the king's command to be done quickly. The decree was also given at Shushan the palace.

✡

Chapter Forty-Three

Reunion

> *And Mordecai went out from the presence of the king in royal apparel of blue and white, and with a great crown of gold, and with a garment of fine linen and purple: and the city of Shushan rejoiced and was glad.* (Est. 8.15 KJV)

In Queen Esther's quarters, she and her attendants were waiting for Mordecai to arrive. It had been a tense and trying time for all of them, and the fasting had been especially hard for young women living in a palace unaccustomed to going without food and drink for three days and nights.

Much rejoicing occurred when Esther related to her maidens Haman's failed and evil attempts. They were gathered to celebrate Esther's success, Mordecai's promotion, and Haman's demise. Presently, they were waiting for the arrival of Mordecai and the opportunity to meet the queen's cousin who in her own way referred to him as *Dod*. She explained to them that it was a word of endearment used by the *Yehudi* for a close male relative. They were also waiting to enjoy a celebratory meal prepared and ready. Secretly, Esther had her own special agenda for Mordecai, and each minute that passed was much too long.

Finally, a rap at the door, a squeal from Roxanna—ever the energetic and bouncy one—and Mordecai was standing in the doorway. Esther and her attendants all gasped at his appearance. He was cloaked in royal blue and white. Underneath the cloak was a fine garment of linen and purple made especially for him by Davzadi, the royal tailor, and on his head a great crown of gold.

Esther ran into his arms with unashamed joy and love. Then she introduced each of her attendants. With pride she told Mordecai how they had listened to stories from the scriptures and grown to desire a God like Hashem. She told him how they and fasted and prayed with her for three days and nights before she went to the king. Mordecai wept with joy and appreciation that Hashem had blessed Esther with such faithful and trusting companions, and favor from all who knew her in the palace.

Another rap on the door, and Esther quickly opened it herself and invited, or rather excitedly pulled in Meradin and Renayar who was holding Darius the Prince. Esther took Darius in her arms and carried him to Mordecai.

"*Dod*, this is your grandson, Prince Darius."

Mordecai was speechless. His mind was spinning as he thought of all the months and years of grieving over the loss of Hadassah. All of the tormenting thoughts of how she had been taken away and lost, and all of the comments from the *Yehudim* community that Hadassah had not been spared from the palace. All of it fell at his feet like shattered shards of glass and then melted away.

He took the child in his arms, kissed him, and blessed him.

> "*Behold, children are a heritage from Elohim, the fruit of the womb a reward.*
> *Like arrows in the hand of a warrior are the children of one's youth.*
> *Blessed is the man who fills his quiver with them!*
> *He shall not be put to shame when he speaks with his enemies in the gate.*"(Psa 127.3-5)
>
> *Prince Darius, Hashem Elohim bless you, and keep you:*
> *Hashem Elohim make his face shine upon you, and be gracious unto you:*
> *Hashem Elohim lift up his countenance upon you, and give you peace.*(Num 6.24-26)

The prince grabbed at Mordecai's beard and giggled. He was fascinated by the crown and in wonder at the solemn faces of his mother and her friends. Everyone was wiping tears from their cheeks and something like an invisible cord pulled them together in hugs and thanksgiving.

Suddenly Leeza, Roxana, Ariana, Farah, Daria, Nima, Yasmin, Roya, Zahra, Hargaza, Saroya, Esther and Mordecai burst into laughter as Darius said, "Food! Hungie!"

"The Prince has spoken! Let us eat," said Mordecai.

Later that night after Darius was put to bed, the attendants had gone to their beds, and Mordecai had left the palace to prepare for the move into his new home, Esther sat on the side of her bed and opened the small scroll Mordecai had made for her. She looked at it with love and appreciation. She carefully unrolled the thin, delicate paper and in his fine script he had copied from the scriptures one of their favorite Psalms.

> "Hallelujah!
> Happy is the person who fears Hashem,
> > taking great delight in His commands.
> His descendants will be powerful in the land;
> > the generation of the upright will be blessed.
> Wealth and riches are in his house,
> > and His righteousness endures forever.
> Light shines in the darkness for the upright.
> He is gracious, compassionate, and righteous.
> Good will come to the one who lends generously
> > and conducts his business fairly.
> He will never be shaken.
> The righteous one will be remembered forever.
> He will not fear bad news;
> > his heart is confident, trusting in Adonai.
> His heart is assured; he will not fear.
> In the end he will look in triumph on his foes.
> He distributes freely to the poor;
> > his righteousness endures forever.
> His horn will be exalted in honor.
> The wicked one will see it and be angry;
> > he will gnash his teeth in despair.
> The desire of the wicked leads to ruin." (Psa 112)

Below the scripture he had written his own private message to her:

Hadassah, my daughter and My Queen:

I know you have wept many tears and wrestled many times about the promises of Hashem concerning children, blessings, and heritage.

I know you felt that you had lost everything Hashem promises for the righteous. But this is what you must remember: Hashem chose you to save His beloved, chosen people from the evil devices of an enemy. He ordained you to be as the mother of the people in Shushan and in all of the other provinces of Persia. He sent you into a place you did not want to go, He gave you a life you did not want, and many nights you wept in despair and confusion wondering why Hashem chose you to be here.

But this is the promise to you. You will be a shining light—as the scripture says, "Light shines in the darkness for the upright." You will be as a star to show others throughout all generations that those who put their trust and hope in Hashem, will go where He sends them—and will do what He sent them to do—in trust and obedience; even to face a King who could easily take their lives. You were obedient and loved Hashem's people and your kindred enough to say, 'If I die, I die.' They will learn of you and know that Hashem will keep His word and fulfill their destiny.

Your Cousin,
Mordecai

✡

Chapter Forty-Four

Rumors and Gossip

The eyes of the LORD are on the righteous, And His ears are open to their cry. The face of the LORD is against those who do evil, To cut off the remembrance of them from the earth. The righteous cry out, and the LORD hears, And delivers them out of all their troubles. The LORD is near to those who have a broken heart, And saves such as have a contrite spirit. (Psa 34.15-18 NKJV)

When Mordecai left the palace that evening on the king's steed, most of the community were in their homes and did not see him. That was just fine with Mordecai. He had had enough excitement for one day.

There was still much talk among the villagers about the man they had thought was a huge success and one to be admired by everyone who sought to get advancement in the world. But the account of Haman was putting a different light on one who would do whatever necessary to advance himself, even to plot murder.

There was much speculation about Zeresh and her sons and their families. Soon everyone knew Haman had been hung on a gallows he had ordered to be built to murder Mordecai the *Yehud*. It was also now wide-spread knowledge that Mordecai's adopted daughter was the beautiful Queen Esther and she was the owner of Haman's house by gift from the king.

Zeresh and the entire family had been removed in a day from the house, lock, stock and barrel, so to speak, and had seemed to disappear somewhere unknown. The people of Shushan were astounded by all of this, and many began to wonder about the God of the *Yehudim* who some *Yehudi* were proclaiming had ordained it all. The recent displays of sackcloth and ashes and public prayers were not forgotten, and some wondered about the power of the ritual. Many desired to learn more about the process.

When the new decree of King Ahasuerus was received, it brought with it a realization no one could ever have imagined. Obviously, the king had changed his mind and was, in a way, diminishing the first decree by adding to it with the second.

Leaders in the community held small meetings to question what they should do in light of the new decree. Those who continued in determination

RUMORS AND GOSSIP

to take up arms against the *Yehudim* were slowly losing numbers. Many of the poorer people who for years worshipped Baga for his promises of wealth and prosperity were seriously considering becoming believers in the God of the *Yehudim*. Those who believed in Him, in recent days had certainly gained great favor, honor, and wealth from the king. *Was it the result of their god?* some wondered. This caused many discussions, divisions, and questions that finally led them to determine to seek out the *Yehudi* men and women to get more history and facts to determine if what had happened was just a coincidence, or was it actually a blessing from the unseen God of Israel. Many wondered if it were possible to become part of the *Yehudim* so they could be blessed by a God who answers prayers, blesses his people, and loves them.

———————— הַפְסָקָה ————————

The morning sunlight did not find Mordecai in bed. He had slept well, had a good breakfast of fresh eggs from the hens, olives from his trees, grapes from his vines, and butter from his goats. Feeling very contented and blessed, he was settled into his favorite chair with the scroll for the day in his hand. A knock on his door startled him.

Carefully laying aside the delicate scroll, he went to the door and opened it to see Rabbi Joseph-ben Gideon.

"*Boker tov*, Rabbi." He moved aside and waved him in.

The rabbi touched the *mezuzah*, kissed his finger and entered.

"*Shalom boker tov*, Mordecai."

"Would you like something to drink, Rabbi?"

"*Toda raba*," he said taking the cup.

"My *Ach*, there is quite an uproar among our people. I came to ask you to meet with the men and as many of the women who would like to be there."

"I don't understand, Rabbi. An uproar? About what?"

"Maybe I am using the wrong word. It's not an uproar of anger . . . Hashem knows we've had enough of that!"

He grinned then quickly lost it.

"There are so many questions about the events at the palace, and we are hearing all kinds of rumors and gossip. Some of it makes sense, but a lot of it is just unbelievable. I have told the *achim* that I would ask you to come this morning and clear the air, so to speak. Give us the account from your own mouth."

Then with a tone purely of astonishment, he asked, "Is Hadassah really Queen Esther?"

Mordecai couldn't help but laugh. "She is, but I think it best if I go so I can answer questions from everyone. That way, you will not become one of the gossipers."

Both of them laughed and the rabbi set his cup down, grabbed Mordecai's hand and asked, "You will come?"

"Is one hour from now a good time?" asked Mordecai.

"*Toda lekha, achy.* (Thank you, my brother.)"

"*Bevakasha, ach* (You are welcome, brother.)"

———————— הַפָסָקָה ————————

After the rabbi left, and Mordecai started to get dressed for the meeting, he debated if he should wear the clothing and the ring the king had given him.

If I wear it, am I being proud and haughty? Will the achim see it as an act of pride? That would not be good. But if I wear it, it will be evidence and proof that what I am saying is true. What is best for the situation I am in? And to whom should the gift of the clothing and the ring be accounted? The King of Persia, or the King of Kings?

The debate settled, he dressed and headed for the meeting.

On the walk to meet with his brethren Mordecai was cheered by the people who clapped their hands and celebrated the humble scribe who had been highly honored by the king. Most of them had seen the gallows built in Haman's courtyard for the execution of Mordecai. They knew Haman was hanged by order of the king on the gallows he built to hang Mordecai. Those who watched Haman parade Mordecai, remembered the lack of enthusiasm, respect, or volume he used when acting on the king's behalf.

Upon entering the meeting with his *Yehudi achim*, the room was eerily quiet. Mordecai made his way to the front to face the men and answer their concerns and questions. Suddenly, someone from the back yelled out.

"Long live King Mordecai!"

The room exploded into laughter. Mordecai fanned out his royal blue cloak, bowed and slowly turned around, which drove the laughter higher.

Once the levity had settled, the questions came in rapid fire.

"What happened to Haman?

"Why was he hanged?"
"Did you get to see Hadassah?"
"Did you have anything to do with the new decree?"
"What are you going to do on the thirteenth of Adar, Mordecai?"
"Did you see the prince? Does he look like the king or the queen?"
"Are you really moving into the house that Haman lived in?"
"Do you know where his family is?"
"How did you feel about the parade for you?"
"What's your answer for what has happened so quickly?"

Mordecai looked at Rabbi Joseph-ben Gideon and all he got from him was a shrug. So Mordecai held up both hands and once it became quiet enough to be heard, he spoke.

"Let's start at the beginning. Shall we?"

———————— הַפְסָקָה ————————

Feeling confident that he had answered their questions and explained what he could, Mordecai had some questions for them.

"Now I have a few questions of my own.

"Is there anyone in this room who has any doubt that our united prayer brought deliverance to us from the decree that Haman devised?"

The room remained quiet.

"Is there any doubt that Hashem protected the *Yehudi* maidens from being taken into the palace when we put our trust and faith in His deliverance? Maybe we didn't see chariots of fire, but they were there."

Heads nodded and it was evident that they knew Hashem had intervened.

"Is there anyone in this room that believes Hadassah, our Queen Esther, was not appointed by God to become the queen for just a time as we are in, and to speak on our behalf and to expose an enemy?"

Some suddenly squirmed, but no one answered.

"*Achim*, we must understand that there will be those who will try to rise up and kill us. Haman was not the only enemy of the *Yehudim*. His ten sons and his close associates will undoubtly surface and join forces to attack us. They will come with a vengence. There are many more who will come from the shadows. So in a little less than nine months it will be the thirteenth of Adar. We must not fail to pray. We need the same power that worked on Zerubbabel's behalf when he and the captives returned to Jerusalem during the reign of Cyrus and worked to finish the tabernacle. Remember what Hashem Elohim said to Zerubbabel.

"*Not by might nor by power, but by My Spirit, says El-Shabaoth, the God of Armies.*'

"We may feel like we are facing a mountain, but remember the rest of that message to Zerubbabel.

"'*What are you, O great mountain?*
Before Zerubbabel you will become a plain.
Then he will bring forth the capstone accompanied by shouts of
"*Grace, grace to it!*"'"

The men jumped up and began clapping their hands, shouting victory and praising Hashem in unison until the very building shook.

✡

Epilogue

The king's command and law went into effect on the thirteenth day of the twelfth month, the month Adar. On the day when the Jews' enemies had hoped to overpower them, just the opposite happened. The Jews overpowered those who hated them. (Est 9.1 CSB)

The *Yehudim* in Shushan assembled and in the cities in all the provinces of King Ahasuerus to attack those determined to destroy them. No one could stand against them because the peoples of all nationalities were afraid of them. All the nobles of the provinces, the satraps, the governors and the king's administrators helped the *Yehudim* because they were seized with fear of Mordecai who was prominent in the palace; his reputation had spread throughout the provinces, and he had become more and more powerful.

When the thirteenth day of Adar ended, the *Yehudim* had struck down with the sword, killing and destroying 500 enemies in the citadel of Shushan. Because Haman's ten sons Parshandatha, Dalphon, Aspatha, Poratha, Adalia, Aridatha, Parmashta, Arisai, Aridai and Vaizathahad hated the *Yehudim* and sought revenge for Haman, they had surfaced with their own allies, but they were also killed. The *Yehudim* did not take their goods as spoils.

At the end of the day a report was made to King Ahasuerus concerning the enemies in the citadel of Shushan.

King Ahasuerus said to Queen Esther, "The *Yehudim* have killed and destroyed 500 men and the ten sons of Haman in the citadel of Shushan. We do not know what they have done in the rest of the provinces. What is your petition now? Tell me, and it will be given to you. I will grant your requests."

"If it pleases the king," Esther answered, "give the *Yehudim* in Shushan permission to perform this day's edict tomorrow; and also, let Haman's ten dead sons be impaled on poles and displayed."

So the king commanded Esther's request to be done, and the edict to allow the *Yehudim* to assemble and protect themselves from their enemies was extended for the fourteenth of Adar. Also, according to Queen Esther's request, Haman's ten sons who had been killed were impaled and put on public display.

On the fifteenth, the *Yehudim* in Shushan held a day of feasting and rejoicing for their deliverance from their enemies.

When the report was received from the other provinces, 75 thousand enemies of the *Yehudim* had been killed, but their goods were not taken. On the fourteenth, the provinces and the *Yehudim* in the rural villages around Shushan rested and made it a day of feasting and joy.

———————— הפסָקה ————————

Mordecai recorded all these events. Queen Esther and Mordecai sent letters to all the *Yehudim* throughout the provinces of King Ahasuerus and it was written down in the records of the Medes and Persians.

EPILOGUE

TO ALL PROVINCES OF KING AHASUERUS FROM INDIA TO ETHIOPIA:

HAMAN, THE SON OF HAMEDATHA THE AGAGITE, PLOTTED AND DEVISED AN EVIL SCHEME AGAINST THE YEHUDIM TO DESTROY THEM. HE CAST THE PUR (LOT) TO DETERMINE THE DAY FOR THEIR RUIN AND DESTRUCTION. QUEEN ESTHER CALLED THE YEHUDIM TO THREE DAYS OF FASTING AND PRAYER IN SHUSHAN. THEN SHE WENT BEFORE THE KING WHO WROTE ORDERS GIVING THE YEHUDIM THE PERMISSION TO ASSEMBLE AND DEFEND THEMSELVES AGAINST THE EVIL SCHEME HAMAN HAD DEVISED, AND HIS EVIL PLOT CAME BACK ONTO HIS OWN HEAD.

THEREFORE, CELEBRATE ANNUALLY THE FOURTEENTH AND FIFTEENTH DAYS OF THE MONTH OF ADAR AS THE DAYS OF PURIM, TO OBSERVE THE TIME WHEN OUR SORROW WAS TURNED INTO JOY, AND OUR MOURNING INTO A DAY OF CELEBRATION WHEN THE YEHUDIM GOT RELIEF FROM THEIR ENEMIES. PURIM SHALL BE TWO DAYS WITH FEASTING, JOY, AND GIVING PRESENTS OF FOOD TO ONE ANOTHER AND GIFTS TO THE POOR, AND IT SHALL BE OUR ESTABLISHED CUSTOM OF OBSERVANCE FOR US AND OUR DESCENDANTS AND TO ALL WHO JOIN US IN EVERY GENERATION EVERY YEAR, IN THE WAY PRESCRIBED AND AT THE APPOINTED TIME. PURIM SHOULD NEVER FAIL TO BE CELEBRATED BY THE YEHUDIM— NOR SHOULD THE MEMORY OF THESE DAYS OF FASTING AND LAMENTATION DIE OUT AMONG OUR DESCENDANTS.

QUEEN ESTHER, QUEEN OF PERSIA
MORDECAI, VICE-REGENT TO KING AHASUERUS

———————— הַפְסָקָה ————————

All of his (Mordecai's) *powerful and magnificent accomplishments and the detailed account of Mordecai's great rank with which the king had honored him, have they not been written in the* Book of the Historical Events of the Kings of Media and Persia?

Mordecai the Jew was second only to King Ahasuerus. He was famous among the Jews and highly esteemed by many of his relatives. He continued to pursue prosperity for his people and to speak for the well-being of all his descendants. (Est 10.2-3 CSB)

Made in the USA
Columbia, SC
04 June 2022